BROWN BLOOD

THE EVOLUTION OF AN URBAN

CHRISTIAN

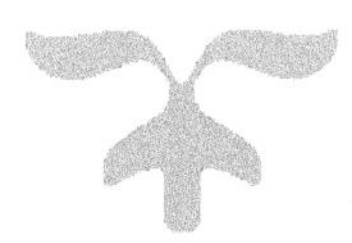

An Autobiography

by

Curtis White

DEDICATION

I dedicate this book to my mother, Phodie Elizabeth White. At the time of her death, I was ten years old. Shortly thereafter, she visited me in a dream and spoke these words, "I just came back to let you know that everything is going to be all right." She faded from my dream as quickly as she appeared and has not shown herself since. I am the remainder of her earthen trinity. My older brother Robert and my younger sister Bernardette have gone on to join her.

I further dedicate these writings to my wife Sandra and our three children, Jillian, Jessica, and Justin. They are my confirmation that my mother's spoken words to me have come to fruition. Thanks be to God! I thank Him for His infinite Grace and Mercy.

Table of Contents

VI

ABOUT THE AUTHOR

So, where do I begin?

In My beginning *was abandonment and* **Abandonment** *begot poverty,*

Poverty *begot murder,* **Murder** *begot death,* **Death** *begot molestation,*

Molestation *begot incest,* **Incest** *begot sexual promiscuity,* **Sexual Promiscuity**

begot disease, **Disease** *begot hunger,* **Hunger** *begot God's word and* **God's word**

begot **Jesus.** *He is our Alpha and Omega, so don't look back eternity has no time for that.*

In The beginning *was the Word and* **the Word** *begot Jesus,* **Jesus** *begot faithfulness,*

Faithfulness *begot goodness,* **Goodness** *begot gentleness,* **Gentleness** *begot joy*

Joy *begot kindness,* **Kindness** *begot love,* **Love** *begot peace,* **Peace** *begot patience*

Patience *begot self-control,* **Self-Control** *begot hunger,* **Hunger** *begot Fruit*

*– **Fruit of the Spirit** – Fruit that has not allowed me to hunger anymore.*

During my early childhood, the smell of happiness was freshly cut grass, bales of hay, and long-stem wildflowers. Adjacent to that smell was the sound of poverty. A sound orchestrated by the different instruments used to catch the rain as it dripped through the holes in the roof of our house.

Several years later the unthinkable happened – the death of my mother. A few years after her tragic, untimely, unfortunate, unanswered, and unnatural death my twelve-year-old self and seven-year-old sister were catapulted from a small southern town named Lumberton into a sprawling metropolis called Manhattan.

We landed in the loving arms of a cousin who introduced us to a man named Jesus. In later years, the smell of happiness wafted up from the exhaust fumes concentrated on the lower level of the New York City Port Authority Bus Terminal. The sound of poverty had become the hollow noise of banging on cold pipes, begging the super to send up heat. Having neighborhood junkies pour into me, to stay in school and not to become like them.

Still later, that smell of happiness morphed into the scent of genuine leather covering the interior of my luxury car. The sounds of poverty had dissipated into songs of praise, but not before I began worshipping the secular provider who paid my salary. Believing that they alone were the ones who allowed me to acquire and enjoy my earthly treasures.

Unknowingly, I had allowed my bosses to become my God. To my co-workers, leaving the protection of the teamster union to become a member of management was due to my belief that the Company could and would offer me more security. My blood had to be brown, UPS brown to believe that. I had become a Company man. Everything that I did at work was to please my bosses. God was still there in the mix, but He was no longer primary in my life.

Where is God right now in your life? What company's blood is running through your veins? Think about it. It may not be a company at all. Who do you seek to please most? Unknowingly, who do you worship? Any blood other than that of our Lord and Savior, Jesus Christ is tainted. All of us can, will and do acquire tainted blood at some point in our lives and none of us are without blemish. Brown blood is indigenous to our humanness, manifesting itself whenever we begin to worship the carnal things in life. Examine yourself, what idols have you allowed to give you Brown Blood?

It is another one of Satan's tricks, to take our eye off of the prize. Who are you aiming to please? No matter what job you have or don't have, take the time to examine yourself. Learn to recognize the symptoms of brown blood. Have you allowed something or someone other than our Lord and Savior, Jesus Christ to become your God?

This delusion is another of Satan's clever distractions to get us to believe him. To believe that the tenets he seeks to establish in this world, will lead to our total happiness and contentment. However, it is only the shed blood of our Lord and Savior, Jesus Christ, that can save us. Remember, Satan's mission is to steal, kill and destroy – full stop!

Our belief in Christ enables us to experience complete joy over total happiness and to have eternal life over temporary contentment. Satan had wrapped me into what seemed to be a Gordian knot. I was unhappy, unfaithful, unhealthy, unfulfilled and depressed.

The writing of this book is my attempt to share with you how God untied that knot. To reverse engineer, if you will, God's grace and mercy extended to me throughout my life. To identify the root cause of why I received so much grace and so much mercy. To

illustrate how God worked around and through me, to dispense His grace and mercy to me.

But what about my salvation? I asked myself, what saves an individual from birth, until such time that he or she accepts Jesus Christ as their Lord and Savior? I discovered the answer to this question was delivered way back on Calvary. It's the shed blood of Jesus Christ, but why didn't I know that?

In my discussion with Assistant Pastor Jan D. Webster of the Trinity Baptist Church in the Bronx, she tells me that "God is and has always been there. It is more of a lack of awareness on your part and not God's lack of presence."

Is it like the poem, Footprints In The Sand, I asked?

Yes, exactly like that, she said.

FOREWORD

To die from natural causes, the way that I see it is to die from old age. My intention here is not to open this statement for debate. I say, in today's world, to die from old age is to die un-naturally.

When the opportunity to die with such dignity and grace is taken away, and life is unwillingly snuffed out, it is very likely that the person died un-naturally.

However, had the propagation of death by other means for the Negro became so prevalent that death at such a young age seemed to be natural in the realm of the rural white South? My answer is yes!

When do Black Lives Matter? My mother's life did not matter to that coroner any more than it did to her killer. Unbeknownst to the coroner, there was no yelling, cursing or screaming, only quiet pleading.

However, I do not believe that her death was the work of medical silent killers like high blood pressure or diabetes. Was her life not worth looking into, or is that done by request only?

Foreword

To the coroner, this young married black thirty-eight-year-old mother of three named Phodie died, and I quote, "Apparently Died Suddenly Due to Natural Causes." Really?

We know that her life mattered to her ten-year-old son who heard something that fateful night but saw nothing. We know that it mattered to her five-year-old daughter, who was left motherless, defenseless and molested.

With no obvious signs of causation, with the exception of just being another Negro, the coroner decides to rule her death as due to "natural causes." What would natural causes look like for a thirty-eight-year-old black female?

Maybe he thought her death to be typical for black women and, therefore, natural. Could "natural causes" have meant a heart attack, stroke, aneurism or something else entirely, like maybe perhaps, he was confused and was speaking about her natural hair?

What could have piqued the coroner's interest enough even to have thought about a cause? Cause ain't nobody asking any questions and ain't nobody getting any answers.

Had an autopsy been requested because we know that one was not performed. What about her husband, Bill? Did he ask any questions, or perhaps he was the silent killer? So, how did Pho-die

die? Who knows, and both parties that do know have taken that answer with them to their graves.

Something wasn't right that night, and I knew it, but what I didn't know was how to process it, so I didn't. Something or someone caused her death, and I believe that it did not happen naturally.

How can I be a witness to something that I did not see? She loved me enough to let me know that despite it all, everything would be alright.

If anything, I think that we all can agree that her death seemed to be anything but natural. This untimely occurrence catapulted the lives of my sister and me into the unknown of the living. Is death ever timely? Yes, but only when it occurs from old age.

At the time of my mother's death, I was ten years old, and Bernardette was five. At ages twelve and eight, we were plucked from a dire, small southern rural situation and set down in a frightening, unfamiliar Metropolis with slightly better surroundings.

In between that time, God was standing in the gap, but I was unaware of his presence.

That being the case, I dared to have wanted more out of life and dared to believe that I could have it. I had no entitlements, or did I? Shortly after arriving in New York, both of us were baptized.

Pastor Rick Warren says, ***"Why is baptism so important? … it is because it symbolizes God's second purpose for your life: participating in the fellowship of God's eternal family. Baptism doesn't make you a member of God's family; only faith in Christ does that. Baptism shows you are part of God's family."***[1]

I believe agreeing to be baptized was our first step toward changing the trajectory of our lives. The second step in changing this trajectory for me was an opportunity to earn a free college education. The potential to earn a free college education had become my dream. I saw this as my ticket to a better life.

Bernardette was defiant and wanted no part of my dream. She yearned to be back with Bill and regain her uncontested freedom. It is said, that home is where the heart is, but I just wasn't feeling it.

In my mind's eye, the "crying window" allowed us to reach the next tier of our lives. In a strange sort of way, crying relieved

---

[1] Warren, Rick. The Purpose Driven Life. (Zondervan, 2022), 120

tension and offered hope. The "crying window" had given us the strength to forge ahead into a frightening new future.

Bernardette cried, while I wept. Had we gained the rites of passage? What were the demarcations of our evolving lives? They were both biological and religious affirmations, something that she and I both had participated in as we were ushered into puberty.

Rick Warren says, ***"The Spirit of God uses the Word of God to make us like the Son of God. God's Word generates life, creates faith, produces change, frightens the Devil, causes miracles, heal hurts, builds character, transforms circumstances, imparts joy, overcomes adversity, defeats temptation, infuses hope, releases power, cleanses our minds, brings things into being, and guarantees our future forever!"***[2]

I discovered through Google that, ***"The concept of rites of passage was first explicated in 1909 by Arnold van Gennep (1873–1957) in his book Les Rites de Passage. While the title of van Gennep's book is usually translated into English as "The Rites of Passage," it might be better translated as "The Rites of Transition" as his study dealt with the ceremonies that accompany the transitions individuals make between various life stages." Van Gennep then distinguished three sequential stages of rites of***

---

[2] Warren, The Purpose Driven Life, 186

passage: rites of separation (séparation), rites of transition (marge), and rites of incorporation (aggrégation). Taken together, he called these the schéma of the rites de passage. While the three stages characterize all rites of passage, van Gennep claimed that they are not equally emphasized in all ceremonies or by all cultural groups. For example, the element of separation is accentuated in funerary rituals while transition, which marks the period when an individual is removed from one status but not yet admitted to another, is most prominent in initiation ceremonies. Rites of incorporation are emphasized in marriage."

Yes, there was separation and yes, we transitioned into puberty and yes, we both enjoyed the rites of incorporation through marriage. *"While the three stages characterize all rites of passage, van Gennep claimed that they are not equally emphasized..."* I understand and agree.

What I've found to be most liberating is that as I moved through each of these periods, I was allowing myself to be led by the Holy Spirit and thus drawn closer to God.

However, ***Dr. Norman Geisler writes that, "The unpleasant truth is that even though I have an inherited sin nature (Eph. 2:3),***

I have no one to blame but myself (i.e., my Self) for my personal moral actions."[3]

Having transitioned from "Footprints In the Sand" to "No Weapons formed Against Me," I can joyfully say that from the rising of the sun, to the going down of the same, God is worthy, He is worthy, He is worthy to be praised!

My prayer for you the reader is, that as you transition through the accounts of my life, you will be enabled to discover your own Footprints. And, be equally able through your steadfast faith to identify and prayerfully dismantle those Weapons formed Against you knowing that you too, can be saved.

Pastor Rick Warren states "If you really desire to be used by God, you must understand a powerful truth: The very experiences that you have resented or regretted most in life – the ones you've wanted to hide and forget – are the experiences God wants to use to help others. They are your ministry!"[4]

---

[3] Geisler, Norman. Chosen But Free. (Bethany House, 2001), 29
[4] Warren, The Purpose Driven Life, 247

PART 1

Natural Causes (Running Ditches and Riding Trees)

FOOTPRINTS IN THE SAND

One night I dreamed I was walking
along the beach with the Lord.
Many scenes from my life flashed
across the sky. In each scene I
noticed footprints in the sand.
Sometimes there were two sets of
footprints, other times there was one
only. This bothered me because I
noticed that during the low periods of
my life, when I was suffering from
anguish, sorrow or defeat,
I could see only one set of footprints,
so I said to the Lord,
"You promised me Lord,
that if I followed you, you would walk
with me always. But I have noticed
that during the most trying periods of
my life there has only been one set of
footprints in the sand.
Why, when I needed you most, have
you not been there for me?"
The Lord replied,
"The times when you have seen only
one set of footprints,
my child, is when I carried you."

Pastor Rick Warren declares that, ***"You must begin with God, your Creator. You exist only because God wills that you exist. You were made by God and for God – and until you understand that, life will never make sense."***[5]

Phodie Elizabeth Williams, what an unusual name. I've never known anyone else, anywhere else, with the first name PHODIE. She was born in July 1927 and "died" in July 1965. She was birthed at home on the south side of a small southern town called Lumberton in the state of North Carolina. Her first born was named Robert, and he came into this world in April of 1943. Yes, she was a teen mother, sixteen to be exact.

A cousin reported that Robert's father left town soon after she became pregnant, never to be seen again. Robert's father may have been running from more than an unwanted pregnancy. This was also during the height of World War two, a global conflict that lasted from 1939 to 1945.

World War II was by far the deadliest conflict in history, resulting in an estimated 70 to 85 million fatalities, mostly among civilians. My father, Curtis White Senior, was a soldier during this time and was stationed at Fort Bragg, North Carolina. Fort Bragg was named after North Carolina native Braxton Bragg, who was a

---

[5] Rick Warren, The Purpose Driven Life, Zondervan, (2022), 17-18

Confederate general in the Civil War and was associated with being a slave owner.

The fort was redesignated Fort Liberty on June 2nd of 2023. The 2021 National Defense Authorization Act mandated the name changes of Department of Defense assets that commemorate the Confederacy.

This post was one of nine Southern Army bases named after Confederate leaders being renamed after the 2020 killing of George Floyd.

The other bases are being named after individual heroes and heroines, but the Fort Bragg naming committee pressed for the name Liberty as symbolizing the post's mission (Jun 16, 2023, taken from <u>http://washingtonpost.com</u>).[6]

The origin of my father was said to be somewhere in Texas. He was my mother's first husband.

From that union, I, Curtis White Junior, was born in October of 1954. He fathered my sister Bernardette, born nearly five years

---

[6] By The Associated Press Updated March 3, 2025 6:06 pm. <u>WASHINGTON</u> — Defense Secretary Pete Hegseth has, for the second time, reversed the renaming of a U.S. military base, saying that Fort Moore in Georgia should revert back to being called Fort Benning.

The move reflects an ongoing effort by the Pentagon to overturn the Biden administration's 2023 decision to remove names that honored Confederate leaders, including for nine Army bases.

later, in January 1959. He left home sometime after Bernardette's birth. I have no idea why and wonder if my mother knew why he left. I don't remember him, and I've only seen one picture of him.

He is dressed in a black suit. My mother is seen smiling in the background. Both of them are standing in what seems to be someone's front yard and he too was smiling. He appears to be a tall, slender man with a dark complexion, broad shoulders and processed hair. Years after he abandoned us, our mother married again. His name was William Powell, another soldier.

At the time of my birth, Lumberton had a population of under ten thousand people. The first home that I remember living in was located on Front Street. Front Street was situated in the heart of the south side of town. It was not a paved road, nor were a lot of other roads at that time. Our house was a small center-block home. It was that standard battle ship gray color with a tiny front and back porch. I have a picture of my mom and me sitting on the front lawn.

She is wearing a pair of cuffed plaid shorts and a white summer blouse. She is sitting on the grass, leaning to one side, with her legs extended out in front of her. Her arms are spread out and placed slightly behind her, with her hands buried deep into the lush green grass. Her eyes are somewhat squinted as they try to avoid looking directly into the bright morning sun. Her head is slightly tilted as she smiles for the camera.

I was happily sitting opposite her with my arms wrapped around both my legs, which I had drawn up to my chest. I had on a pair of shorts and a t-shirt. My back was to the sun, and we were both smiling. I appear to be four, maybe five years old.

I vaguely remember the inside of the house, but I do recall a bassinet in the hallway. That would have been for my baby sister, Bernardette. I also recall a huge green tractor-trailer parked outside in front of our house. This particular memory has always stood out for me, and I'm not sure why. It was a dark green tractor-trailer with the word Mayflower written on it in big yellow letters.

I also remember seeing three colorful snakes together in our backyard once. They had colorful rings around them. My mother told me that they were king snakes. We did not kill them. She said they were good to have around because they kept all the other snakes away.

Ironically, this would be the same street (Front Street) many years later, where I would have another close encounter with a serpent. An encounter, which had I not been careful with, could have had fiery eternal consequences for me.

Mr. Benny Lee, I think he may have been a relative, also lived on Front Street. He had beautiful plum trees in his back yard. They were large, dark, purplish plums, almost black. The leaves also were very dark, almost as dark as the skin on the plums. He had several of these trees. The tree closest to the backdoor to his house yielded the smaller, more colorful plums. There was only one tree of this kind.

The colors of the plums from this tree were red, yellow, green and orange, and they were half the size of the black plums. They were sweet, but the black plums were the best. He would not allow anyone to enter his yard to pick them up. Most of them fell to the ground and rotted away. When I visited, I got all that I wanted.

I'm told that Front Street was one of the more affluent streets in the black section of town. After all, the only black doctor in Lumberton lived on our street. The corner house is where Dr. Robinson lived and worked. His office was attached to his home. It was a big white house on the corner of Front Street and the Fairmont Road. The Fairmont Road was the main thoroughfare in the Negro section. I had only been inside his office once. For what, I don't remember. I do remember it being a cold and quiet place.

On the other side of the Fairmont Road opposite Dr. Robinson was our neighborhood supermarket, Cash & Carry. It was white-owned. Various other small businesses dotted the roadway. There was a barber shop, a gas station, a two-story candy store, a fish store, a café, a tire shop and a gas station, all black-owned.

The owner of the tire shop had only one fully developed arm. His other arm seemed to have stopped growing at his elbow.

However, that deformity did not hinder his ability to perform his work. Watching him work on repairing tires was amazing. Not knowing that he was missing half and arm, you would never suspect him not having it.

Sandy Grove Baptist Church and First Baptist Church were the two most prominent churches on the black side of town. I had limited exposure to one and no experience with the other. I vaguely remember going to Sunday school a few times at Sandy Grove. I remember one Halloween night, sitting on the steps of Sandy Grove Baptist Church. I was not comfortable there. Actually, it was very scary.

There was a joke about a man who used the graveyard as a shortcut to get to his friend's house. One night, he had accidentally fallen into a freshly dug grave. He was unable to get himself out and started complaining out loud that it was cold down there. A drunkard who happened to be walking through the graveyard that night heard the man complaining. The man who had fallen into the grave kept saying over and over again that it was cold down there. The drunk walked over to the open grave, looked down on the man and said, no wonder you're cold, you dun' kicked all the dirt off you, as he continued on his way.

There was also McCormick Chapel, an AME (African Methodist Episcopal) church. It was off the beaten path, and although near the end of Main Street, it was nowhere near the main road, which was the Fairmont Road. It was smaller than either of the Baptist churches but still larger than most other houses of worship. It had beautiful stained-glass windows and a certain serenity about it. I had only been inside once but often hunted birds in the huge hedges that grew behind it.

Across the street from McCormick Chapel lived the Blue brothers. One day, a bunch of us boys decided to have a bb-gun fight. We started shooting at each other. We continued to play until one of the boys was shot exactly between his eyes. At that point, all of us realized how dangerous this could be. We stopped shooting at each other immediately, and that game never surfaced again.

Also, on Fairmont Road was the elementary school that I attended. The W.H. Knuckles Elementary School. At that time, it was called the South Lumberton Elementary School. It was initially called the Thompson Institute, which was formed to educate blacks in the post-Civil War era. The school trained teachers and pastors who worked all over North Carolina and the country. It was renamed the South Lumberton Elementary School in 1950 and, in 1994, became W.H. Knuckles Elementary School, named after the Rev. William H. Knuckles, who served as principal of the Thompson Institute for 30 years. Dr. Knuckles passed away in 1942.

At the northern end of the Fairmont Road on the right-hand side of the road was Spivey's Hardware Store. Although located on the black side of town (supposedly, the wrong side of the tracks), this store was also white-owned. The store's check-out counter was located at the back of the store. As you entered, just past the front door on the left side was a live black talking parrot. Everyone who came into the store had to walk past this bird. But, get this.

Whenever the parrot saw a black face, he would say loud and clear – "Here comes a nigger." I was a little kid, but I was big enough to know that was not right. I thought it so ironic that a black bird owned by a white man called black people nigger. I remember standing at the cage, staring at the bird. He was blacker than me. Another person of color came into the store, and again he announced to his keepers – "Here comes a nigger." Now, in retrospect, it really would have been amazing if that bird had said, here comes ANOTHER nigger.

Spivey's was a stone's throw from the railroad tracks. When a train came through town, you could hear its whistle blowing for miles. Standing on the tracks as I often did, you could see for miles in each direction, and the railroad tracks always seemed to converge somewhere in the distance.

On the other hand, freight trains were no optical illusion and were not to be played with. I could watch them for hours; most would be miles long. They could really mess-up traffic. When this occurred for any significant amount of time, they would have to break the train. This would also allow for freight cars to be taken on and off from the seemingly endless line of containers.

One time, I remember a huge tobacco warehouse fire just off First Street near a neighborhood area called the Bottom. It was a gigantic fire. From a distance, I observed the flames consume the warehouse, and all that was within it. Telephone poles were burning as electrical power lines fell to the ground. It was a spectacular fire.

Seaboard Street was the name of the street opposite Spivey's Hardware Store. It ran parallel to the rail road tracks for about a quarter of a mile, then made a ninety-degree turn to the left and went off into a neighborhood that we called the Field.

Seaboard Street had the steepest decline when you turned onto it from Fairmont Road. It gradually leveled out after about one hundred feet or so. It was low country, and they literally sat in a dirt bowl. Sugar Lane, located behind First Baptist Church, was even worse.

Seaboard street is where our cousin Persaver lived. We called her Aunt Persaver. Aunt Persaver's only daughter was named Weebee, and she met an untimely death. I'm told that she died at an early age, losing her fight with alcoholism. She left behind three children, Ronnie, Bobby and Jean. Aunt Persaver owned a green and white house that sat close to the ground but not up on stilts.

Persaver's sisters, Ms. Lonnie and Ms. May, lived in the first two houses on Seaboard Street. They were old, raggedy wooden houses that sat on stilts and leaned ever so slightly to one side. They seemed like they were about to fall down. The roads were all dirt, and when it rained, what a mess it made. This area flooded quickly and often. There is nothing fun about being poor. Who said, I've been rich, and I've been poor. I like rich better.

The railroad tracks divided the town. The area for the Negros was called the Southside, which also included the Bottom. Sugar Lane was another area near the tracks behind First Baptist Church. When flooding was eminent, Sugar Lane was the first neighborhood to go under because it was the closest to the river.

All of the houses on Seaboard Street faced the tracks. From my experience, the flood waters never covered the Fairmont Road or the railroad tracks. This, to me, made them the highest points in town. The railroad tracks sat well above Seaboard Street.

I'm unsure why Aunt Persaver had such a nicer home than her sisters. I heard it said that she was the recipient of a large insurance settlement from her husband's accidental death. Her sisters were very destitute. Aunt Persaver later moved across town away from the tracks and, I'm sure, to slightly higher ground.

Natural Causes

I'm not sure how long we lived on Front Street. Then we moved. If I had to guess, I would say that this was around the time that my father, Curtis Sr., left us. To my knowledge, our mother did not have a job. If we did not own that home, and apparently, we did not, we had to move. She could not have afforded to stay there.

So, we moved to Powell Street. There weren't many houses on Powell Street, and on the opposite side of the street, there were no houses at all. That side was all over grown with small trees and other vegetation. I remember being on that side of the street, trying to get at some small yellow plums. I was walking on these mounds of sand.

Suddenly, I was attacked by hundreds of red ants. They were stinging my legs and arms. It was really bad. I knew not to go there again. We lived in the last or next to the last house on that street. At the end of Powell Street, the road opened out to the Lumbee Homes. Powell Street was paved like all the streets that ran through the complex. Across the street, diagonally from us, lived a cousin.

I don't remember the exterior of the house on Powell Street. However, I do remember our brother Robert being in the kitchen one morning. He was preparing to cook something. I remember watching him strike a match and light the stove. It appeared like he shook the match out. I saw him toss the "outed match" into the garbage can.

13

<u>Natural Causes</u>

I don't remember a fire, but the fire department did come. I remember being held back by one of our cousins who lived across the street. I was screaming and trying to go back inside our house to save my toys. I was taken across the street to their house. I don't remember how much damage was done.

This is also the same house where I choked on a piece of meat once while eating supper. I panicked, jumped up and ran outside. Someone caught me and dislodged it. I don't remember if this took place before or after the fire.

Around the corner from my cousin's house were the Sanders. I'm not sure if they were relatives or not. There was a little juke joint off to the side of their house. The structure was half the size of their backyard barn and had a jukebox within it. It was a small rectangular building with a dirt floor. I was not allowed inside. I remember watching Robert dance. From the outside, I could see him dancing with two girls at the same time. They were swing dancing. Boy, could he dance.

There was also a barn at the back of the house. I remember playing in the barn, playing around the bales of hay up in the loft. I can almost remember the smells of hay, grass and wild flowers. I'll call it the smell of happiness because I enjoyed playing there so much.

Natural Causes

Frank was a little boy who lived next door to us. Frank, I remember, had a very interesting complexion. He wasn't black or white, and he didn't appear to be Indian. I did not know what he was. He was just different. He and I would always play in the dirt under his house. We were always burying something or digging to find something.

The games we played were all very simple, and most were "may-likes." These were games where you pretended to be some thing or some person. If it was cops and robbers, you had to "may-like" you were one or the other. May-like was another way of saying, let's pretend that you are.

We played in red dirt. It was red dirt with a fresh damp, wet smell. It was unique, but I'm sure it was the same as the dirt across the street, minus the sand and the ants. I also remember his family's clothes flapping in the wind on the clothes line out in his back yard. Off in the distance, you could see the back of W.H. Knuckles elementary school.

There wasn't much traffic on Powell Street or any street aside from the Fairmont Road. Powell Street was short, maybe a quarter of a mile long. As said earlier, in the end, it opened up to a development called Lumbee Homes. Powell Street was one of the few paved streets on the black side of town.

<u>Natural Causes</u>

One wintery day, I remember a lot of people, both old and young, roller skating on Powell Street. I thought nothing of it then. It was just something people did. But over the years, I've thought about how nostalgic that was. There is something very serene and Norman Rockwellish about it. I only remember that happening once. It was beautiful. Precious memories of that time always conjure up those nostalgic smells of happiness.

So, at some point after the fire, we moved again. Back across town, we went. We moved into a house on Washington Street next to Ms. Ester. She was a big-time bootlegger. She sold liquor, and her customers' cars would always be all over her yard. Her yard was uneven and had many mud holes in it, as did the street. Unlike Powell Street, Washington Street was not a paved road.

When it rained, it was a mess. Ms. Ester sold sealed liquor and moonshine. Sealed liquor was state-regulated and legal to buy; Moonshine was not. Moonshine went by several other names, such as white lighten, stump hole and, of course, corn liquor.

My mother would send me to Ms. Ester's house from time to time to get one thing or another but never to get liquor. There was a side door to her house that opened to her kitchen. I would always enter at the side door. From the kitchen, I could see some of her customers. They would be laughing, talking, drinking and smoking.

Ms. Ester was always cooking or frying something. A good fish sandwich could also be had.

There was an over grown vacant lot between our houses. I remember one evening when I was standing on our front porch facing the lot. I started to sing. I can't remember the song, but I do remember singing my little heart out. After I finished, I took my bows and thanked my pretend audience. What a performance!

Across the street from Ms. Ester was Linda's house. Linda had a big house also. In her back yard was a gigantic pecan tree. One day, a pecan fell from high-up in the tree. The pointed, sharp end of the nut hit her in the top of her head. She grabbed her head and screamed. She started crying. She was bleeding, but she ended up being ok. I liked Linda.

Some years later, Linda and her family moved across town to Sunset Heights. That was a new private housing development on the black side of town. The same development that Aunt Persaver had moved too. The streets in her development were named after one of the fifty states. They lived on Nevada street.

One morning, a few of Linda's brothers and I were playing baseball on a field behind her house. Someone hit a long high fly ball. Her brother was running backward to catch it. When he realized that the ball was hit over his head, he turned around to run faster. Just as he turned, he ran into a tree.

After hitting the tree, he fell to the ground. He did not get up right away. We all ran over to him. He was lying on the ground screaming, holding his face. There was a nail sticking out of the tree, and when he hit the tree, the nail went into his eye. We carried him to his mother's car. She rushed him to the hospital. I don't remember if he lost that eye or not.

Our house on Washington Street was an ugly, dark brown wooden house. It had both a front and back porch. This house sat high off of the ground. Not on stilts but a few feet above the ground. We had no indoor plumbing. Our toilet was in the backyard, about twenty feet from the house.

It was literally a hole in the ground covered by a little shack with a bench in it. The bench covered the pit and had a hole cut out in the middle of it for anyone who wanted to sit down to do their business. It was your typical outhouse.

The smell was horrible. There were no lights, heat or water. If you were not able to make it to the outhouse or if it was at night, you used specific pots inside the house to relieve yourself. These pots or pot had to be emptied the next morning, and guess whose job that was. The color of our pot was red and white.

When it rained, especially if there was thunder and lightning, you stopped doing everything. We were made to lie down and told to go to sleep. The Lord is doing his work, we were told. Also, when it rained, our roof leaked. We had to place pots, pans, buckets and jars in several places throughout the house to catch the dripping water.

During thunderstorms, you had to be quiet. We would lay there in total silence and listen to the rain hit the roof. I would also listen to the different sounds each drop made when hitting their empty vessels throughout the house. As the storm raged outside, I found those sounds to be soothing. Dripping water falling into pots, tin pans, glass jars and buckets. Plop, plop, ping, ploop, ploop, splash, the house leaked everywhere. They were the sounds of poverty.

I was pretty independent for a little kid. Once, I was ironing some clothing in the kitchen. I plugged the iron into one of those multi-socket holders. There were several things already plugged into it. Even at that young age, I thought twice about plugging one more thing into that socket.

It just didn't look safe, but I did it anyway. The ironing cord was insulated with cotton. Shortly after I plugged in the iron, I heard a pop, and the insulation started to burn away. There were no flames. It was as if someone had lit a fuse.

I was holding the iron in my right hand. My eyes followed the disappearing insulation until it reached the iron. I literally received the shock of my life. It knocked the iron out of my hand,

and I received an electrical burn on my right wrist the size of a matchbook. A burn that I have 'til this day. The house did not catch fire, and I don't remember receiving any medical attention.

Another memory of that kitchen was once having some oysters. We had gotten a foot tub of fresh oysters from someone. They had not been washed off and still had the mud and stilt on them. They were put on a flat pan and baked in the oven. Baked just enough for them to open wide enough to insert a knife and force the shell completely open. They were good, but you had to be very careful not to get any of that gunk and grit in your mouth.

I only remember going to the beach once. Carolina beach was the beach for colored folks. What I recall about that experience was not very pleasant. It was late afternoon as my mother, and I walked along close to the shore. I remember the waves being pushed violently toward the shore by heavy winds.

No one was in the water. The sky was dark and gray. The waves crashed against the beach with such force, causing the water to foam as it rushed quickly back into the sea. The waters seemed to be angry and there were white caps everywhere. It was scary, and I wanted no part of it.

At home, we got our water from a hand pump in the back yard. I remember having to prime the pump. Pouring water into that pump sometimes seemed to take forever, but it was worth it. Not that we had another choice.

That was the best water. It was ice cold even on the hottest of summer days. We had no running water inside the house. The pump was our only source. God only knows how old that pump was. It was a brown, rusty old pump. But it really didn't matter how old it was; it did its job.

There were a lot of kids in the area. I don't remember my brother Robert living with us during this time. One day, some older boys were playing catch with a baseball. They were throwing fast balls to each other. Carelessly, I walked between them and was hit on the side of my head. I was dazed but did not lose consciousness.

Those same boys molested me by trying to get me to suck their penis. This took place in our neighbor's house, Ms. Ester. One of the boys, I believe, may have been her son. Perhaps both were. She suspected something was going on and told us to go outside. It never happened again. That is the only time I remember entering and exiting her house through the front door.

We lived beside a ditch. Our house was the last house on the street. I remember one time the chain gang came through. These men were all chained together, cleaning out the ditch with shovels. I watched them from our front living room window. I remember seeing a man on a horse. He held a long gun across his arms as he watched them work. The prisoners wore either black and white or gray and white striped jumpsuits. They were all chained to one another. They worked very quietly. I never saw that again.

The kids in the area loved to play in the ditch. We called it "running the ditch." The ditch was very wide near the top on the opposite side of the road from our house. To run the ditch, you would start at the top, run down one side and up the other. To do this successfully, there had to be very little water in the ditch. We would do this repeatedly, trying to increase our speed with each run. It was a lot of fun.

The object of this game was to see who could run the ditch fastest. There was also a field of straw beside the ditch. We would tie the straw together and make above-ground tunnels. The straw was a golden blonde color and grew to be three or four feet tall, nearly as tall as we were. I remember the straw being shiny and smooth, almost silky.

To help keep the mosquito population under control, the town of Lumberton would dispatch trucks to drive though residential neighborhoods, spraying an insecticide into the air. We called it the mosquito truck. The spray was a fine blue mist. One of the most dangerous and stupid things we did as kids was to follow behind the "mosquito truck." The mosquito truck would drive slowly through the neighborhoods late in the day/early evening.

It sprayed a blue chemical mist into the air. We would follow behind the truck, running and jumping in the mist. We could only do it for short periods of time because it was difficult to breathe. I don't remember anyone getting sick or a rash or anything.

God only knows what we were inhaling and getting onto our skin. Not to mention, what could be the long-term effects of having ingested that stuff. I'm sure if any parent would have seen us, they would have stopped us from doing that.

There was a dog in the neighborhood that we all played with. One day it was in our back yard. He came onto our back porch. I was playing with him, slapping his snout back and forth with my hands. As he was backing away from me, he slipped off the porch and fell on his head.

He rolled back onto his feet. He shook his head several times but had this weird look on his face. Looking at me, he began to growl and foam at the mouth. I slowly backed into the house, bringing Bernardette with me. I remember someone coming; they said to shoot the dog because it had rabies.

Another time, I had a beautiful black puppy. I don't remember where it came from. At one time, I had a black dog named Queenie. She was beautiful with jet-black curly hair. It could have been one of her puppies. I don't remember. This puppy was sick. It had diarrhea that would not stop.

<u>Natural Causes</u>

I remember carrying it by both front paws, holding it out in front of me as I walked. I took it to the outhouse and dropped it in. I watched it as it struggled to stay afloat. I was not proud of that moment. I didn't know what else to do.

I owned a bb gun. It was a Daisy Air Rifle. I shot a pigeon and broke one of its wings. It fell to the ground, and I was able to catch it. I brought it home and placed it in my room on top of a trunk on top of my dresser. It was as high as I could put it. Very close to the ceiling. I spread out some newspaper to cover the top of my trunk. I fed the pigeon worms, bread and water. It was well out of the reach of my dog Queenie.

Each day, I would rush home to see how my pigeon was doing. It started to walk around and exercise its wings. Queenie was aware that it was up there. I would tell the bird to stay up there. I would tell Queenie not to bother the bird.

One day, when I returned home from school, Queenie had bloody feathers stuck in the corners of her mouth. I knew she had eaten my pigeon. She had been waiting for that day. Little did I know that a year or two later, I would have eaten that pigeon myself.

South Lumberton, aside from being the Negro section, I later discovered that it was also geographically located in a flood plain. During one of the more serious floods, I remember wading in water slightly above my knees. I was sent to the store to get something.

<u>Natural Causes</u>

There was water everywhere. It did not come into our house. However, water did cover the roads and fields all the way to Fairmont Road and in all directions. If the Fairmont Road wasn't covered with water, nor were the railroad tracks.

I didn't have any toys, but I remember having gotten a battle ship gray small steam shovel for some occasion, either my birthday or Christmas, I forget which. I loved this toy and would play with it outside on the side of the road for hours.

It had a stainless-steel crank handle with a mechanical arm that would scoop-up dirt. I played outside in the dirt a lot. I've always been intrigued by construction equipment and those gigantic earth movers, cranes and thangs.

Jimmy was a school mate of mine and lived at the end of Washington Street. He actually lived on the K&B Road. We all grew-up saying, the Kennin' Big Road. It's really the Kenny and Biggs Road or the K and B Road. Jimmy's family bought a television and invited me to come watch the Wizard of Oz with them.

The Wizard of Oz was broadcast on television for the first time on Saturday, November 3, 1956. I'm not sure as to when Jimmy's family got their television but his was the only family that I knew of that owned one. We sat around on his living room floor, watching it in black and white. That was a big, big treat for me, and I was mesmerized.

We never owned a television set. The next time I had the pleasure of watching television was years later at someone's house out in the country. Bill and I were coming from Fort Bragg. I remember sitting in the living room of this house, waiting for him. The television was playing an episode of the Twilight Zone. The story was about a giant alien in a small western town. We left before it finished and I never got to see the ending. Not knowing how that episode ended haunted me for years.

The street behind Washington Street was named Spearman Street. I remember the first house on that street being vacant for a long time. It was an attractive home made with reddish/orange bricks. The windows were very low to the ground. The family that finally moved into it was from Baltimore, Maryland.

The girl who lived there was cute, and she liked me. It was a family of four. It was her, her mother and father and her older brother who moved in. One night, I was at her house. She and I were in the kitchen. We were kissing by the sink. I had my eyes closed and her back was to the kitchen window.

I opened my eyes and saw her father and brother outside looking in at us. I panicked, ducked down and quickly made my way out through the kitchen and through the back door. Not knowing if they were following me, I ran all the way home.

After that, I always felt that her brother and father were looking for me. I'm not sure if they were or not, but from then on, I went to the store the long way. I didn't go anywhere near their house. Several months after that, I was told that they had moved again to a different state. Boy, what a relief.

On that same street, there lived a couple who argued all of the time. They were unbelievably loud. You could clearly hear them from the street. We knew the woman as Ms. Tippy, and she seemed to be a little bit crazy, anyway. Truth be told, I am not so sure that her husband was all there either. They did not have any children. Their house had a tin roof on it and a fireplace.

When the arguing got really bad my friends and I would find bricks and heave them onto their tin roof. It made such a loud noise that the arguing would stop instantly. You could hear the brick sliding off the roof. There would be peace and quiet for a moment. When they realized that the world was not coming to an end and that the bricks were no longer on the roof, they would start arguing all over again. We would throw another brick and run.

The Barnes lived further down the road from Ms. Tippy. They had a tiny home and four children. Mr. Barnes was a truck driver for the Pepsi-Cola company. He was a skinny, mild-mannered, quiet man. Mrs. Barnes was a hefty, robust housewife. The children were; Linda, the only girl, Donald, the oldest boy, Charles and finally, Johnnie.

Johnnie had Down Syndrome. We did not know that term then. We all called Johnnie retarded. Like his father, Johnnie was very kind and mild-mannered, too. Johnnie knew everybody in the neighborhood. He always called me by my full name. He would always say, "Hello, Curtis White Junior."

He had a fat tongue that was deeply creviced, and he smacked his mouth when he ate. Johnnie's statue was short and stubby. He walked with his feet turned outward. No one bothered Johnnie and likewise, Johnnie never bothered anyone. He was also as strong as an ox. You did not want to get him angry.

The Barnes had pretty much become my guardians. They were my protectors. I began to hang around with them. We had become a gang.

Opposite the Barnes were the Fords. They had two sons. The father, Mr. Ford, was a barber. This was his side hustle. He would give you a haircut in his garage on a Saturday morning for 50 cents. It was a lot cheaper than Clawson's barber shop on the Fairmont Road. I've gotten plenty of 50-cent haircuts from Mr. Ford.

Just past the Fords was Stacey Mae. She lived with her mother and father. She also had a brother. Stacey Mae was nice and always quiet. Years later, I'm told that she got into a fight with her brother and that she either stabbed him to death or stabbed him, and he died as a result of the wound.

I'm also told that she claimed that it was an accident. It had to be bad either way, murder or manslaughter. She went to prison for it. One summer, many years later, my sister pointed her out to me as she walked through the neighborhood. I never got to talk to her.

At the end of Spearman Street, lived Mr. Pernell. He was a cousin. He and his wife had six children. At one point, we all went to the same school together. Some of them I got to know personally, like Sammy, Ann and Vicky.

Mr. Pernell was a dedicated husband and father. I later learned that he proudly served as a lead foreman for the Seaboard Railroad Company (CSX). He retired after forty years of service. He was considered a "Gandy Dancer." He coordinated songs in a rhythmic pattern while laying down railroad tracks. According to Wikipedia:

"Gandy dancer is a slang term used for early railroad workers in the United States, more formally referred to as

section hands, who laid and maintained railroad tracks in the years before the work was done by machines.

"Section hands were called gandy dancers for the synchronized "dancing" movements of the men using a long "lining" bar, called a "gandy." The name is said to be based on the name of the company that manufactured them to lever track rails into alignment.

"The term "gandy dancer" is allegedly a combination of the name of Chicago-based Gandy Manufacturing Company, a maker of track-lining tools, and the description of the railway workers' dancelike movements."

As a member of the Sandy Grove Baptist Church, Mr. Pernell served as a deacon, choir member, and Sunday School Superintendent. He was also a member of the Robeson County Baptist Union. Pernell was a mans', man. He was certainly one of my heroes. In his retired years, he dedicated himself to visiting nursing homes and delivering the message of Jesus Christ. His appearance reminded me of Frederick Douglass with his nearly all-white wiry hair and full beard.

Deacon Pernell died on September 22, 2018, at the ripe old age of eighty-nine. I attended his funeral. Due to his popularity, finding a church large enough in the area for his funeral was a challenge. His funeral was held at the First Baptist Church in

Fairmont, North Carolina. This church was larger than any church that I knew of in Lumberton. There was standing room only.

It was the largest funeral that I have ever attended. The procession to the Powell cemetery had to be fifty cars long. As I drove in the procession, all the oncoming traffic would pull off to the side of the road. Some people would exit their vehicles, stand and watch. I didn't think that this public display of homage was still exhibited. It's a show of respect from the general public, total strangers. I was surprised but pleased to see that this practice was still in existence.

I remember the first and only time that I saw my mother naked. I had come home from school, and the back door was locked. She came to the door to let me into the house. She was taking a bath. I was surprised that she came to the door naked but thought little of it. I also have a picture of her in a beautiful floral dress. She's standing on Washington Street next to a car parked in front of our house. The picture is black and white, but I visualize her dress's colors as black, gold and tan.

The final move for us was only one street over from Washington Street. We moved to 134 Page Street. It was a smaller house but a more modern one. It had indoor plumbing and an indoor bathroom with a bathtub. There was a small front and back porch. In the backyard was some kind of fruit tree, and further back, a canal crossed our yard and ended in a farmer's field a quarter of a mile away.

The summers were super-hot, and the winters were mild. One summer night, I was walking home from the store. A box of matches was one of the items that I had purchased. I stuffed the box of matches into my back pocket. I was wearing a pair of tight dungaree shorts. It was so hot that night that halfway home, the matches self-ignited in my back pocket.

Not knowing what happened, I took off running. What a scare. I must have run a half mile before I realized that I was not on fire and that no one was chasing me. Jesse Owens couldn't have caught me that night. Thankfully, I was not harmed, and the fire remained contained within the matchbox. Boy, was it hot.

A path ran from the recreation center to the canal behind our new home. The Faulks and the Hoopers had become our newest neighbors. The path ran beside each of their homes and stopped at the canal behind our house.

To cross the canal, people placed planks of wood across the shallowest section. The only other crossing option would have been to walk a half mile to the Fairmont Road which had been built over the canal. On the other side of the canal was a section of town referred to as "the Field." This neighborhood was known for its violence. I only knew of one family that lived in the field, the Moodys.

I remember one day riding in the car with Bill. Riding with us was a lady I did not know with a little girl about my age but younger. She must have been the lady's daughter. Anyway, her daughter and I were sitting in the backseat. Her daughter told me that she had a scar on her leg and asked me if I wanted to see it. I was completely indifferent but said okay.

Unashamed, she raises her dress to her waist to show me the scar on her upper thigh. I see her underwear and a big gash on her right thigh. I never asked her what happened. I was too embarrassed and tried not to look at it too hard. I thought one of us was going to get yelled at, and it probably would have been me, but nothing was said.

We dropped them off at the Moody's house. The Moody's were big-time boot-leggers, too. They lived in an area we referred to as the Field. I never went into the Field because I had heard of so many bad things happening there.

There were no street lights, so it was pitch black at night. You had to know where you were going, or you would get lost. It is said that people have been known to go into the Field at night and never come out. I heard that after dark, the police didn't go into that section, either.

One day, Bill told me a girl was coming by the house to see me. It may have been the same girl from the car; I'm not sure. I did not believe him at first, but then he convinced me that she was really coming. I refused to believe it and was both excited and scared.

I climbed this huge tree across the street from us. I climb almost to the top. I remember looking around while I was up there. I had never been so high in the sky before. I could see for miles. The girl did come with her mother. Bill had no idea where I was. I could see him calling for me. I didn't budge. I waited until they left, and then I climbed down. It was more scarier climbing down than it was climbing up.

After moving to Page Street, the Bostics moved into our vacated Washington Street address. This is when I met Clara Mae. She was the oldest of five children and about five or six years older than me. I was always at their house, which is how our friendship was forged. She kept us all in line.

I recall seeing her boyfriend, Preston, around, and I remember her first pregnancy. I didn't know then that they would eventually marry and have more children, just as I didn't know what my fate held for me. Together, we all played in the ditch, including Clara Mae. This was my new family: the Bostics, the Barnes and the Faulks.

Clara Mae's mother didn't like the fact that I would go fishing alone. She thought that it was too dangerous. One late afternoon, I was going fishing. She saw me and asked where I was going. I told her, "Fishing." She said, "Not by yourself. You go on back home; I will take you fishing with us tomorrow."

So, she started taking me with her. I remember one trip she took me to the power plant. It was literally the Robeson County Electric Company. The plant was located just off a section of the Lumber River.

There was a parking area but then you had to walk quite a distance to the river. I remember a lot of people fishing there. They would all be lined up along the water. I remember seeing men in small boats out on the river. Everybody was catching fish. The fish were all small, about the size of your hand. It was a lot of fun, and I wasn't on some river bank fishing all alone. I had plenty of company.

During another trip, we fished in a different section of the river. There was a flat wooden footbridge lying across the top of the river. It actually lay on top of the water. I had never seen anything like it before. You had to hold onto thick ropes on each side as you walked across. The water was moving quickly, which made the bridge sway.

It looked very scary. No one crossed it. I would have never crossed it on my own. The fishing was good. I fished along the edge of the river near the trees that were growing up out of the water. Those quiet places proved to be excellent fishing spots.

Page Street ended where the K&B road began and vice versa. At the juncture of these two roads was a curve. A very dangerous curve. The two roads (K&B and Page Street) were paved. Page Street was only about one-half mile long. On the other hand, Kenny and Biggs Road was probably more than five miles long and as straight as an arrow.

Cars would fly on this stretch of road. One evening, a car was travelling so fast that he blew through that curve and ripped the porch off of one of the houses. Thank God no one was on the porch at that time. This was not the first of such accidents on this curve.

Socially and economically, moving from Front Street was a step down for my mother and us. Each subsequent home was worse than the one before. However, this move to Page Street was different. It was several steps up for us for a few reasons.

She met and married William Powell. He was a soldier and was still active with the U.S. Army at that time. He was a Mess Sergeant stationed at Fort Bragg, N.C. His income and benefits were directly responsible for our uplift. As a result, the house that we moved into was much better than the others. The roof didn't leak, and we had indoor plumbing.

Aside from knowing William Powell's military stats, who was he? All I know is that he was a soldier and fought in Vietnam. I know nothing else about him. Where was he from? Who were his folks? Had he ever been married? Did he have any kids anywhere? How much did my mother know about him? We will never know.

Bill, as he preferred to be called, would take me to the Fort Bragg army base with him sometimes. It was very exciting. I remember once watching the 82nd Airborne Division practicing. Seeing them repel from helicopters and the different aircraft types was exciting.

We did our shopping at the PX. That's what the military grocery store was called. I remember life at this time being good. I remember eating dinner together as a family. For the first time since leaving Front Street, I felt loved and secure.

Bill would bring home food all of the time. I particularly remember the boxes of milk. It came in a large plastic bag inside a cardboard box with a rubber hose attached to it. The hose had a clip on it. The box would fit in the bottom of our refrigerator. I would lie on my back on the kitchen floor, put the hose in my mouth, unclip it and drink until I was content.

On Sunday mornings, although we were not in church, I remember hearing gospel music coming from the radio that sat on our dining room table. More than likely, it was blasting the sounds of either the Five Blind Boys of Alabama, the Dixie Hummingbirds, James Cleveland and the Angelic Choir or Mahalia Jackson. It would definitely be Sunday morning when you heard them.

One time, I heard the song, Don't Mess with Bill, by the Marvelettes, which had achieved popularity in the early to mid-1960s. He had convinced me that the song was about him, that he wrote it and that it was my mother singing it.

One time, on our way back home from Fort Bragg, he stopped at a friend's house. I sat in the living room watching television. This was my second time ever watching a television. I was glued to it. The show was The Twilight Zone.

A giant alien had invaded a small western town and terrorized a woman living there. The alien walked on top of houses and overturned cars. She reported all of this to the town sheriff, who drove out to her place to investigate.

Before the show ended, Bill was ready to go and I never got to see the ending. I never forgot that episode. Even as an adult, I would search for it. I did not know the name of the episode, and I only knew that it was from the Twilight Zone. Many years later, I found the episode and finally got to see the ending.

The sheriff found the alien standing in an open field. He shot it several times, after which the wind started to blow. However, the air was coming from the giant alien. Turns out, the alien was just a big, giant balloon because it was deflating. Supposedly, this is what walked on the roof of her house and left a huge fingerprint on the overturned police car. But how could that be if it were only a balloon? It doesn't make any sense. The episode ended with the now ever so familiar, "Welcome to the Twilight Zone."

I remember 134 Page Street well. It was smaller than the house we had moved from on Washington Street but more modern. From the front porch, you entered the living room. Opposite that to the left was the door to our parents' bedroom. Then, behind the living room was the dining area. Opposite that was a pot-belly stove in the middle of the house. I remember having to make the fire each morning during the winter.

It would be a layer of newspaper followed by a layer of kindling wood, then a layer of coal on top of that. I had to light the newspaper first. That stove had to heat the entire house, and it did, but barely. Slightly to the right of the stove was a cot against the far wall.

That's where Robert would sleep when he was home. Past that area was our bedroom and then the bathroom. There was no door to our bedroom. There was a bed on each side of the room.

Bernardette slept in one and me in the other. You had to walk through our bedroom to get to the bathroom.

Now that I think about it, I realize there were only four doors in the entire house. The front door, our parents' bedroom door, the bathroom door and the back door. To get to the back porch, you had to go through the kitchen. Comparatively speaking, it was a tiny house, as were all of our homes.

At some point, we got new neighbors. The Faulks remained, and this new family moved into the house on the other side. They had moved in from somewhere out in the country. The boy's name was Frankie, and the girl was named Connie. Their parents would dig a pit in their backyard, kill a hog, gut it, and roast it over an open pit. I was not used to seeing that. We lived within the city limits, and only country folk did stuff like that. Yeah, they were country.

Connie was a chubby girl. One day at school, she had a bad body odor that became obvious to everyone. Teachers were allowed to whip you in school. Connie did not have an assignment ready, so the teacher started to whip Connie with a strap.

The whippings took place in front of the class. Connie started jumping and running around in circles. The funk that came from her was fierce. The class never wanted Connie ever to get whipped again. It was very embarrassing for her and extremely offensive to us.

<u>Natural Causes</u>

The canal in our backyard was too wide to jump across. The section behind my house was maybe two or three feet deep. It was teaming with fish. I played in and around that canal a lot. It ran from the farm down to where it connected with the river again.

A section of it ran underneath the Fairmont Road. One day, while playing at that section, I stepped on a broken glass bottle. I sliced open my right bunion. I wrapped it with a rag or something, and it eventually stopped bleeding. Again, no hospital, no doctor.

Cyril White's café was the only black-owned restaurant I knew of. Her café was on Fairmont Road, right beside the canal. It had a long green counter with little round green stools that spun around. Opposite the stools were small cubicles.

There also used to be a nightclub next door to the café called the psychedelic shack. Walking by, if the door was open, you could see people dancing. It was a wooden structure with a dirt floor and a jukebox. It was much like the juke joint I used to watch Robert dance in at our cousin's house but much, much larger.

My best friend, Swindell and I caught a huge catfish once in that canal. We had to carry it home in a foot tub. Coot's canal was the most populous fishing area. There was a small candy store there called Coot's. This was at the intersection of Lovett Road and Chicken Foot Road. After a good rain, the water in the canal would rise, as did the river.

This would bring a lot of fish inland from the river. I've seen as many as fifteen to twenty people fishing along both sides of the road at the canal. If you followed and walked along Coot's canal, it was the shortest and most direct route to the Cutlar Moore Bridge from that point on. It was not a popular shortcut because the paths were very narrow and overgrown with bushes. Also, there were a lot of snakes and mosquitoes.

One evening, while walking, coming out from the canal, I stepped on the back of a snake. I was leaving the canal because it was getting dark. I was barefoot, and the grass was knee-high on each side of the path. I had to carefully watch each of my steps. I was putting one foot in front of the other. I was walking along carefully, watching the path, and as my next step was going down, I saw the snake. He was moving slowly across the path.

I could not see its' head or its' tail. It was too late to stop my foot from going down. I stepped on its' back and felt its' muscles curl up under my foot. I jumped sky-high and ran the rest of the way out to a clearing near the road. Another time, a snake fell out of a tree. It was a harmless green snake. Sometimes, people would walk around with them in their pockets. I was never one of those people.

An old lady by the name of Ms. Mamie J. started me fishing. She lived a few houses up from us on Page Street. She would take me fishing with her. I would carry the bait bucket and the hoe. I would use the hoe to dig for worms, which was also our defense against snakes. Ms. Mamie dipped snuff. She would always spit on her bait for good luck once it was on the hook.

At first, I would never fish. I would just dig for worms and assist Ms. Mamie. She would carry her own poles. She had four or five of them. They were called cane poles. I guess it's because they resemble sugarcane stalks. They grew all over the area. After cutting them down and stripping off the leaves, we would place them on the rooftops to dry out in the sun. Drying out made them tough and strong.

Freshly cut, they were all green, both the stalk and leaves, but they turned a brownish tan after being in the sun and drying out. She and I always fished at the Cutlar Moore Bridge. The fishing there was great. One morning, we went there, and I wanted to fish. I did not have a pole, and I thought, of course, she would lend me one of hers. I was wrong.

She gave me some fishing line, a hook and a sinker. She told me to find my own pole. I was surprised at her. That was not right. I remember finding a long limb. It was about half the length of her poles, but I still caught some fish.

I remember this particular tree that grew horizontally over the river for about five or six feet then started growing straight into the air. I always wanted to walk out on it, but it was covered with a lot of slippery green moss. I knew better than to try walking out on it. I always wondered what caused it to grow in such a unique way.

One day, while fishing in that same area, the water along the river's edge appeared to turn black. Hundreds, if not thousands, of baby catfish were swimming upstream. It was amazing. They were about an inch long, and all of them were jet black. It was so beautiful.

On the opposite side of the river, fish were jumping. Somehow, through the years, the river's flow encircled this small stripe of land and made it an island. I have never seen a person on it, and maybe once or twice, someone in a boat fished along its' edge. Overall, the state notes the Lumber River as a scenic river. It really is beautiful.

Another time, while fishing with Ms. Mamie, a thunderstorm arose suddenly. First, the wind started blowing very hard, then came the rain, followed by thunder and lightning. I was so afraid of getting struck by lightning or a falling tree. I left Ms. Mamie and ran to the nearest house. She was calling for me to come back to help her. She was a large old woman who waddled when she walked. She could not move very fast.

She wanted me to wait for her. I left her on the river bank as she was gathering her poles. The nearest house was about a quarter of a mile away. We used their yard as a shortcut to the bridge. I ran onto their porch. The people who lived there were at home but said nothing about being on their porches.

I'm sure they knew I was there because of the storm. Ms. Mamie finally caught up to me there. She was a mess and definitely not happy. Why didn't you wait for me, she demanded. I don't think that I said a word, but in my mind, the Lord was doing his work – I was supposed to be quiet.

Ms. Mamie had a nice brick house. I've never seen her use the front entrance to her home. The front of her home was almost entirely overgrown with shrubbery. She had pretty much confined her living to her bedroom near the back door. I always entered her house there. She once sent me to get something from her living room.

The living room had a fireplace, and her dining room was very nice. Everything was covered in plastic. Her kitchen appeared to be fully functional. She had all sorts of plates and glasses in all of her cabinets. I don't know if she had any children or was ever married. Years later, I'm told, she died from a fire in that same bedroom.

When it comes to fishing, Ms. Mamie had me hooked. I loved fishing, and I started going alone when she could no longer go. After the death of my mother, fishing became a means to feed the family. I would go after school and on Saturdays.

No one fished on Sunday. That was taboo. People just didn't do it. We were told that if you went fishing on Sunday, you would pull up the devil and go straight to hell. That was convincing enough for me not to go.

At the Cutlar Moore Bridge, I also learned how smart some fish really are. The Lumber River is designated as one of the natural and scenic wonders of the State of North Carolina. The water in that river has always reminded me of a bottle of Coke or Pepsi Cola. In the sunlight, it's lighter at the top and gradually darkens as you go down the bottle. It's the same with that river. The water appears to be clearer near the top and gradually darkens as the water deepens, and of course, that's due to less sunlight.

One day, I had a string of fish in the water. I noticed once in a while, they would start splashing around. When I looked at them, the restlessness would cease. I removed them from the water. I noticed that one of the fish had bite marks on it. It was bleeding. I put the fish back into the water. My intent was to wait until whatever it was to bite the fish again, and I would yank whatever it was out of the river.

The fish on the string was to my right, and my fishing rods were to my left. The sunlight also hit the water from my left, allowing me to see several feet below the surface. While looking at my rods as they hung out over the water, I noticed a pair of beady black eyes staring at me from under the water.

It was a large black fish. This black fish was watching me. I couldn't believe it. When I became distracted, it would swim over to my fish on the string and try to take one. Isn't that amazing?

So, I waited, pretending not to pay attention to my fish on the string. When they started flopping around again, I yanked them out of the water, pulling this large black fish still latched onto a fish with them. Wow!

That black fish knew to watch me when it was safe to approach the fish on the string. It also knew that the fish were tied up and could not escape. He would try to take one when he thought they were unattended.

The fish on the string also sensed danger because they tried to free themselves by flopping around. Absolutely amazing! Had I not observed this with my own two eyes, I would not believe it. Well, at least I learned that I could outsmart a blackfish.

From this experience, I began to look for some semblance in other forms of nature. I found it amongst trees. Trees try to give each other room to grow. They sense each other's presence and contort themselves into positions for the best growth, making decisions as to how best to survive.

Beside Ms. Mamie's house, there was an empty lot. It was overgrown with small trees, grass and straw. All of us loved to play in that lot. We called one of our activities "riding trees." We would climb any tall, skinny tree to the top. Then, at the top, we would rock back and forth in an attempt to get the tree to sway.

At the right moment, we would kick our legs out, hang from our arms and let our weight and gravity slowly bend the tree toward the ground. We would let it go when we got very close to touching the ground. It was also fun to watch the trees snap back into position, swaying back and forth. Then, we would start the climb all over again.

Life was better for us as a family on Page Street. I was doing ok in school. I attended W.H. Knuckles Elementary. It is a two-story brick building. Mr. Jones was a very popular teacher. He kept a Spaulding rubber ball on his desk at all times. If he caught you talking or not doing what you were supposed to, he threw that ball at you with all his might. He did not care where it hit you, and nearly all of the time, it would be a headshot.

After the death of my mom, I remember one comment made on my report card. It said 'Curtis is doing well however, he tends to daydream quite a bit.' I remember that comment, and it was true. Shortly after the death of my mother, school was no longer my priority; food was. I would be looking out of the window and be a million miles away from that classroom. Not sure of what exactly I was thinking about but you would have to agree, I had a lot to think about.

I had a pair of boots with taps on the heels. They were square-toed leather cowboy boots. The school hallways were covered with tile. Those metal taps against the tile floor made quite a noise. They could hear me coming from a mile away. They made me tip-toe whenever I had to leave the classroom.

The lunches at school were like dinners. We had fried chicken, collard greens, mashed potatoes, liver smothered in gravy, cabbage, string beans, corn, fish, cornbread, and so on. Not to mention a whole array of desserts.

Lunch was 15 cents a day, seventy-five cents for the week. You were given a lunch card with the days of the week perforated. You would have to tear off a stub each day.

I remember a boy named Calvin sold me his belt for 15 cents. Then he changed his mind and wanted it back. I refused to give it to him. He told the principal. The principal gave me 15 cents, and I gave Calvin back his belt. One day, Calvin removed his shirt for some reason. When he did, I saw his whole bare back.

My God! There wasn't one square inch of smooth skin on his back. I asked him why he was scarred-up so badly. He said that his parents would beat and hit him with any and everything. Belt buckles, sticks, bricks, pipes, etc., and whatever they could get their hands on at the time. I could not believe my eyes. I really felt sorry for him.

The smells of the early mornings were fresh and clean. It was that of wild flowers and freshly cut green grass. The silence and the peacefulness made early mornings special for me. Years later, the song, 'A Beautiful Morning,' became one of my favorite songs.

I liked getting to school early in the morning. Weather permitting, the boys would always play marbles. I was pretty good. The girls would stand around and watch. You always wanted to impress them or at least one of them.

The summer heat could, at times, be almost unbearable, especially around noon. I don't think there was an air conditioner in my entire school. Air conditioner, you say, what is that? I remember Stacey Mae. She fainted once in class. I cried. I thought she had died.

Sometimes, it would get so hot that the heat waves coming from the paved roads looked like water on the road's surface in the distance. Sometimes, the paved roads would get so hot you could not walk on them with your bare feet.

<u>Natural Causes</u>

I remember "health day" at W.H. Knuckles elementary. I had two teachers, Mrs. Thompson and Ms. Best. They were checking the students to see if they had on clean underwear. Ms. Best checked me. Each boy had to unzip their pants, and she would, with a ruler, part your zipper and look. I did not have any underwear on that day. She laughed and called Mrs. Thompson over to also take a look.

They both had a good laugh. Needless to say, I was mortified. I think about how traumatizing that must have been for me. It was certainly a form of abuse. I never forgot that.

As an adult I wanted to confront Ms. Best about that experience. I wanted to check her underwear to see if her underwear were clean. I learned from Mr. Jones that she had left that school district years earlier. I really wanted to let her know how that affected me.

Down the road from the school was the Lumberton recreational center. It was a good place for kids to gather after school. There were games, indoor basketball, ping pong tables, etc. Outside, you had swing sets, monkey bars and other stationary toys.

There was also a baseball field. The home plate area was nicely fenced in, and there were sets of bleachers to the right of home plate. One summer, I joined the little league. I played the center field position. At one game, someone hit a fly ball to center field. I was backing up, ready to make the catch, and I tripped over a clump of dirt. Of course, I missed the ball. I was laughed at and booed.

My friends, the Barnes, felt so bad for me. After the game, when we got close to my house, they hoisted me up onto their shoulders. They made it seem as if my team won the game, or I at least caught the ball. It was all done so that Bill would be proud of me and to make me feel better about myself. I'm not sure if that impressed anyone at all, except me.

I remember that time of my life. I needed attention and sought his. Home life was in shambles, and I needed to belong to someone. I remember starving for attention. At one time, and for a very short time, I thought about setting the Hooper's house on fire. It really scares me to think that I seriously considered doing something like that. I could have become an arsonist. My God!

The Barnes filled that void. I began hanging around them a lot and had no fear. They had become my protectors along with the Bostics.

One Saturday morning, I was there for baseball practice. An Indian boy had his pony there. It was a pinto color – brown and white. He let me pet him. He was racing his pony up and down the field. On one of those runs, the pony stepped into a hole and broke its leg.

Natural Causes

I remember the pony falling and getting up but being unable to walk. The kid was crying, saying that his father was going to have to put the horse down. I did not know then what that meant. It meant that his father would have to kill it. I was not around for that.

One day, Bill was going to give me a whipping for something that I did or did not do. I now have no idea which one it was. I decided that I could outrun him. So, I took off running. He caught me so quickly that it made my head spin. I remember the size of the muscles in his legs. That was not a wise decision on my part, nor did I ever try to outrun him again.

When our mother was alive, Bill would check my homework daily after school. One day at school, my friend Carl and I discovered carbon paper and what it could do. We placed the carbon sheet in my notebook and started writing all the bad curse words we could think of. That night, while checking my homework, Bill comes across this sheet.

I had forgotten all about it. What's this he asked. I blamed my friend Carl. Bill said, ok, let's go. He made me show him where Carl lived. He knocked on the door. Carl's father answered the door. Bill introduced himself and stated what I had told him. Carl's father called Carl to the door. Carl blamed me, and I blamed Carl. I got a whipping all the way back home. Life was good back then.

One evening during dinner, Bill cut some fresh green pepper over his rice. I asked for some. He said you won't like this. I said that I still wanted some. He cut some for me and put it on my rice. After tasting it, I did not like it. He made me eat every morsel. Bill was an excellent cook. He used to make a dish called cornmeal mush. I loved that dish.

One time, we had gone to visit someone far away. We drove there. On the trip back home, crossing a long bridge, the wind blew the car sideways a little, and I screamed. He yelled at me and called me a little girl.

My mother took exception to that and said to him that I was frightened and that I was just a little boy. He was visibly annoyed.

As far as I know, my mother never worked outside of the home. She was always there. I had very little interaction with my sister. She was too small to follow me around, and I was always out of the house. Bernardette was always left at home with my mom.

I have very sparse memories of any direct interactions with my mother. I remember her always being around but never being there. I was never lonely, but I was always mostly alone, especially when hunting or fishing.

Our mother, Mrs. Phodie Elizabeth Powell, died at the age of 38. At the time of her death, I, Curtis White, was ten years old, and my sister, Bernardette White, was six years old. Some years later, when I became a young adult, I obtained a copy of my mother's death certificate. Where it says, **Cause of Death:** this is what is written. "Apparently Died Suddenly Due to Natural Causes – No Physician attended her prior to Death." The year and date - July 6, 1965.

How does one die suddenly of natural causes at age 38? It happens maybe at age 98 or 108, even 88, but not at age 38. And for the record, my mother had never been sick.

The night before she "died," I was at home. Someone was in her bedroom with her. It was a man, and I believe that man was William Powell, our stepfather. I could barely hear his voice. I heard her quietly pleading. No, Bill, don't do that. There was no arguing or scuffling. I could barely hear them. What she was asking him not to do, I'm not sure of. At some point, I heard him leave. I finally fell asleep.

At daybreak, my mother summoned me. She had removed herself from her bedroom. She was now lying on the couch in the living room. Bill was not there. Curtis, she said in a very calm voice. Go tell Ms Baker to come take me to the hospital, I'm sick.

It was very early in the morning, just after the break of dawn. Ms. Baker lived on Washington Street, one street over from us. Her house was very near to the Fairmont Road. I knocked on the door and window several times. No one responded. I was unable to wake anybody up, so I returned home.

In my absence, someone had called an ambulance. I say that because, shortly after returning home, one arrived. I'm not sure at what point she passed. As far as I know, she may have died while I was gone. I remember her being put into the ambulance.

Mrs. Phodie Elizabeth Powell, my mother, died sometime later that morning or that day. The next time I saw her, she was in a casket. I didn't know what to do with the information I had overheard the night before. So, I did nothing with it. The coroner said she had "apparently died suddenly due to natural causes," but I knew better.

Her funeral was held at Sandy Grove Baptist Church. I remember Bill holding our hand as we walked down the center aisle approaching her casket. His left hand held mine, and his right hand held Bernardette's. I remember looking into her casket. While staring at her face, she winked at me. I was amazed. I could not believe it.

As Bill pulled us away from her casket, I struggled to look back at her again. I was crying, trying to look back to make sure that's what I saw. I was dragged reluctantly back to my seat. There was no doubt in my mind that she had winked at me. And now, some sixty years later, I maintain that she had winked at me. In the twinkling of an eye, she winked at me.

Philip Yancey states that **"The Spirit of God has resources of sensitivity beyond those of even the wisest mother. Paul says that Spirit lives inside us, detecting needs we cannot articulate and expressing them in a language we cannot comprehend. When we don't know what to pray, he fills in the blanks. Evidently, it is our very helplessness that God, too, delights in. Our weakness gives opportunity for his strength. Now, the Holy Spirit lives inside us as a personal seal of God's presence."**[7]

I've only dreamed about my mother once since her death. Bernardette and I were playing in the front yard at 134 Page Street. I looked up and saw her walking toward us. She was coming down Page Street, walking along the road's edge.

I jumped up and started screaming mama, mama. I was so happy to see her. As she approached us, she told me, I just came back to let you know everything will be all right. She never came into the yard. She just kept walking past us and the house until she faded away.

At this time Bill had either retired from the Army or was kicked out, I'm not sure which. We no longer went to the PX out at

---

[7] Philip Yancey, Where is God When It Hurts? (Zondervan 1990), 236

Fort Bragg. He began drinking heavily. I would come home from school and find him sprawled out on the floor.

I remember having to step over his body. Careful not to step on him, not that he would have known the difference. I have no idea who was looking after Bernardette. She had not started school yet. She would be left at home alone with Bill or perhaps across the street with the Hoopers.

Things turned ugly fast. We began to run out of food quickly. I would go fishing and I would clean them and fry them. My fish fed all of us. Bill would eat more than we did. I would also hunt birds. I remember this time when I killed a white swan on a canal that ran beside McMillan Funeral Home. The current kept it in the middle of the stream. I was praying that it would drift to the edge so I could get it.

I remember running beside the canal as far as I could, hoping it would eventually come close enough to the edge for me to grab it. It stayed in the middle and never drifted to either side. It was dead. I had killed it. I watched it, with its head slumped over until it floated completely out of my sight.

I was so disappointed. That bird would have made a great meal for days. We ate a lot of birds – cherry birds, blue jays, robins, pigeons and sparrows. It was against the law to kill the North Carolina state bird, the all-red cardinal.

Natural Causes

In addition to hunting birds with my bb gun, I would prop up a flat board with a stick. I tied a string around the stick and put some cornmeal under the board. The string had to be long enough to bring into the house. This was during the winter. We would watch the board from the living room window. We were out of sight, and the birds would go under the board to eat the cornmeal.

I would yank the stick away. The board would fall on the birds. They all tasted really good. I would clean them and fry them. The robins were the best because they had sweet meat. Trying to make a meal out of them was tough because they were so small.

A lot of the kids had bb guns. One day, we started shooting at one another. We were playing at a friend's house over on Main Street. One of the Blue brothers peeked around the corner of his house and was shot right between the eyes. This scared us enough never to play that game again.

I remember one morning. We had absolutely nothing to eat. I went to our neighbor, Mrs. Faulk. It was early in the morning. She had about thirteen kids herself to feed. She answered the door. I told her that we were hungry and had nothing to eat.

With sadness in her eyes, she said wait here. After a few minutes, she returned to the door with two hard biscuits. She said if you put some water on them and heat them up, they will be fine. She had nothing else to give me. I thanked her. I think a lot of people thought that because Bill was in the house, we were okay. We were not okay. We were starving.

If someone offered me a meal, I would take it. Swindell became my best friend. His mother would always make room for me in the morning at breakfast. Like the Faulks, she had a lot of children, too. They all sat on a long bench. Each morning before school I knew that I could always get breakfast there. She would say, ok, everybody scooch over a little and make room for Curtis. She was an angel.

Theirs' was a big house. It was black and white and sat on the corner of Page Street and the Fairmont Road. It used to be a funeral home. The outhouse sat in the backyard as far as it could from the road. The boys would always go out there to masturbate. It was a good location for that because you had a 360-degree view through the cracks between the boards. You could always see if someone was coming. Outhouses were still fairly common back then.

During the spring and summer, I would take food from people's gardens. Sometimes, it would just be me, a box of salt, and a field of tomatoes or cucumbers. I also picked berries, strawberries, blueberries and blackberries. Those I would sell. Fifty cents a jar. Pecans were only available in the Fall.

I would also sell the fish that I caught from time to time. I would accept whatever was offered, fifty cents or seventy-five cents. It would never be more than a dollar. The exchange would go something like this: hey, son, how much for that string of fish you got there, boy? I'll give you seventy-five cents for 'em. I never negotiated. I didn't know that I could, especially with an adult, nor did I know how to. Whatever was offered, I accepted. It wouldn't be the last time I failed to negotiate something better for myself.

One day, I came into the house. It was very hot outside, and I was very thirsty. I opened the refrigerator. It had one jar in it, which held a clear liquid. Of course, I thought it was a jar of cold water. I grabbed it and took one big gulp. It was corn liquor. I got sick to my stomach.

I placed it back and looked for something else, anything else. The refrigerator was completely empty, nothing in the freezer, nothing on the door, nothing anywhere. Not even an ice tray. I remembered the days not too long ago when our mother was still alive. Our refrigerator was full and overflowing with military milk and honey.

Directly across the street from us lived the Hoopers. Several kids lived there with an old Indian woman. Their house was twice the size of ours. It sat high off the ground and had a nice front porch with a swing on it. The back porch was very small. It had a lot of wood and boxes of newspapers on it. I had been inside their house a few times.

What I remember most was the night I turned on the light in their kitchen. When I turned on that light, I must have seen a thousand roaches. Huge ones, medium-sized ones, small ones. They were dark brown, light brown and blonde colored.

I had never seen so many roaches before in my life. It was as if the floor moved. I wondered how they could eat anything in that house. I guess we didn't have roaches like that because we didn't have anything for them to eat.

Debbie, one of the girls who lived there, became one of Bernardette's best friends. She also had a younger sister and an older brother. Old lady Hooper had funny color eyes and long, stringy black and gray hair. She also dipped snuff. Dipping snuff was very common among women.

Snuff came in small round tin containers. Snuff users would deposit a pinch of snuff into either corner of their lower lip. Needless to say, it made your teeth and gums look horrible. Most of the old ladies I knew dipped snuff, like Miss Mamie. For men, the nicotine habit was chewing tobacco or smoking cigarettes.

One day, while playing at home in my room, my raised window slipped out of place and came crashing down on one of my fingers. I was leaning out of the window. Both of my hands were across the bottom. When the window slipped, I yanked my hands back as fast as possible.

The bottom of the window slammed down on the pinky finger of my right hand. The tip of that finger nearly came off. The skin and fingernail had all been peeled back. I could see what I thought was the bone. Someone got old lady Hooper from across the street.

She got an old black felt hat that had spider webs on it. She took a small knife and scraped away some of the felt along with some of the spider web. She stuffed it under my nail and into my flesh. She pulled the skin and fingernail back over it.

Then she poured a blue liquid from a jar on it. There was a bee floating in this blue liquid. It did burn a little. Finally, she wrapped it really tight with some string. She told me not to take the string off. It took a long time for it to heal, but it did, beautifully. The cob-web and felt were never removed.

The window pane was shattered. I'm sure Bill could not afford to have the window repaired and he didn't. So, he boarded it up. He nailed narrow strips of wood across that section of the window. One night, while in one of his drunken episodes, someone tried to break into the house through that window.

The person started pulling the boards down. My bed was right next to that window. I remember hearing the first board snap and seeing that person's fingers wrap around the next board. Screaming, I ran to Bill, trying to wake him up. Shaking and calling his name did no good. He would not get up from the floor. Thank God, hearing me trying to wake him up, the person ran off.

We did have a rifle in the house. It was kept somewhere on the back porch. Bill told me when I was eleven that the rifle would be given to me on my twelfth birthday. He also carried a handgun. He showed it to me. It had a pearl handle. One day, I found some bullets.

I lined them along the edge of our front porch. With my bb gun, I started shooting the back of the bullets to make them fire. Stupid, stupid, stupid, me. One bullet fired, and the cap from it flew back and hit a bone on the side of my left wrist. I didn't believe anything was broken and wrapped it as best I could. There was a lot of blood and no doctor. God protects who, fools and babies.

One morning, Bill drove to the store. He took me with him. The store was Cash & Carry on the Fairmont Road. For some reason, and it was probably because he was drunk, he told me to drive home. I could not have been more than ten or eleven years old. I got behind the wheel.

<u>Natural Causes</u>

I drove down the Fairmont Road, made a lefthand turn onto Page Street, and headed home. All of a sudden, I see a police car behind me with its lights on. I pull over onto the side of the road. This was the same area of Page Street where my dog Queenie was run over.

Having stopped, I had to now put the car into the park position. I moved the gear shifter from drive to park stopping at each gear in between without my foot being on the brake. When I reached reverse, the car backed up a little and hit the front of the police car.

I forgot to keep my foot on the brake. Bill told the officer that he was teaching me how to drive. The office said that I was doing a fine job, except they could not see anyone behind the steering wheel. The police officer chuckled. He told Bill that he had to drive home, and they let us go.

The largest houses in Lumberton were located on the Fairmont Road. Two of the very large homes were originally funeral homes. Those were the Doug McMillan and the Shaw Funeral Homes. Swindell's family moved into the latter.

Swindell and I became friends after my mother passed. The Fairmont Road was busy back then. Lumberton had two prominent black churches, Sandy Grove Baptist Church and First Baptist Church. First Baptist was at the northern end of the Fairmont Road, and Sandy Grove was near the southern end. If you wanted to be seen, the Fairmont Road was the place to go.

Sunday afternoons were the best. I enjoyed standing on Swindell's stoop and watching the people and the cars go by. I remember having gotten this new paisley shirt. It was dark brown with small tan and purple swirls on it.

It was also short-sleeved and came to a v-point in the front and back. I was so proud of that shirt. I would stand proudly on Swindell's front porch and pray that someone would notice me and say something about my shirt. No one ever did. I just wanted to be noticed and acknowledged.

I often think about that time in my life and how lonely I must have been. How eager I was to have someone acknowledge me. Someone to validate me, someone to notice me. How vulnerable I must have been, but by the grace of God, I survived.

Swindell and I would play this game. Each of us would take a different side of the Fairmont Road. One side was travelling East, and the other side cars were travelling West. Whichever side had the most out-of-state license plates would win. New York plates and Florida plates were the favorites.

I was extremely independent. In retrospect, after my mother died, I had little to no parental guidance. At eleven years old, I did pretty much whatever I wanted to do. I was always with the Barnes' children. I spent most of my time with them. We become almost like a gang. I didn't realize it then, but my independence was beginning to get a little out of hand, and it was just a matter of time before I got into some real trouble.

One night out at the recreation center, this older boy was teasing me about my mother dying. I told my friends, the Barnes, about it. We circled him at one section of the field. We started beating him up. He was on the ground hollering.

We had him surrounded, and I wanted to get my licks in. I was wearing my square-toed leather cowboy boots. The ones that had the taps on them. I found an opening, drew my foot back, and kicked as hard as I could into the middle of the circle.

We heard this gut-wrenching scream come from him. We all knew that something bad had happened. Everybody backed away. He was lying on the ground in a fetal position, holding his face. We all ran and left him there on the ground. I'm not sure how much time elapsed after that before Bernardette, and I were moved to New York. I never knew what became of the guy that I kicked.

After becoming a young adult, one summer, I was home visiting. I went to the candy store on the Fairmont Road. There was a man beside me at the counter. I noticed that he had a huge keloid between his eyes. Was this the same person I helped beat up that night at the recreation center?

I don't even remember who it was, but I bet this was the guy. With a scar like that, it had to be him. For a moment, I thought about asking him about his scar. I thought better of that idea and said nothing. Wow, but I'm sure it was him.

One late summer night, I was near the recreation center with some friends. The center was located just outside the property line of the Lumbee Homes and a short distance from the Dr. Knuckles Elementary School. My friends and I were somewhere between the two and noticed a pair of headlights at the end of the road. As we moved closer we could see that the driver of that vehicle was not in it and had left his door open. Whoever the driver was, also did not take the time to turn his motor off. He left the car on and running.

As we walked toward the headlights, I saw a man kneeling in front of the car. Another man was standing over him. He was repeatedly punching the man on his knees in the face. The man on his knees was semi-conscious and wobbling. The man standing over him would not let him fall to the ground.

He would steady him with his left hand to keep him from falling to the ground and punch him with his right fist with all of his might. Someone yelled for him to stop. He said no, he pulled a gun out on me. With each punch, blood would fly everywhere. His face was a mess. He was bleeding from his mouth, eyes, nose and lips. That man probably beat him to death.

There was no one there who could stop him from punching the other man. We stayed there until the police arrived. They cuffed the man doing the punching, and then we all walked away as the other man lay face down on the ground, waiting for an ambulance. We were not sure if he was dead or alive as we moved on.

Our favorite swimming hole was in a small lake called Dr Kings. It was back up in the woods. It was a pretty place. The water in the area where we would swim was clear to the bottom. Bright pebbles and sand covered that section of the lake bottom, so you could see your feet. We always swam naked. No one had any swimming trunks. One day, a group of us were swimming. Two native American men came to the lake.

They were drunk or at least had been drinking. They started firing their pistols into the air. They ordered us out of the water. When we came out, they started shooting at our feet, telling us to run. We ran into the woods, stark naked.

As we were running, I noticed, for the first time, that all of the trees were the same. They were all pine trees, and the pine nettles that covered the ground were soft but slippery. We hid behind the trees and waited for them to leave. After they left, we went back, gathered our clothing and headed home.

To get to Dr. Kings, we would walk along a truck path at the edge of this nearby farm. This was the same farm the canal in my backyard ran to. We had to walk past a watermelon patch before branching off into the woods.

One day, returning from the lake, one of the older boys decided to crack open some watermelons. He would pick one up and slam it to the ground. Nope, he would say, this one ain't ready. He would pick up another one and do the same thing.

The farmhouse we could see was about a half mile away. Right behind us was a really small center block house. It had no windows, and we weren't sure what purpose it served. It did have what appeared to be electrical wires running into it.

We see a pickup truck and a cloud of dust speeding down the other side of the farm, heading towards us. We didn't think much of it. Walley, the oldest boy, had stopped busting open melons. The truck speeds past us and comes to an abrupt stop.

A white man jumped out. He has a blackjack in his hand. He grabbed Wally and hit him over his right eye. I was the littlest one in the group. I ran far out into the field to my left. My friend Swindell ran around the truck through a briar patch on the right. The farmer reached for him. He grabbed him but could not hold on to him. Swindell defecated all over himself but kept it moving.

We all got away. We teased Swindell all the way home. Walley got an instant knot on his forehead. I don't think that knot ever went away. Other than that, we were all ok. The farmer, apparently satisfied that he had taught us a lesson, turned his truck around and returned home. Thank God that farmer didn't bring a gun with him.

Once, while hunting I came upon a real log cabin. Unless you were right up on it, you would have missed it. It was deep in the woods and covered by all the plant growth. I found it to be fascinating. I went inside. I was careful not to touch anything. It was one large room with a dirt floor. I could see where the fireplace had been. Plenty of sunlight was filtering through the hundreds of cracks between the logs.

I could see how the logs were cut and fitted together. Hardly any of the filler between the logs was left. I did not see any utensils at all. Yes, it was both dangerous and foolish for me to have gone in alone. After all, one wrong move and it could have all collapsed on top of me. I probably would have never been found.

In the fall, the farmer would allow us to fly our kites on his land. The only hazard was the high-tension power lines that ran across his field. I was taught how to make a kite without using any glue or staples. First, you had to get the right sticks. You only needed two of them, and they had to be strong but hollow. You would put one stick across the other to form a cross and bind them together with straw. This was now your frame.

Place your frame on a few large pages of newspaper. Fold the newspaper to cover the frame. Use very small twigs to pin the newspaper to the frame. Toothpicks would be perfect for this if you had any. If not, wood splinters worked just as fine. For the tail, we would use very narrow strips of cloth taken from old rags, sheets or pillowcases.

The cloth from the towels was much too heavy. One day, I flew my kite so high I thought migrating birds would hit it. I almost ran out of twine. The wind was blowing away from the high-tension lines. It was the perfect day to fly a kite.

This was the segregated South. Pre-1965. Pre-civil rights movement. At this point, nearly every moment of my life had taken place on the south side of the railroad tracks. Every person that I'd interacted with was either black, white or native American.

My teachers, preachers, doctors and local store owners. Black people owned gardens but not farms. We owned candy stores but not department stores. We owned fields of land but rarely acres of land. White people did not live on my side of town. Most of the Native Americans lived out in the country.

<u>Natural Causes</u>

The downtown Lumberton area consisted of 2 movie houses, 1 courthouse, 1 jailhouse, 1 trailway bus station, 1 gas station and various other stores and shops. As you walked around, it was common to see signs that read: Whites Only or "No Niggers Allowed" or Negros enter through the rear. All store owners and shop owners were White and quick to remind you of your place in their world.

The only time that I would go into town was on Saturdays. On Saturday we got to go to the movies practically free. You needed to have six Pepsi cola bottle caps to get in. Pepsi was king on Saturdays. We had two movie houses. The Carolina Theatre and the Riverside Theatre.

Blacks were only allowed in the Carolina movie house. I say that because it was the only one, we ever went to. Negros had to use the side entrance, and we were only allowed to sit up on the balcony. We were not even allowed to enter the main lobby.

A separate entrance for blacks was located on the side of the building. You had to walk up a long flight of steps to reach the balcony. I remember looking down from the balcony onto their bubbling soda fountains, glass-enclosed candy counters and voluminous popcorn machines. Everything was so fresh, polished and sparkling clean.

On the other hand, the black and brown people were served from cardboard boxes. Our candy counter was a big brown cardboard box. Our sodas, as well as our popcorn and cotton candy, were pre-poured and pulled from a big brown cardboard box. We should have been thankful that they even let us see the movie.

However, the movies that were shown were great. King Kong, the original, was everyone's favorite. Tarzan was another favorite. After the movie we would all drift back over the bridge and back across the railroad tracks – to where they told us we belonged. Where we chose to live without having been given a choice.

At night, from our house on Page Street, you could see the glow of the tall ballfield lights at the recreation center. It was an indication that a game was going on. I would always go. Not so much to observe the game but to play with my friends.

I was always gone. I was this skinny kid who could be found just about anywhere and at just about any time. It's said that God takes care of babies and fools. I think that I was a lot of both.

My mother had a brother named Lafayette. He was very dark like me and Bernardette and he lived on the other side of the Fairmont Road. He had enlisted in the Army when he was younger. When he was honorably discharged, he started his own business. He was a sign maker. He made signs for all kinds of businesses. I heard he was a gifted artist.

He got married after returning home from the Army. It was reported that his wife tried to poison him. There should be an article about it in the black magazine Jet. She failed to poison him, and they ended up getting a divorce. I never learned any more about it.

Growing up, I never remember seeing my Uncle Lafayette and my mother together. I was allowed to visit him but I never remember ever seeing him at our house, at any time. Whenever he would see me and Bernardette, he would grab us and rub his face against ours. The hairs on his face felt like steel wool bristles. We would holler and squirm to get down. That made him laugh out loud.

I had been in Lafayette's house only once, which may have been after his death. There was a screened-in front porch. All the furniture in his bedroom was dark, solid, polished cherrywood. In the master bedroom there was a huge and hideous portrait of himself over his bed. I have the feeling that he did that portrait himself. That alone said a lot about him.

The furniture in his living room was marble and majestic red cherry hardwood. Everything was very masculine. There was a study, a kitchen and then a back porch. Behind his house in his backyard, he had a much smaller house built. Our Aunt Eva lived there.

There was also a huge pecan tree back there. When I was a little boy, I would visit her from time to time. She would encourage me to take some pecans home. Her house had no electricity in it. Everything was done by candlelight. I remember her being really, really old.

Then there was Aunt Anna, her sister. She lived in a house a few streets over from Lafayette. Aunt Anna raised chickens. She would have a black kettle of boiling water in her backyard. She would grab a chicken by the neck and wring it off in two seconds flat.

I remember seeing chickens run around her backyard without heads. She would throw them into that kettle of boiling water. This made it easier to remove the feathers. We would have fried chicken not too long after that. Her cornbread was flat and hard.

One very early morning, I was coming home from one of their houses with my dog Queenie. There were hardly any vehicles on the roads. Queenie and I crossed the Fairmont Road and turned onto Page Street shortly after.

A powder-blue pick-up truck also turned onto our street. Queenie was on one side of the street, and me on the other. I called to her to come beside me. As she crossed the street to join me, the truck driver sped up and ran her over. I could not believe it.

I looked up at the back of the pickup truck as he sped away. I could see that it was a white man. He had a big grin across his face as he looked back over his shoulder through his rear window. There were no witnesses. Queenie was still alive but badly injured.

Crying, I picked her up and carried her the rest of the way home. She died hours later. I buried her in our backyard by the canal.

One afternoon, in front of our house, something weird happened. It appeared as if there was a large crack in the sky. People were gathering near the end of Page Street just past our house to look at this "crack" in the sky. The sky was a beautiful blue with no clouds anywhere. It was as if the sky had been sliced open with a very sharp knife.

On the inside, it was pitch black. The crowd watched this opening for a long time. It never moved or changed position. Nothing ever went into it or came out of it. Eventually, it just closed up, and that was it. I am not sure what happened or why it happened. I never heard anyone talk about it, but that's not to say it didn't happen.

Sometimes, I used to lie down in a field and look up at the sky. I would occasionally see a plane. They were so high in the sky, leaving thin lines of white smoke behind them. I would always wonder where they were going. Similarly, years later, I would question thin lines of white lights at night. These would be the headlights of cars streaming along the FDR Drive in New York City.

My Field of Dreams

Clothed in my field of dreams, lying horizontal to the world, straw twig held, between my teeth,

as I glare up into the silence. My thoughts cancel each other out, though not random at all.

A lone plane you see, I see, streak across this deep blue sea. Beyond my touch, but within my reach,

it unapologetically crosses my cone. Leaving behind thin white lines inviting my eyes, to a place unknown.

As time expired, and death transpired, I bolted up-right to see where I was headed.

My mother foretold what my future would hold, no details she shared with me.

Having gotten my attention and with no further mention, she moved on to a

destination unclear. Would she need wings to return or be self-propelled, within her new atmosphere.

Natural Causes

I had arrived at a place that demanded a pace, much faster than what I had been living.

Headlights alight, on an East River drive, that could never remind me of home.

I had landed on a rock, skipping across waters that promised a new beginning.

But, when I was submersed, all of my worse acts began to melt away.

Now my view was of a different hue, with blinders long removed.

I could see ships and boats and miracles up close, even on the waters of the Hudson.

But, behind that screen was an ungodly scene, of people who could not be trusted.

They were full of dope with little hope, being led to a path of total destruction.

With my eyes now closed, and my hands folded, I searched again that deep, blue, sea.

79

Natural Causes

I could see unveiled to me, highways and subways,
concrete and steel and people sealed, with the Holy Ghost.

I saw bright lights and experienced a wondrous zeal, felt by
different persuasions.

I heard of a Man, who never once conceded, And His name
alone, was just as strong. He was just what I

needed. Running my race, at such a fast pace, I risked
leaving a lot on the table. But what I've unclothed, in

My field of Dreams is that, this Man is fully able. Far from
home, but never alone, He will never leave you forsaken.

By Curtis White

At some point, Bill met a lady, and she came to live with us. Her name was Ms. Mert, and she had two little boys, Vincent and Duckie. They slept in my bedroom. The two of them shared a bed. If you wet the bed Bill would give you a whipping.

Duckie used to get a whipping almost every morning. He was the youngest. I could see in Duckie's face that he was confused and not quite believing that it was him who had peed in the bed.

One morning, I was awake early but had not gotten up yet. Vincent was also awake. He did not know that I was not asleep. I

80

saw him dragging his brother Duckie onto the wet spot of the bed, where he had peed. So, Duckie was not the one peeing in bed, after all, it was Vincent. I never exposed him. They did not stay with us long. I'm not sure why, but I don't think it had anything to do with bed-wetting.

Then, a lady named Ms. Alice came to live with us. She had bow legs and wavy hair. There were no kids with her. However, she enjoyed drinking alcohol, too. She drank a lot of beer. I remember her speaking to someone about Bernardette.

I was looking at her as she said to that person, "This girl is messed up on the inside about this much." She touched her thumb to the first joint of her index finger, indicating about an inch.

Extending her arm and shaking her hand, she repeated the words, about this much. I wasn't sure about what she meant by messed up. By her expression, though, I knew that it was something bad and it had to do with her private parts.

How bad I didn't know. I also didn't know if she did anything about it. Robert, at this time, was living in New York. Was he responsible? He was the only one that I suspected. Bill was always home drunk. Perhaps he did it. It could have been anybody or several people.

Conditions were perfect for this kind of abuse to occur. There was no parental supervision; she was all alone behind closed doors with an alcoholic. The house was always a mess, and things were just chaotic, all the time.

Not to mention, I was abused outside our home before any of this took place. Bernardette was a prime target for any sexual predator. She didn't stand a chance.

Alice confirmed what I had always suspected. So, what now? Alice moved in and was now our new "Mom." Things didn't change much for me. That summer I had gotten sick and was apparently running a fever. I remember Alice literally rolling me up in an army wool blanket in the middle of the summer. This, she said, "will break your fever." Those Army wool blankets were no joke.

They were greenish-brown in color, fairly thin, but super warm. No heat escaped them, and no cold penetrated. I remember actually thinking that this woman was trying to kill me. I wiggled and squirmed until I finally broke free from it.

I'm not sure if it broke my fever or not, but I nearly passed out. I guess it worked. However, I never trusted her again after that. There was a home remedy for everything. Everything except child abuse.

<u>Natural Causes</u>

We were not taken to the doctor for anything. Dr. Roberson was the only black medical doctor on our side of town. I was in his office once. I remember being all alone, sitting on a bench in his waiting room. I believe I was there to get a shot. For what, I don't remember.

However, I do remember a school trip once to some kind of health facility, but no one declared it health day. After arriving, we never went inside the facility. They made us line up outside and no one was checking to see if we had on clean underwear.

We had to open our mouths as we filed past a white nurse who placed a sugar cube onto our tongues. Part of this sugar cube was pink. I assumed that it was a pink drop of medicine. I remember them saying how important it was for us to have this; every kid got it.

I remember the summer Robert came home to tell us that we would live with Aunt Louise in New York. We had a cat named Tang-Tang. Because Robert didn't like cats, he took Tang-Tang away from us.

He drove her out into the country and let her go. He had no right to do that, and it let me know how little he thought of us. It was just another reason for me not to like him.

We cried and were upset with him for having done this. Approximately a week later I heard a faint cry of a cat under our house. It was Tang-Tang. She managed to find her way back home. She was emaciated, but she survived. I cried and hated Robert even more.

I had a large boil on the back of my right thigh. I had it for a while. It just kept getting bigger. Ms. Alice or whoever stayed with us then would put a slice of raw potato on it. She said that it would help bring the boil to a head.

My leg began to draw up. I could not straighten my leg out. The boil was about the size of a golf ball. Robert said, before we go to New York we have to take care of this boil.

I remember him running very hot water into the bathtub. He made me sit in the tub of hot water and stretch my leg all the way out. This took a while because the water was really hot. I gradually sank my lower body into the water and fully extended my right leg. After several minutes, the boil popped.

I recall the warmth of the water and the relief from the pain. There was blood and pus in the water. My leg felt so much better. He put bandages around my thigh. I could walk again, with a limp but not a hop. I never saw a doctor. It, too, healed on its own, leaving an indentation on the back of my thigh.

We did not go to church. God was oblivious to me. I vaguely remember experiencing Sunday School at all. I now think, Lord, you made me, and after the fall of Adam and Eve, you never made me less. My mother loved me, but how did I not know that, for at the same time, Jesus was loving me, and I did not know that, either.

As I now think about that time, I write:

<u>Lord, I Found You</u>

God, I was not searching for You. However, through Your
divine plan,

I found You. I don't remember being called down through
the cosmos,

All to settle down in the womb of the woman you'd chosen
to be my Mary.

However, having set all things in motion, You ordered my
steps.

I realize now, Holy Spirit, that You, were there all the time.

It is the Giver who gets credit for the gift, not the receiver.

So, until my acknowledgement and acceptance of you God,

Satan will continuously try to take Your place.

However, the good news is that You Lord,

You will always have the final victory.

By Curtis White

Pastor Rick Warren states, ***"God wants to redeem human beings from Satan and reconcile them to himself so we can fulfill the five purposes he created us for: to love him, to be a part of his family, to become like him, to serve him, and to tell others about him."***[8]

Bernardette and I were going to New York. I remember thinking that I never got the rifle, that .22 rifle that Bill had promised me for my twelfth birthday. We didn't get to say goodbye to our friends. No more running ditches and riding trees. Would Clara Mae miss us? It was the summer of 1967. I was turning thirteen that year, and Bernardette had just turned eight that January.

What did Bill have to say about us leaving? I don't ever remember him saying anything. I doubt if Bill had even been asked if it was okay with him that we leave. Who had talked to him? Did he know that we were being taken away? Did he even care? I don't remember us saying goodbye. He was the only father that we knew but not the only father that we had. God was standing in the gap but we were not aware of Him.

---

[8] Warren, The Purpose Driven Life, 282

Of God, Timothy Keller writes, "*…a Father who gives us everything he has: first his Son to die for us, and then his Spirit to live within us…*"[9]

I've also written a few reasons as to why we should love our fathers, especially the fathers who have stayed in the family. And those who have accepted and fulfilled their responsibilities.

Father/father

HE/he supplies all of your needs. Love

HIM/him, for who He/he is, give

HIM/him all the glory, honor and praise.

HE/he deserves it, with all due

REVERENCE/with all due respect.

If reciprocal responsibilities have now been fulfilled,

strive to understand that,

WE/HE are the HOLY TRINITY.

Rebuking all demons,

with the shield of the HOLY SPIRIT.

---

[9] Timothy Keller, Preaching, (Penguin, 2016), 56

Now, I understand and shout to the world

my belief in JESUS CHRIST, my acceptance of

the Apostle's Creed, as I welcome Thee.

By Curtis White

Pastor TD Jakes states "An amazing thing happens when we learn how to bless the Lord – how to praise, worship, and exalt His name. We become more willing and able to bless our wives and children! In giving God what He wants, we are better able to give others what they truly need and desire from us."[10]

---

[10] T. D. Jakes, So You Call Yourself a Man, (Putnam Son's, 2004), 76

PART 2

THE TRANSITION
(AN UNSELFISH LOVE)

Author Philip Yancey writes, "The Spirit of God has resources of sensitivity beyond those of even the wisest mother. Paul says that Spirit lives inside us, detecting needs we cannot articulate and expressing them in a language we cannot comprehend. When we don't know what to pray, he fills in the blanks. Evidently, it is our very helplessness that God, too, delights in. Our weakness gives opportunity for his strength. Now, the Holy Spirit lives inside us as a personal seal of God's presence."[11]

It was the summer of 1967 and we were New York City bound. Our brother Robert told us we would stay with Aunt Louise. Bernardette and I only knew of one Aunt Louise. That was Louise M., the daughter of our one-time next-door neighbor in Lumberton, Ms. Ester.

This lady from New York would bring her daughter Stephanie with her whenever she came to Lumberton. She lived in New York City, in East Harlem, to be exact. Her address was 425 east 106th Street between 1st Avenue and the FDR drive. They had a two-bedroom corner apartment on the fourth floor.

Stephanie's building had an elevator, as did all of the buildings like hers. Coming from where I come from, I had never

---

[11] Yancey, Where is God When It Hurts? 236

been in an elevator before. But, also, coming from where I had come from, there were a million other things that I had never seen or done before.

After several times of riding the elevator alone, once I pressed all of the floor buttons before getting off. I just wanted to see what would happen. I was accused almost immediately of pressing all the floors by one of the maintenance workers. I denied it and have always wondered how he knew it was me.

Stephanie's bedroom was like something out of a fairy tale. The entire room was pink and fluffy. Her bed had a canopy, and everything matched. The bedspread matched the canopy, and the sheets matched the bedspread. The carpet matched the walls, and the curtains matched the lamp shades. I had never seen anything like it. The only thing missing was Sherly Temple.

The smells were magnificent. They were light and airy, sweet and fruity. She had stuffed animals everywhere. I remember the scented soaps in the bathroom. I would press them against my nose and inhale deeply. Her window faced a highway that ran parallel to a river. I remember looking out of her bedroom window at night and seeing the streams of car lights on the highway.

As they zipped by, I wondered where those streams of lights were going, just as I had wondered about the planes that painted the very thin white lines across the skies of Lumberton. It would be many years later before I could answer with any certainty where those cars could have been going.

Her building was nice, clean and tall. In that area there were a lot of buildings exactly like theirs. All having been made of the same color light brown bricks. Louise M. and her husband Willis had one daughter named Stephanie. Stephanie knew Louise P., who was a close friend to her family. She affectionately called Louise P. her Aunt Weezie. Stephanie was a little younger than me but older than Bernardette. Bernardette and I did not know Louise P.

So, when we were told that we were coming to New York to live with "Aunt" Louise, we assumed it was Stephanie's mom. We were happily excited. However, the euphoria did not last long. After a few days of staying with Stephanie, Robert told us we would leave Stephanie's house. He told us that we would no longer be staying there with them. It was devastating news, and I hated him for delivering it.

He told us that we would live with another "Aunt Louise." I remember Robert saying, "She's a cousin you don't know."

I said, "I thought we were staying with Louise, Stephanie's mother."

He responded, "Yes, I know, but her name is Louise, too."

I remember how disappointed I was.

<u>The Transition</u>

I felt betrayed, but what could I do? His lie did make our trip to New York easier. It made things a lot less complicated for him as well as for us. I was 12 years old, soon to be thirteen. Bernardette was five years younger than me. Our mother had passed away nearly two and one-half years earlier.

Louise P. is of no relation to our stepfather, William P. This was a traumatic experience, to say the least. I didn't remember ever having met this other Louise. I believe our first meeting was in Louise M.'s car as we were being driven to her apartment.

I remember there was a disagreement in the car between the two of them about something. I think it may have been over money, but I am not sure. We did not know it at the time, but that would be the last time we would ever see Louise M. and Stephanie again.

Helen was Louise P.'s first name. She hated the name Helen. I did not discover this until years later. She was a small-framed woman. As a child, she had been severely burned. While playing in the house, she had fallen into a lit fireplace. She was burned on the right side of her face down to her knee.

Ninety percent of the scars you never saw because her clothing covered them. Those scars that you could see were clearly burn marks. Her burn marks reminded me of a quilt with all of its squares sewn together like patches.

Like Stephanie, Aunt Lou also lived in Harlem, but she lived on the Westside. Helen Louise P. lived on Amsterdam Avenue at 131st Street. Her apartment was above a group of store fronts on the avenue. The buildings were only two stories tall, and you had to walk to the second floor. The bathroom was located outside the apartments at the end of the hallway and had to be shared with the other family on the floor.

When you entered the apartment, there was a tiny bath tub that was attached to the kitchen sink. It was partially covered with a drainage board for the dishes. The living room followed next, which was sparsely furnished. Her bedroom was straight to the back.

Her apartment was what is called a railroad flat. It was an apartment with a series of rooms connecting to each other in a line. The whole apartment was dark and drab. Being a sleep-in maid, Aunt Lou only had to come home on weekends.

There was no canopy in her bedroom, but everything was neat and clean. The smells were nondescript. They were not light and airy, sweet and fruity. She had curtains to her only bedroom window. There were no stuffed animals anywhere.

A big gray metal gate covered her bedroom window. Was this gate to keep her inside the apartment, or was it to keep someone on the outside from coming in? I wasn't sure. The window in Stephanie's room had no gate covering it.

The Transition

We started calling Cousin Louise, Aunt Louise just because it sounded better than Cousin Louise. At the same time, Aunt Lou stopped us from saying yes ma'am and no ma'am. She called it singing. She told us that not saying ma'am was not being disrespectful and that we were to continue using Mr. and Ms. or Mrs. to show respect.

Our neighbor was another single female with a son who was younger than Bernardette. Aunt Lou raved about how smart this kid was. She said he could read the ingredients on food packages and different medicines. He wore very thick glasses, not that wearing thick glasses and talking funny authenticated his gift.

We did not stay in that apartment long. Not because of this kid but because the apartment was too small for the three of us. Bernardette slept with Aunt Lou, and I slept on the couch. Sometimes, we made pallets and slept on the floor. Aunt Lou spoke of having to sleep on the floor many, many times growing-up in the south.

For the few weeks that we lived there, I only remember venturing outside alone, once. It was to go to the park across the street. Amsterdam Avenue was a very wide and busy two-way street. I noticed that across the avenue were those same tall, light brown brick buildings. They were very similar to Stephanie's with a slight difference.

<u>The Transition</u>

These buildings had colorful terraces in the middle of each floor. Red, green, blue and yellow were the colors. One day, I asked Aunt Lou if I could go to the park. She said yes. I bought a bunch of green grapes and ventured over. She cautioned me to cross the street at the traffic light.

Standing at the corner of 131st Street and Amsterdam Avenue, I noticed how hilly the avenue was. To my left, the avenue gradually sloped down to 125th Street and then gradually started to rise again to its peak at 116th Street, which was at Columbia University.

In the other direction, the topography again gradually rose, peaking at the summit of 140th street which was near the entrance to City College. There exists a valley between the two schools which was 125th Street. Little did I know that I was just a few blocks from the world-famous Apollo Theatre and just up the block from Jimbo Burgers.

I made it safely across the avenue. I entered the park and shared my grapes with one of the neighborhood boys. I don't remember playing any games or playing on any equipment. I do remember the absence of trees. I saw absolutely no trees on my side of the avenue and very few in the park. Where was the grass, and where were the trees? I never got to visit that park again, not that I would have wanted to.

Aunt Lou felt stressed because school would be starting soon, and she wanted us to be in a larger place before then. She had only one bedroom and now two kids, a girl and a boy. A boy who, in a matter of months, would be a teenager. We definitely needed a larger apartment.

Our stay on Amsterdam Avenue was very short-lived. It was mid-August, and we had only three more weeks left before school would start in New York City. Classes were well underway in North Carolina.

As stated earlier, something happened between Louise M. and Louise P. We never visited or saw them again. To the best of my knowledge, an argument had taken place between them. I asked Aunt Lou what happened. She quickly told me that it was none of my business. I dared not to ask again.

I thought that they were such good friends. I would wonder how Aunt Lou could sever such a "friendship" so quickly and so completely. Unfortunately, years later I would see and experience this type of odd behavior from her again, repeated against me.

Aunt Lou quickly found us another apartment. Our new address was 2059 Webster Avenue in the Bronx, the South Bronx. And, like the Harlem apartment, there was no elevator. Although, this was a five-story walk-up. Bernardette and I were still in culture shock. The noise, so many people, garbage everywhere and no trees or grass. We were two frightened little kids. It was so unlike Stephanie's place. How we wished that we were still there.

Our apartment was on the second floor, apartment 2E. It faced the back of the building, and unlike the Harlem apartment, this apartment was larger. It had two bedrooms with a separate bathroom inside the apartment. Thank God that the outhouse did not exist in New York City. There was wall-to-wall linoleum, just like the other place.

I like to refer to it as a right-handed apartment. When you entered, all of the rooms were to the right of the hallway. The bathroom was first, and then came the kitchen. The hallway emptied out into the living room. Further to the right was our bedroom. A little further back and to the center was a pair of French doors that opened out into Aunt Lou's bedroom.

The bathroom was simple enough. The water to flush the toilet was held in a wooden box above our heads, close to the ceiling. You only had to pull the chain to flush the toilet. Thank God that the water replenished itself automatically. Bath or shower, both were performed in the tub. The tub sat on the floor, supported by four small feet that resembled lion paws.

The small kitchen sat between the bathroom and the living room. It held a small four chaired table, a small refrigerator, a small four-burner stove and a sink to wash dishes. Cabinets sat above the refrigerator, stove and sink. There was a window opposite the table. The window overlooked the stores next door. This window faced north. There was no fire escape at this window. To the left of this window in the corner were the steam pipes.

In the winter, if the pipes were cold, so were you. If the pipes were warm, heat was on its way. If they were cold, Aunt Lou would bang on them with something, anything hard. This was how we communicated to the super that the apartment was cold. It was an informal request for heat.

Sometimes, it got so cold in the apartment that we had to turn on the stove. All four burners blasting with the oven on and the oven door open. This was very dangerous. At times, we were very cold but very careful. We wore lots of clothes. Thank God that the cold wasn't that extreme too often. I'm not sure which was better, this or having to build a fire inside a pot-belly stove.

The hallway emptied out into the living room. It was sparsely furnished. It had a sturdy couch with six legs. Plastic slip covers protected the fabric. There were two end tables with matching lamps and a coffee table. Opposite the couch was a stereo console. It had a built-in zenith television. For the first time we had a television within our living space. A record player was fitted next to the television with record albums stored beneath it.

I remember seeing and playing the albums of Aretha Franklin, Brook Benton, James Brown, et al. At the end of that wall was another window. This window faced east. Very little direct sunlight entered this window. There was no fire escape at this window, either. You could see the roof tops of the other buildings across the avenue. You could also see the top of the only tree on the block. It was a somber view, even with the sun shining.

Inclement weather made it even more dismal. Once we started school, this became our "crying window." This window had a wide windowsill. It was wide enough to hold a medium size kitchen pot. A pot to catch the falling snow. Aunt Lou would make the best homemade ice-cream, something we had never experienced before. Sometimes, the pot would also catch some of the soot in the air from our buildings' coal-burning furnace. Of course, when that happened, it rendered the entire pot of snow useless.

Further left past the "crying window" was one of the walls to our bedroom. Bernardette and I had to share a bedroom. Aunt Lou was not happy with this arrangement. I would soon be a teenager. She felt that we needed and should have our own separate rooms. She could not afford a larger place. This apartment had to suffice.

Aunt Lou bought us bunkbeds. Bernadette slept up top. There was a clothing closet at the end of our beds. I enjoyed reading comic books. I never threw any of them away. I would bind them into stacks of twenty-five or more and store them in the top of our closet. Our room came painted with a funny color, sort of a light pea-green color. I'm not sure why, but that color stands out vividly.

Aunt Lou's bedroom was the last room in the apartment. Her room had a set of the classic French-doors. She hung curtains on them, and they were pinched in the middle. It looked really nice. Her dresser was against the left wall. Opposite this was her bed. The room had a big window. Like the Harlem apartment, it too was protected by big gray metal gates and on the other side was the fire escape.

Beyond that, you could see huge rocks, and the skyward view was of the tops of more buildings. Two stories below Aunt Lou's window was a small cemented court yard. This area could only be accessed from the basement or, God forbid, via the fire escape in an emergency. The court yard belonged to the super.

Protecting all of our worldly possessions was the infamous police lock at the front door. It was the Fox Style Floor Mounted Police Lock. It was a long iron pole, pointed at one end and curved at the other. It reminded me of a hockey stick and was perhaps five times heavier. The pointed end fitted into a metal plate that was installed on the floor. The other end fitted into a lock mounted on the door. I understand that these locks are no longer in production.

The Transition

With a turn of the key, the pole would shift from side to side, locked to unlocked. At that time, it was supposed to be the best house lock money could buy. Even the police couldn't get past it. I vaguely remember some talk about making them illegal. It was additional protection supported by two other traditional locks already on the door. This was something that Bernardette and I were certainly not used to. We had come from a place where our doors were never locked, closed yes, but locked, no.

Leaving apartment 2E, you stepped out into the hallway which was covered with decorative ceramic tiles. They lined each hallway area on every floor. There were five floors with five apartments on each floor. These small tiles formed intricate designs. The edges were supported by marble boarders. The stairs were also marble pierced by wrought iron fencing. This fencing was topped with a hard wood banister. I found the tile designs to be attractive.

There was a large window at each landing of the staircase. Each window held frosted opaque wire mesh glass. It didn't matter; remember, there wasn't much of anything to see on the other side, anyway. The view would have been of roof tops and other buildings. The walls were thick and solid. In retrospect, I would say that this was pre-WW II construction. Each marble step was slightly worn down in the middle. Undoubtedly, due to thousands of footsteps pressing down upon them over the years.

The Transition

The front of the building was constructed of reddish bricks and beige stones. I did not see any buildings like those that Stephanie lived in and none taller than five stories high. Outside, a tall black wrought iron fence confined the garbage area. Wooden steps led down to the basement. This is where the super lived. These wooden steps also led to the cemented courtyard seen from Aunt Lou's bedroom window.

A fire escape also serviced those apartments on the front. It draped down the front-middle of the building. On the ground floor, there existed a narrow hallway enclosed by a set of double doors that led out to the stoop. Once on the stoop there were three or four long dark gray marble steps that allowed tenants to the sidewalk.

To the right were other five-story walk-ups. Some had store front street level businesses. A cleaner, a pool hall and Smitty's barber shop. To the left was a liquor store and a delicatessen, which covered the corner. These two establishments had nothing built above them. They were single-story buildings. I worked for all of them except the pool hall and liquor store because I wasn't old enough. Even so, I was allowed to hang out in the pool room from time to time.

On the sidewalk between the liquor store and our building was one tree. It was the only tree on the block. It was the oddest and saddest thing I had ever seen. Coming from where we came from, you can only imagine how sad this must have been. Not seeing any grass or trees. As time went on, whenever I saw a clump of trees anywhere, it made me home sick. We really were living in a concrete jungle.

In front of the deli was a city bus stop. Most of the time, we played on the sidewalk between the cleaners and the deli. We were not allowed to go outside much. And nor did we want to. We did not go out to play for quite a while. We were too afraid and Aunt Lou too protective. We had only been living in the city for a few months. We had not made any friends and only knew kids at our school. It was fall, and we noticed the weather getting cooler. This would be our first New York City winter. Boy, did I miss that Carolina sun?

Aunt Lou tried to make winter as fun as possible. She would buy 500-hundred-piece puzzles. The three of us worked on them together. It was fun, and I enjoyed it. She encouraged us to read a lot. Although her education never got pass the eighth grade, she pushed us to excel. If Aunt Lou didn't know the answer, she would find it. She really enjoyed crossword puzzles. She tackled them all, from the New York Times to the Daily News.

The New York Times and the Wall Street Journal are huge newspapers. I would read the Times at home but get frustrated because of the size of its pages. Aunt Lou started teaching me how to fold it. Learning this technique enabled me to seamlessly keep track of my stories and gave me the ability to read this oversized newspaper in tight spaces, like subway cars.

Knowing how to fold it made all the difference. By the time I started college, I was proficient in reading the New York Times anywhere, either standing or sitting. To read that kind of newspaper in any crowded location is an art form. I greatly appreciated being made aware of nuances such as this.

Aunt Lou was smart, sassy and fearless. She was no pushover. If something wasn't right, she would be in your face making it right. She taught me many things that I would never learn in a classroom.

Webster Avenue was very busy and it was also very dirty. There was garbage everywhere. Across the avenue was a Pepsi-Cola distribution plant. It reminded me of Mr. Barnes from Lumberton. Further down the avenue on that same side were several auto shops.

Toward the middle of that block was another apartment building, and it, too, was a five-story walk-up. One block east was Park Avenue which was also, the path of the Metro-North commuter railroad. Unlike the D-train these rails carried folks north of the city, to the suburbs which were well beyond my reality. Initially, we moved around a lot. Aunt Lou was scrambling to get settled.

Within two months we lived in two of the City's five boroughs. The remaining three, Brooklyn, Queens and Staten Island we never resided in.

Aunt Lou had already accomplished one goal: to have us stabilized and in a larger apartment by the time school started. Now, she had to find another job. Prior to taking us, she worked as a sleep-in maid on Long Island. She had to give that up now.

She quickly found another job in Brooklyn, working on an assembly line. It was in a factory that made ink pens. She came home every day with ink all over her hands.

She had to be at work at 8 am. This necessitated her having to leave the apartment before us. She explained the circumstances to me. She told me that she needed to rely on me. Each day, I had to get Bernardette and myself to and from school.

I was petrified and hoped that it didn't show. I understood my responsibility and knew that she was counting on me. Once again, I was the man of the house, but this time, it was not by default. I also knew that I had to protect Bernardette and was better able to do so. With all that was going on I still knew and believed that we were still in a better place.

What made Aunt Lou decide to raise two children that she barely knew? Who did she discuss this with, the other "Aunt

Louise," our brother Robert or perhaps her male friend CJ? I'm sure she had a discussion with God. Aunt Lou knew Jesus, but did Jesus know Aunt Lou? Who partitioned her to take us? Was it Robert, was it Louise M. or perhaps the Holy Spirit? What an extraordinary thing for her to do. Whatever it was, I will be forever grateful.

Aunt Lou was in her mid to late thirties. She was single and had no children of her own. Prior to us, I'm told that she treated Stephanie like a daughter. Aunt Lou was in the prime of her life. She gave up her life for us. Why? Someone told me that she didn't give up her life. Her life did not begin until she took us. Wow! That is powerful. What made her do it?

I believe that Aunt Lou had come to the Red Sea place in her life, as written by Annie Johnson Flint – ***"Have you come to the Red Sea place in your life, where in spite of all you can do, there is no way out, there is no way back, there is no other way but through? Then wait on the Lord with a trust serene till the night of your fear is gone; He will send the wind, He will heap the floods, When He says to your soul, "Go on." In the morning watch, 'neath the lifted cloud, you shall see but the Lord alone, When He leads you on from the place of the sea to a land that you have not known; And your fears shall pass as your foes have passed, you shall no more*** *be afraid; You shall sing His praise in a better place, A place that His hand has made.* "[12]

Aunt Lou was one of our many rams in the bush, but what does that mean – having a ram in the bush.

Pastor T. D. Jakes tells us that **"God is responsive only to those men who are willing to fall on their faces before Him, completely yielding everything to Him, and placing themselves in utter reliance upon Him."**[13]

Let us examine the book of Genesis chapter 22. God tested Abraham's faith and obedience. The Lord instructs Abraham to take his only son Issac, whom he loves so much, to the land of Moriah and sacrifice him as a burnt offering.

Along the way, Issac raises a question, "Father, Issac asked, we have the wood and the flint to make the fire, but where is the lamb for the sacrifice? God will see to it, my son, Abraham replied.

And they went on. When they arrived at the place where God had told Abraham to go, he built an altar and placed the wood in

----

[12] Sanders, J. Oswald, Spiritual Leadership (Principles of Excellence for Every Believer). (Moody, 2007), 133

[13] Jakes, T.D., So You Call Yourself A Man? (Albury Publishing, 1997), 76

order, ready for fire, and then tied Issac and laid him on the altar over the wood.

And Abraham took the knife and lifted it up to plunge it into his son, to slay him. At that moment the Angel of God shouted to him from heaven, Abraham, Abraham.

Yes, Lord! he answered. Lay down the knife' don't hurt the lad in any way, the Angel said, for I know that God is first in your life – you have not withheld even your beloved son from me.

Then Abraham noticed a ram caught by its horns in a bush. So, he took the ram and sacrificed it, instead of his son, as a burnt offering on the altar." Abraham named that place "Jehovah Provides."

Aunt Lou had an extra key made for the apartment. She put that key on a string, placed it around my neck, and told me not to remove it or lose it.

Aunt Lou would get us ready for school each morning. She had to travel to Brooklyn so she had to get us up early, very early. She would do Bernadette's hair. She made sure that we had a hot breakfast. She would make sure that we had all of our school supplies. Checking homework and bathing would always take place before we went to bed.

<u>The Transition</u>

Aunt Lou would kiss us goodbye each morning. After she left the apartment, Bernardette and I would hold hands. We would stand there in the living room at the "crying window" and say how we wished that we were back home. Holding hands, we would cry with tears streaming down our cheeks. We were terrified of New York and walking to school alone in this strange new land called the Bronx.

<u>If You Had Any Idea</u>

If you had any idea / of my reality

and voice of reason

You would not want / to walk in my shoes

And, if you had any idea / of my fragility,

you would cry me a river

Does it matter / that I'm a motherless child or

what it takes for me to get out of my bed each morning

Should you have any idea / of where I come from, my Alpha, my

Omega

Why does the caged bird sing, he knows that he is

the apple of HIS eye

The Transition

but the caged bird does not sing

because he is happy

he cries

how do you mend a broken heart

If you had any idea / you would know

that his song comes from a different place.

By Curtis White

When it was time to leave, we'd wipe our faces with our hands, take a deep breath, put on our game face and leave. We never had any problems, and no one ever bothered us. It wasn't easy, but we did it. But I knew that we were in a better place.

We were loved and cared for. Why did Aunt Lou do this for us? This question has always haunted me. I missed the grass and the trees, the hunting and fishing and swimming naked in the lakes and rivers and at Doctor Kings Pond. I missed Clara Mae.

New York City had our heads spinning! One day, coming home from school at around noon. Loud sirens started to go off. I began to run home. I didn't know what to do. I kept watching the skies for planes, bombers, etc. I had never heard anything like this. Were we under some kind of attack? Was this a warning? Was this an air raid? I must have looked half-crazed. No one paid me any attention.

I noticed that the other people were not excited. They carried-on as if nothing was happening; I stopped running and continued home hurriedly. Someone later told me that it was some kind of test. I never did find out what that was all about. It was soon forgotten. Nor do I remember it ever happening again.

My first time riding the subway was a near disaster. Aunt Lou was taking me to the dentist. It was during rush hour. The D-train was our nearest subway. I remember the subway ride home. We were at the 125th Street station. The train doors opened. Aunt Lou pushed her way onto the train, thinking that I was right behind her.

I remember her yelling for me. I was still on the platform in la, la, land. Her arm parted the people. She grabbed me by the collar and yanked me into the subway car. She yelled at me. I could see the panic in her face. She warned me to stay right next to her. People around her nodded their heads in agreement. I was embarrassed. **Welcome to New York.**

Aunt Lou had a sister who lived in Baltimore, Maryland. Mildred was her name. She, her boyfriend and her son De'Andre came to visit us in the Bronx. This would be our first-time meeting

The Transition

Aunt Mildred. She was a small frame woman like Aunt Lou with a very distinctive Baltimore accent.

Her boyfriend Gilbert was a well-dressed, odd-looking man with a head shaped like a fish. He did not drink liquor and was as quiet as a church mouse. They say that opposites attract, and this was certainly the case here. Aunt Mildred was a loud-talking alcoholic. She and Gilbert seemed to balance each other out.

Their mother's name was Essie Mae. I was told that she, in addition to also being an alcoholic, was also a very mean woman. Although Aunt Lou had dodged that bullet, she did keep liquor in the house for special occasions and for her friend CJ.

Once, while she was away, I decided to have a drink and poured it from an already-opened bottle of Johnnie Walker Red. Back home, this was sealed liquor, the good stuff. I knew that Aunt Lou would notice some missing liquor, so I replaced that amount with water, thinking that no one would ever know the difference. The bottle looked untouched to me but Aunt Lou and CJ knew immediately that water had been added to the bottle. She questioned me, and I admitted that I had taken some. She told me to never water-down her liquor again, and I didn't.

Aunt Lou did not like it when her sister Mildred started drinking because she would become loud and boisterous. Aunt Mildred would argue, curse and act as if she was ready to fight. Her son DeAndre was a few years older than me. His temperament was nothing like his mother's. He was a handsome guy; he was Mr. Cool. I remember the clothes he wore, and I have to admit, he did look good in them.

Anyone could tell that his clothes were expensive. His shoes were top-of-the-line. His suits were tailor-made. He dressed impeccably. I remember Aunt Mildred talking about what DeAndre would and would not wear. I wondered how this guy could afford to dress so immaculately. I had an idea how, and a few years later, I would find out.

P.S. 28 was the first school that we attended in New York. Unlike Professor Knuckles elementary school in South Lumberton, P.S. 28 was made of stone and was five stories tall. Schools in Lumberton had names, not numbers. If P.S. 28 had a name, I did not know it. I only remember being in the main office once. That was when Aunt Lou was registering us. Aunt Lou and I were both upset that I was not placed in the sixth grade.

My southern report card supported and recommended that I move on to the next grade. The principal of P.S. 28 said that the southern schools were not as advanced as the northern schools. Because of this, I had to repeat the fifth grade. It was their policy, we were told. This made me very upset.

<u>The Transition</u>

I vowed to make up that lost year. I had six years to do it. Aunt Lou told us that she never made it past the eighth grade. She had since learned the value of a good education. She made sure that we did, too. She made sure that we had the resources necessary to be successful.

My first day at school was beyond intriguing. Miss Haran was a tall, lanky Irish teacher. She was very nice, extremely pale and very goofy. Her front teeth were very bucked, and she had a slight hump in her upper back.

My classroom was like the United Nations assembly. I didn't know this many different kinds of people existed in the world. Some students had squinted-eyes, others had long jet-black hair that ran down their backs, others had freckles across their faces with red hair and still others with jet-black hair standing straight up in the air. There were some black children with cut marks on their cheeks. I wanted to know more about each of them and their cultures.

They were Spanish, Chinese, Cuban, Irish, Jewish, Italian, African and Mexican to name a few. Talk about New York being a melting pot! My head was spinning. Coming from where I came from, you were either black, white or American Indian.

I'm sure that they found me equally odd. The girls thought my southern accent was funny. You talk funny, they would say. One girl, named Linda told her brother or cousin that I was annoying her and I probably was.

They waited for me one day after school. She and two boys. They confronted me about bothering her. A small crowd had formed. One of the boys got down on the ground behind me, on his hands and knees. The other boy pushed me backward. I almost fell over him. Everyone laughed, and then it was over. I was embarrassed. Bernardette questioned me about it all the way home. I made her promise not to tell Aunt Lou.

We lived a full three blocks from the school. Between 2059 Webster Avenue and P.S. 28 was Tremont Baptist Church and Echo Park. Tremont Baptist Church is a beautiful stone-gray building of worship. It has large stained-glass windows and sits on a hill. Echo Park is on that same hill but opposite the church.

Aunt Lou joined Tremont and immediately got us involved with the church. We became members, and shortly thereafter, Bernardette and I were baptized. Aunt Lou encouraged us to get baptized, and we did. Reverend Rutland was the pastor at that time.

I remember the day that I was baptized. I remember changing and putting on my white robe. I remember wading into the baptismal pool. It was filled with warm water. Reverend Rutland stood there welcoming me. I remember him saying something to me and then the words, I now baptize you in the name of the Father, Son and Holy Spirit.

With one hand, he covered my mouth while pinching my nose closed. He told me to close my eyes and cross my arms over my chest. I remember being lowered backward into the water. I remember a warmth covering my entire body. Was this warmth from the water, or was this entirely something different?

I was completely submerged and raised out of the water. Assistants wrapped me in a towel as I exited the pool. I remember hearing praises, shouts of amen and hallelujahs from the witnesses. I was baptized, but I did not fully understand the ramifications of what had just taken place.

Not sure of how I should feel, I questioned myself. Should I feel differently, talk differently, or think differently, I didn't know. I felt the same but questioned if I should feel the same. I was happy that I had done it and now awaited my transformation.

Dr. James T. Jefferson states, ***"The difficulty is we are dealing with the choice between heaven and hell and many of us are not really aware of that; and many of us don't believe that is the case. The sinfulness of our human condition has blinded us to the reality of sin and its consequences of eternal damnation. We have devised our own way of thinking and eternity is not a part of*** *it. Some of us are so accustomed to sin that we are not aware of what it has done to us.* "[14]

I knew I had been saved physically, and Aunt Lou had done that. But had I been saved spiritually? I knew that what I had done was something good but I really did not understand how good.

Rick Warren writes, *"Baptism doesn't make you a member of God's family; only faith in Christ does that. Baptism shows you are part of God's family."*[15]

The benefits of my spiritual salvation would be incalculable, and Jesus had done that.

He goes on to say, *"If you haven't been baptized as an expression of your faith in Christ, do so as soon as possible, as Jesus commanded."*[16]

For many years, the devil kept me unsure of my salvation. People would ask me if I were saved, and I would always say yes, not really knowing/believing that I was. Saved from what? Saved by what?

---

[14] Jefferson, James T., One Night In Bethlehem. (It Is Written, 2023), 110

[15] Warren, Rick. The Purpose Driven Life. (Zondervan, 2022), 120

[16] Warren, The Purpose Driven Life, 121

The Transition

Benny Hinn states, *"From the moment you accept Jesus as Savior, it is the Spirit that gives you the will, the strength, and the desire to obey God and live the Christian life. Without Him it is impossible."*[17]

Being saved starts the process of sanctification. I didn't have a clue. The devil would say, if you are really saved, you would not be doing this or that. So, I doubted my salvation even though I believed all the elements necessary to be saved.

Dr. Jefferson shares that *"Jesus, His birth, His life, His ministry, His death and resurrection, were all a part of God's plan to save sinners who heard the message of salvation and believed. Remember, it was God who loved the world and because of that He devised a plan to save sinners without going against the sinners will. He accepted only those who came to Him believing the gospel indicating their hearts were touched and their minds were made up to accept His invitation to salvation and eternal life with Him in Heaven."*[18]

Reverend Rutland soon thereafter retired. A young black minister by the name of Dr. Robinson replaced him. Dr. Robinson came to us with a lot of credentials. He was well-educated, well-

---

[17] Hinn, Benny. Good Morning, Holy Spirit. (Thomas Nelson, 1990), 170

[18] Jefferson, One Night In Bethlehem, 112

119

spoken and full of ideas. Dr. Robinson asked me to be his altar boy. That was something completely new to me. I did not know what that entailed. He explained it all to me and Aunt Lou.

He also formed a youth choir. Miss Lucy L. was the choir director. I joined the choir. I couldn't carry a tune in a bucket. I was told that my voice was an alto. Whenever we sang, she would place me between two of her sisters, Janet and Oscar, both of whom were also altos. They were supposed to keep me on note. It worked, some of the time.

Being an altar boy was an honor. I felt special, privileged and blessed. Most of the church members thought I would pursue a religious career in theology. Dr. Robinson was very encouraging. He kept telling me how special I was.

This made me nervous because I was fearing and anticipating some kind of sexual approach. It never happened, and I finally learned to relax around him. Being baptized meant a lot to me. I was a Christian and believed in Jesus Christ. I was also saved and did not know it.

My duties as an altar boy were to open the Sunday morning service. I would announce the opening song and read the selected scripture. This was all done from the pulpit. One morning, as I stood before the congregation, I spotted the two boys who roughed me-up at school.

The Transition

Had God made my enemies my foot stool? To my surprise, there they were sitting before me. I looked directly at them from time to time. Finally, they got up and walked out of the church. This was not my intended goal but I must admit, I felt vindicated. I never saw those boys again, nor did I ever say anything more to Linda.

Mrs. Ferguson was a long-standing member of Tremont. She and her husband did a lot for the youth of the church. They had two small boys themselves. Once, she and her husband provided tickets to an event hosted by the New York Knicks, an NBA pro basketball team. At this event, you got to sit at a table with one of their players to talk and ask questions.

Our player never opened his mouth. Neither did I. He just sat there like a lump of coal. I remember thinking to myself, what a waste of time. Wasn't this supposed to be exciting and uplifting? I suppose it would be if you were a basketball fan, which I was not, but I was excited and thankful for the opportunity.

It afforded poor inner-city kids, such as myself, the opportunity to get up close and meet a pro sports figure. My pro sports figure sat there with a frown on his face and with his arms folded. What a disappointment he was. He didn't interact with any of us and never introduced himself. It would have been better for me if he hadn't come at all, or should that be the other way around?

121

<u>The Transition</u>

Our choir director, Miss Leach and Aunt Lou became fast friends. Occasionally, on Sundays, we would get invited to their apartment. She lived with her three sisters. They lived at 1700 Grand Concourse, a doorman building with an elevator. This was a big deal for the black folks that I knew. She had to be rich, I thought.

The Grand Concourse was the crown jewel of the Bronx. At that time, it still flaunted doormen buildings, furriers, jewelers, doctors, lawyers and people with money in general. Yeah, Miss Leach had to be rich to be living there. The doorman was white and wore a uniform and cap.

Whenever we visited her, he would have to announce our presence and get permission to let us go up to their apartment. Never mind that it took four working adults (she and all of her sisters) to afford such an address. This was my assumption, and I was probably right. School and church had become our life, and Aunt Lou made it fun.

She also introduced us to bowling. We learned to like it, and it helped with our boredom. She was an avid bowler herself and belonged to a league down at Webster Bowl. We did not go outside to play for the first eight or nine months. We were still new to New York, trying to adjust.

I thought about Lumberton every day. I missed Lumberton so much, but I knew deep down inside that we were in a much better place. I missed my friends, the grass and the trees. I missed fishing and hunting.

It was these memories that sustained me. It was these memories that put me to sleep each night, for years. I longed to talk to Clara Mae. I had no way of reaching her, nor she me. However, she was always there in my thoughts and in my dreams.

During this time, I gained a lot of weight. According to Aunt Lou's male friend, when we first arrived, I was a scrawny little kid with sores all over my legs. By the seventh grade, I had become this chubby little kid. I was in Junior High School now. Having to walk further to school and no longer being afraid of going outside to play, I began to thin out.

We got to know other families in our building. We got to know Miss Jannie Pickett, who lived on the fifth floor. Miss Jannie was a big woman. She had three children. A girl and two boys. The girl was named Gladys who we all called Kitten. Her younger brother was named Robert P. He was later determined to have Sickle Cell disease.

Jerry was her oldest son and had just come home from Vietnam. Jerry was very nice with a great sense of humor. He had a smile broader than Broadway. He was tall and very muscular with long eye lashes. His eyes reminded me of those of a giraffe. Next door to them lived Linda. Linda had a large family. They were all tall, taller than me. Linda was very attractive.

I remember one day, I was sent to the store and instructed by Aunt Lou to come straight back. I ran into Linda, who was standing on our stoop. I started talking to her. I was rapping hard. I forgot that Aunt Lou was waiting for me.

Aunt Lou got tired of waiting and came looking for me. Aunt Lou gave me a whopping on that stoop in front of Linda. That was the end of that romance. How could I ever face Linda again?

My friend Hubert lived on the third floor. He lived there with his mother. He had a very obedient dog named Lucky. Lucky was a black-and-white mix. I admired how well Hubert had trained his dog.

Hubert was from Cuba, and his uncle Kirby owned the corner bodega on 180th street. I remember it was from Hubert that I learned the word pharmacy. He was surprised that I did not know what that word meant. I was a little embarrassed. It had always been the drug store to me.

He motivated me to start increasing my vocabulary. Hubert was several years older than me. I'm not sure where his mother ended up being relocated. Hubert and I remained close and kept in touch through his Uncle Kirby.

<u>The Transition</u>

Hubert went to Temple University and became a medical doctor. We talked a lot during his senior year. He invited me to his graduation. He also told me that he was getting married the day after and asked if I would be his best man.

The wedding was taking place in Toledo, Ohio. That was his fiancée's home town. He asked if I could drive us there right after his graduation. I had just received my driver's license the week before. I met him at his dorm on the day of his graduation.

Hubert's car was a Peugeot. What the heck was a Peugeot, and how do you even pronounce it? Peugeot, I later learned is a French brand of automobile. I smiled and wondered how Hubert ended up with a Peugeot. It was an ugly dark green box type of vehicle. It looked like its' name, his car looked foreign.

The interior was drab but provided a lot of head space. The most unique aspect was not that it had a manual transmission but that the gear-shift was not on the floor but on the stirring column. This was something completely new for me. I had never seen anything like it.

However, I knew how to drive a stick, thanks to UPS. So, a few quick lessons from Hubert and I was ready to go. I drove the entire trip that night non-stop in a driving rain. Hubert slept the entire trip. God protects babies and fools. We certainly were not babies.

<u>The Transition</u>

They married the next day. I was his best man. Shortly after that, they moved to Washington, DC. His medical residency was at George Washington University hospital. His wife became a corporate lawyer. Somehow, shortly after his move to DC, we lost contact.

Several years later, my wife and I visited them at his last known address. His wife answered the door and stated that she and Hubert were no longer together. She did not invite us in. We appeared unannounced, so we understood why. She stated that, **as** far as she knew, he was still at George Washington University Hospital. They did have a daughter together. We never heard from or saw either of them again.

On the second floor of 2059 Webster was Miss Freida. She was our immediate next-door neighbor. She was a tiny woman and had a little girl. Although Miss Freida and Aunt Lou became friends, we did not interact with them much.

There was a very peculiar family that lived on the first floor. This woman had a mentally disabled son named Harry and a beautiful daughter. Harry seemed to be maybe thirteen or fourteen years old. He had no intelligible speech. He would utter weird sounds and make grunts. Harry was slightly disfigured and would always try to hump your leg if you stood too close to him.

<u>The Transition</u>

His sister was a bit older. She was shy and avoided eye contact. She barely ever said anything and did not appear to be mentally disabled herself. Her mother would beat her often. From time to time, I could hear her cries as I passed their apartment, but I never knew why she was being whipped. The mother was a tough-looking, mean woman. They were rarely ever seen outside of the home.

Across the hall from them was a family that had moved in from the deep south. It was either Alabama or Mississippi. It was seven of them. Three girls, three boys and the mother, Mrs. Lewis. There was Mary, the oldest, then Villittha and Linda, the baby girl. Villittha loved Aunt Lou. I don't know why. She would come by our apartment almost daily to say hello. I grew to like her as well.

Walley, the oldest boy, then Larry and Arthur, the youngest of the boys. After a few years, Mary married a guy named Glen. Villittha was the most popular. She managed to land a good job down on Wall Street at the New York Stock Exchange. Everyone was so proud of her.

Villittha was a local hero because of her job. She wore glasses. She was short, had short hair and a very shapely body. Linda, the baby girl, was still in grade school. Walley went into the ministry. Larry and Arthur both got jobs at the Fulton Street Fish Market. I also did not get to know the other tenants in our building.

There were several small businesses on our block. The barber shop, pool hall, dry cleaners, liquor store and delicatessen. I worked at them all except the pool hall and the liquor store. I was not old enough.

Smithy's barber shop was an interesting place. Standing on my stoop facing the avenue, Smithy's was to your right, on the downtown side of Webster Avenue. I got myself a job there, first shining shoes, then sweeping up hair, cleaning the mirrors, and sterilizing his barber tools.

On Saturdays, I often walked up to the Grand Concourse near Fordham Road to shine shoes. One day, while shining shoes on the Grand Concourse in front of a restaurant, a little white kid would come out of the restaurant, point at my head, say the word black, and run back inside.

I would make an angry face, and he would run back inside laughing. I was careful not to be too obvious. I didn't want any trouble. I quickly realized that to him, it was all a game. He was too young for it to be anything malicious.

Another Saturday, a white woman put her foot on my shoebox and asked me to give her a shine. I was reluctant. I wasn't sure if I could do it without getting the black polish on her white skin. She assured me that if that happened, it would be okay.

<u>The Transition</u>

She went home that day with a black ring around each of her ankles. True to her word, she was not upset and even gave me a tip. I would leave the Grand Concourse before dark and return to the barber shop. No one ever bothered me. I would be ladened with quarters, dimes and nickels. By the grace of God, I never had any problems.

Smithy was a fairly tall man with a yellow complexion and a thick mustache. His legs spread apart from his knees down. He reminded me of a giraffe also. He was married and the superintendent of the building next to ours.

He had two children, a boy named Derek and a girl named Joyce-Ann. Joyce-Ann ended up going to school for nursing, following her mother's footsteps. She had the same leg trait as her father. Derek ended up becoming a drug addict.

Unfortunately, this was a trap that a lot of our neighborhood boys fell into. The same trap that nearly snared me. There go I, but for the grace of God. Smithy had four chairs in his shop. His, of course, was the first chair, and he rented out the other three. His brother Doug had the second chair. Shortly after I started working there, Doug moved back to North Carolina.

Smithy appeared to have had a good business. Saturdays, it would be standing room only with all four chairs busy. Folks would come in and leave their shoes for me to shine. It was not uncommon for me to make forty or fifty dollars on a Saturday.

There was one character who would come into the shop with his boombox on his shoulder. Trying to sing the song, Always and Forever by Heatwave. He knew the words. The only problem; he was a stutterer – and a severe one at that. "… and e-e-e-every da-da-da-da-da-day love me your own spe-spe-spe-spe-special way, melt all, ma-ma-ma-my heart away, wi-wi-wi-wi-with a smile." We would be on the floor with laughter. He did not care.

All sorts of individuals would pass through the shop. Some selling various hot (hot as in stolen) items such as records, tapes, frozen meat and clothing. And others asking Smithy for a dollar or two, which he would always give. One of his barbers was named Roy. He was a thick guy, solid fat.

If anyone was going to McDonald's, Roy always had an order. One day, he gave me his order. I made the purchase and gave him his order. He did not offer to pay me. Someone in the shop cautioned me not to press the issue. That's when I learned that Roy had a prison record and probably didn't mind going back.

The number runner was probably the most popular individual in the neighborhood. Nearly everybody played the numbers. I never developed an interest. Aunt Lou played every day. If someone hit it straight, everybody knew about it.

The Transition

The most I had ever heard of anyone hitting for was sixteen hundred dollars. From time to time, it would be said that the number was changed. It was said that they changed it because too many folks had hit it. There was nothing anybody could do about it except complain.

The pool hall was run by a guy named Sammy. I liked Sammy because he was kind. He would allow us to play pool from time to time. The place was a store front. At one time, it may have been a grocery store. The pool tables were coin operated, 75 cents a game, quarters only.

The quarters were placed into slots on a tray. Then, you would push the tray into the side of the table. The queue balls would drop. It was discovered that if you pushed the tray in really fast, the balls would drop, and you got your quarters back. This technique worked 50% of the time. We could only try it when Sammy wasn't in the room. We got to play a lot of free games.

Working at the cleaners was fun. I volunteered to help when things got really busy. I didn't do much except help to retrieve people's clothes. All the cleaning was done on the premises. I enjoyed watching how they would clean, wash and press each item. The woman who ran the cleaners was the owner's sister. She liked and trusted me. Her name was Ms. Noily, and his name was Lanlo.

<u>The Transition</u>

They were Spanish and very nice people. Only during the summer did I work at the cleaners. I worked at the delicatessen after school and on Saturdays. I worked at the barber shop some week nights and on Saturdays after the deli closed. The cleaners, barber shop, liquor store and deli were all closed on Sunday. One summer, I worked all three jobs. No other kids were interested. I always had money, and Aunt Lou never took any of it. She made me open a savings account at the Dime Savings Bank on Fordham Road.

Sometimes, Aunt Lou would allow me to go shopping by myself. I once bought a few nylon shirts from Bonds department store on Fordham Road. Aunt Lou did not like them. She said that they were cheap and poorly made. She made me take them back. She decided to go shopping with me. Alexanders was her choice department store and was much larger than Bonds. I must admit that the quality and style of clothing and the prices were much better.

My sneakers were purchased from a table top. The laces were tied together. You had to double-check each pair to make sure that you had a left-foot and a right-foot. Also, to make sure that they were the same size. All of my clothes came from Alexander's. I was pleased with the way that I looked. I had to wear a shirt and tie to school each day. I did not look like my cousin D'Andre, but I wasn't trying too. When we first started going to church, Aunt Lou had her friend CJ teach me how to tie a necktie.

<u>The Transition</u>

This he taught me early on. Knowing how to tie a tie was nothing new for me. Most of my classmates wore clip-on ties.

After our first year in New York, Aunt Lou took us back to Lumberton. Our mode of transportation was the Trailway Bus Company. We would ride the subway downtown to 42nd and eighth. The bus terminal was located across the street.

The night before our trip, Aunt Lou would fry-up some chicken and make our sandwiches. We carried a greasy brown paper bag with our sandwich wrapped in aluminum foil with a napkin, some cookies and a soda.

Aunt Lou would purchase our tickets at the station. We would find our gate and get on line. We would be so excited. The hustle and bustle of it all. I remember the smell of the bus fumes. I would inhale deeply. I like the scent. That let me know that we were going home.

The bus station was dirty and had a lot of homeless people in it. The lines were long and often times a second bus had to be put on. We had always hoped to get an express bus. The first stop would be Richmond, Va. Usually, we were not allowed to get off the bus. That was Aunt Lou's rule. To ride a bus that made all local stops was misery. It would take forever to get to Lumberton.

As Aunt Lou would put it, that bus would stop every time a dog raised its leg. Traveling by bus was the only mode of transportation available to us. No commercial trains came to our hometown and certainly no airline did. It really didn't matter because both modes were beyond our means. I did not ride a commercial train or fly on an airline until I was an adult.

Aunt Persaver would pick us up from the bus station. I was this fat, chubby kid. Bernardette had two little pig tails. We looked good. We stayed with our cousin Persaver. She was raising her three grandchildren, Jean, Bobbie and Ronnie. We enjoyed being home. Years later, I was allowed to come home for the entire summer.

Bill had stopped drinking. He had a job as a cook and had to always wear white. He had gotten himself together and had a nice apartment on the other side of town. After talking with him, Aunt Lou allowed me to go home for the summer. He promised her he would get me a job working with him at the restaurant. It was the Johnson family restaurant. No relations to the Howard Johnson restaurant chain. He got me a job clearing tables. I loved it. I was home for the summer, and I was making some money.

I did not know that the tips left on the table were for the waitresses. I thought that they were for me. I took the tips first and then cleared the table. Wow, this is great, I thought. The waitresses complained to my father. They were ready to tar and feather me.

He said to me, "Son, the tips are for the waitresses. You cannot take them."

I said, "Ok. I did not know."

Knowing this made my job a little less attractive, but the waitresses and he were happy that it had been straightened out.

In addition to busting tables, I also had to clean the bathrooms. One morning, while cleaning the lady's room, one of Mr. Johnson's daughters came in. See saw me and continued to unbutton her blouse. She let her hair down and started applying her makeup. She acted as if I were invisible.

I, of course, became very nervous. What if she decided to say that I approached her or she me? Who would be believed? I quickly removed myself from her presence. I did not like that. She put my life in jeopardy, I thought.

We worked long hours. On the way home at night, I would ask him to drop me off at my girlfriend's street. From the Fairmont Road, I would walk down to her house. One evening, as I walked down the road, I saw a guy running away from her house. He was running across the field next to her house. I could not make out who he was. I never asked her about it and assumed he was just another suitor. If he was, I felt good that she told him he had to go because I was coming.

<u>The Transition</u>

Minnie M. was her name. She was tall, dark and real pretty. The first time I saw her, she was walking down the Fairmont Road. I don't remember how I met her, but I did. For the summer, at least this summer, she was my girl. They lived in a brick house. She said that she had a sister. I was never invited into the home, nor did she ever introduce me to anyone. There was a tiny newborn baby boy that I held once. I assumed that it was her sister's baby.

The porch had a light and a swing on it. The swing was suspended from the ceiling and big enough for two people. One night, we were sitting on the swing side by side. She said to me, "I can make you do anything I want you to do." I didn't say anything.

She said it again, looking at me. I could tell that she was serious. A chill went down my back. She said, "You want me to prove it to you?" I changed the subject and acted like I had something important to do. I left and did not see Minnie again for many years.

I would walk home to Parkview Terrace after leaving Minnie's house. It would be midnight or later. I walked along the Fairmont Road. I was warned to be very careful. They said that some white boys were driving around the black side of town throwing rattle snakes from their cars onto black people. I was very careful. It never happened to me, and I was home for the entire summer.

The Transition

One night my cousin Ronnie and I literally stumbled onto the scene of a rape taking place. It was at an abandoned house just off the Fairmont Road and Washington Street. There were as many as five or six guys with this one girl. She was being held down by two of the guys, one on each of her wrists. I did not know her and was told that she had been drinking and had agreed to go with one of the boys to this house for sex. When the other boys showed-up that's when she refused to have sex with any of them, so they raped her.

Benny Hinn says, ***"I felt uncomfortable about things I was doing. That's the convicting power of the Spirit."***[19]

They held her down on the wooden porch as she squirmed and tried to scream. I was not one of her rapists, but I did lay on top of her long enough to whisper into her ear that I was sorry for what was happening to her. I was not at all aroused by what was happening and was not sure if she was fully aware of what was going on.

I could never rape any woman, and I only did what I did to save face with the guys that were there. I realize now that I was trying to protect my own pride. Somehow, I felt that what I said to her would make things better for her. I was a coward, and although

---

[19] Hinn, Benny. Good Morning, Holy Spirit. (Thomas Nelson, 1990), 167

I did not participate in the rape, I did nothing to stop it. I felt awful and so, so convicted.

Rick Warren states, ***"For God to use your painful experiences, you must be willing to share them. You have to stop covering them up, and you must honestly admit your faults, failures, and fears. Doing this will probably be your most effective ministry. People are always more encouraged when we share how God's grace helped us in weakness than when we brag about our strengths."***[20]

Eventually, she was let go. We all went our separate ways and dispersed. I could not sleep at all that night. I made sure that Bernardette and I left the next day, heading back to New York. Bernardette wanted to know what the rush was. I did not answer that question.

My fear was that rape charges would be brought up against us. I was there, and although I did not participate in physically raping her, I was sure that that would not have mattered to any judge or jury. I wanted to be long gone.

As Bernardette and I stood at the Trailways bus station the next day, my heart was in my throat. How could I have witnessed such a hideous act? I could have refused to have had any part in it

---

[20] Warren, Rick. The Purpose Driven Life. (Zondervan, 2022), 247

or at least tried to stop it, but I didn't. I was so ashamed of myself. My cousin told me that she never accused anyone of raping her. That didn't make me feel any better about what happened that night. It should have never happened. It was never mentioned again and I repented and asked God for His forgiveness.

Pastor T. D. Jakes declares that ***"Demons are disembodied spirits. They don't have a body and they don't have a soul – they have no mind of their own or will of their own. Their will is totally subjected to Satan. They are vessels and carriers of Satan's nature. They are filled with his desires, his lusts, his passions, and his unclean thoughts. Because demons don't have bodies, they are seeking one. They are seeking a vehicle through which they can express their lusts and passions for evil."***[21]

Another time that I had come home, there was this family there from New York. They were visiting with the Ivy family on Page Street. I knew the Ivy family. Mr. Ivy was the blackest man in Lumberton. His skin color was incredibly dark. The family visiting him were his relatives, and they had two girls. I met one of the girls while walking around on the Fairmont Road. Her name was Stella. Her sister's name was Elizabeth.

---

[21] Jakes, So You Call Yourself A Man?, 122

I discovered they lived in the Bronx like me and not too far away. The parents were Mr. and Mrs. Robert A. They were very nice, and Stella gave me her address in New York. Upon returning to New York, I told Aunt Lou about them. She knew both Mr. Ivy and thought she knew Mr. Robert A. They lived uptown in the Bronx on 218th Street. I asked permission to start going to see Stella. Aunt Lou said, ok.

The #41 Bx bus would take me there. I only got to see her on Sundays. That was one of the happiest times since I had been in New York. Every Sunday after church, I was headed to 218th Street. The bus traveled up Webster Avenue. Made a right turn onto Gun Hill Road and a left turn onto White Plains Road.

We were now traveling under the elevated subway tracks. Just before the bus reached Gun Hill Road, there was a group of trees on the righthand side. Passing these trees made me feel like a million bucks. This part of the Bronx was different.

There was grass and trees everywhere. I had so missed this. My bus stop was 219th Street. I would walk back a block and then walk across several blocks to her house. They were all attached to well-kept single-family homes. Very neat, very clean. Nothing like what I had left on Webster Avenue.

Sometimes, I would be invited to attend church and have Sunday dinner with them. It was all wonderful. I enjoyed being away from Webster. These were the type of friends that I needed. They were a blessing to me, and I knew it.

Mark Batterson states, ***"The people you associate with will greatly determine how you think. One of the positive values of attending church is that the Christian receives encouragement from other believers there. It's possible to know the characteristics of a person by knowing his or her friends. Peer pressure is often the greatest influence upon the life of an individual."***[22]

The Lord had provided me with a new group of friends; this was another ram in the bush for me. I needed to get away from the folks I was hanging out with on Webster Avenue. I met Stella and Elizabeth in Lumberton, which is six-hundred miles away from New York, and they lived less than ten miles away from me in the Bronx. God is so amazing! My new friends were smart, had jobs, and went to school and church.

They all lived in nice private homes, except for me. I was the only outsider. I didn't think that Stella's sister liked me. She bossed Stella around a lot. I started to challenge her a little bit about that, and in doing so, I discovered that Stella had a learning disability. I tried to help her with her homework and it was a challenge.

---

[22] Batterson, Mark. All In (You are one decision away from a totally different life). (Zondervan, 2013), 16

She clearly had a learning deficit. Discovering this, I realized that her sister Elizabeth saw herself as her protector. I understood and respected that. In the wrong hands, Stella could have easily been abused and misused.

Elizabeth's boyfriend was named David. He was Jamaican and a pothead. She tried to hide his addiction. She did not want any of us to know it. David was a tall, goofy guy. He was very immature. David was a store manager somewhere. He still lived at home and always had money. He bought himself a small two-seater sports car. It was a Triumph TR-6. It had a manual transmission and I got to drive it a few times.

The group of us did a lot of things together. Stella's house seemed to always be the gathering place. We had cookouts in the parks and picnics. We would go to the movies, go out bowling etc. We had a lot of fun, and I was so happy to be away from Webster. I would take Stella to Manhattan on the subway; she loved that. Now and then, we would go to the pool hall on Gun Hill Road and the bowling alley which was on Gun Hill Road, also.

We knew how to have nice, clean fun. Aside from David, there were no drugs and even David never smoked around us. Delores worked at Kentucky Fried Chicken. We could always get a free meal there. Pat, one of Elizabeth's friends was the first to get married out of the group.

The Transition

She married a white guy. It was surprising to nearly everyone. It was not talked about. They kept to themselves. We all met him once. Pat seemed happy. Shortly after that, they had a son. The marriage seemed to be working.

Things came to a head with Stella shortly after we were relocated to Castle Hill Projects. She would come to visit me but did not know when to go home. Aunt Lou would say to me, "Curtis, it's time for Stella to go home."

She would linger and linger. Then Aunt Lou would say to me, "You don't want me to have to tell her, do you?" Lord, I knew that I did not want that. Neither did Stella, but she didn't know it.

I would finally get her out of the house. I would walk her to the bus stop. The bus would come, and she would refuse to get on it. This happened a couple of times. It was a game to her. It's nearly midnight now, and the last bus will arrive soon. If she refuses to get on this bus, I'm stuck with her and cannot take her back upstairs with me.

Out of frustration and anger, I slapped her as hard as I could to impress upon her the seriousness of the situation. I was wrong, and I knew that I was wrong. She had driven me to do something that I had never done before and something that I thought I could never do at all.

My behavior at that moment frightened me, and her behavior was not normal. That, too frightened me. She brought out the worse in me. I knew that I had to break-off the relationship. This was not working and was not going to work. When I started going to college, I stopped going to see her.

Back on Webster, I was too young to work at the liquor store. The delicatessen owner, Vincent D., worked by himself. I remember asking him if he needed any help. He said yes. I told Aunt Lou and she met with him and allowed me to work there. I learned to make sandwiches, slice meat and operate the cash register.

Lunch time was the busiest. One afternoon one of the local junkies who I knew came into the store and stole a bag of chips. I saw him and told Vinny. Vinny said to me, "Go get him, tiger."

I went outside and got the chips back. Of course, that junkie called me everything but a child of God.

One day in the deli, I was slicing some bologna. Suddenly, the bologna turned red. Then I felt the pain. I had sliced off the left front corner tip of my right index finger. Vinny wrapped my finger in towels and applied pressure.

It took a long time before the bleeding stopped. I just knew that Aunt Lou would stop me from working there, but she didn't. The bleeding eventually stopped, and I did not have to get any medical attention. I enjoyed working and was careful never to let that happen again.

The deli owner, Vinny, knew the person who owned the horse stable on Pelham Parkway. They needed help one summer, and he asked me if I wanted the work. I accepted the job. The job was loading horse manure onto dump trucks with shovels and pitchforks. I quickly learned which way the wind was blowing.

I had to take two buses to get there and two to get back home. Getting there was a pleasure. The trip home was always a different story. I smelled like horse poo-poo and looked like horse poo-poo. Everyone on the buses knew it was me. No one wanted me to stand over or near them. I tried to disappear, but I could not. I was embarrassed. That job ended quickly. I never thought to bring a change of clothing.

As I traveled back and forth to the horse stables, I noticed that once we reached the Botanical Gardens, the bus crossed over a river. I loved fishing and had never gone since coming to New York. Very early one morning, I walked from Webster Avenue to the Botanical Gardens. I crossed over the stone wall on Fordham Road with my fishing rods. After crossing the wall, I noticed a police car on one of the paths nearest to the river. I froze.

Peering through the fence, I saw two male officers get out from the back seat of their patrol car together. They were fixing their clothing and getting dressed again. I held my breath. After fixing themselves, they got back into their patrol car and drove off.

What would they have done had they spotted me looking at them? This could have easily been one of those New York Daily News Headlines: Bronx teenager found floating in the Bronx River.

Thank God that they did not see me. After they pulled away, I slid down the embankment to the river and started fishing. I caught nothing but carp and gold fish. Not good. I never fished there again.

So, the only time I got to do some "real" fishing was when I would go back home to Lumberton. I recall the time that Preston, Clara Mae's husband, and I were preparing to go fishing. I was sitting in the back of his car, attempting to remove a hook from the end of my fishing line. The knot on the hook was too tight, and I needed to break the line.

To break the line, we always placed it in our mouths between our teeth and bit down on it really hard. You could hear the line "pop," indicating that it was broken and then yank the line out of your mouth. I did this, but unbeknownst to me, the line had not broken, but I thought that it had. As I yanked the line from my mouth, the attached hook became deeply imbedded in the left corner of my mouth.

<u>The Transition</u>

At first, I wasn't sure of what happened. I tugged on the line several times, driving it further into my flesh. We tried to wiggle the hook out and even considered making a small cut. Thank God we thought better of that idea and headed to the emergency room. The line had to be cut to avoid carrying the pole with us to the hospital.

Preston cut the fishing line, but rather than cut it down near the eye of the hook close to my mouth, he cut it high-up near my forehead. The fishing line was across my face, from the left corner of my mouth to the right corner of my forehead. Everyone who saw us laughed and I said to Preston, "Oh wee, boy, you caught yourself a big one." It was embarrassing. The hook was removed quite easily, and I was given a tetanus shot.

Another time, we were fishing at a wildlife preserve area. A game warden approached us and asked for our fishing license. We each gave him our ID. Because I was from Lumberton, I did not think I needed to have a license to fish, nor had I ever known anyone else to have needed one.

The game warden told us to put all of our fishing gear into the car and follow him into town. He said that the judge would decide my fate. The judge's office was across the street from the jailhouse. The judge said that I was no longer a resident of North Carolina and had to pay a thirty-dollar fine for fishing without a license.

<u>The Transition</u>

Sitting on the bench, we counted our money and only had seventeen dollars between us. We told the judge that Preston was going home to get the rest of the money and would be right back. After Preston leaves, the judge orders the clerk to take me over to the jailhouse across the street. This was a surprise to me.

I was asked to remove all of my personal belongings, wallet, watch, keys, etc. These items were placed into a large manilla envelope. I was then asked to step up to this metal gate. The officer pulled a lever, and the gate opened. I was told to step forward and then that gate closed behind me. That's when I realized that this was the real thing. Wow, had I committed capital murder?

Another gate opened in front of me, and once I stepped forward again, it closed behind me. I now had to turn to my right and was allowed to enter the general housing area with the other inmates. I could not believe it. I was now standing outside of the individual jail cells and facing a group of four or five men at the far end of the floor.

All of the jail cells were open and lined the entire left side of the wall. On the right side was a wall of equal length. It also had bars opening about midway up to pass food trays and other necessary items to the inmates. That passageway also seemed to lead back to the front desk.

The Transition

One of the men yelled out to me, "Hey kid, what are you in for?"

I said, fishing without a license, and they all had a good, hard laugh. With that, I mustered up enough nerve and shot back, "What are you in for?"

He proudly stated I'm in here because I killed my wife. If there had been a hole big enough for me to crawl into, I would have. You could hear a pin drop. I did not have visions of gumdrops. This was now really scary.

It was still early morning, and Preston had not yet returned. I finally walked down to where the others were gathered, knowing I shouldn't have to be in there much longer.

It was now lunchtime, and I began to wonder what was taking Preston so long. He needed only to get thirteen dollars more. We were all poor and to get that seemingly little amount of money, he probably had to go to several people.

The jail orderly came around with lunch. It was on a tray with one hot dog, bun with some pork-n-beans, and a cup of very sweet grape cool aide. I declined it. He told me, "You might as well eat it because you will have to pay for it anyway."

I didn't take it; besides, I was too nervous to eat.

149

<u>The Transition</u>

Preston finally arrives at the jailhouse. He gives the desk officer thirteen dollars, and the officer tells him that the fine is now thirty-five dollars. Preston asks why. The jailer tells him that I had lunch. That's when I heard Preston yell, "LUNCH, you mean that NIGGER ate!"

The jailers laughed so hard that they let me go. I had to let Preston know that I did not order lunch. It was given to me, and I was told that I had to pay for it whether I ate it or not. Now, we had a good chuckle.

As I recall, the summers in the late 1960's were very hot. I had never been in a swimming pool before, but I knew how to swim. I learned that from swimming in the lakes, ponds and rivers back home.

In the swimming pools that I had seen in the South, black people were not allowed to swim in them. One summer, a bunch of us boys from around the block went to the only public swimming pool in the area. It was the Crotona Public Swimming Pool in Crotona Park.

The pool was located at 173rd Street off of 3rd Avenue and was within walking distance, about a mile away. A group of us went one day. The pool was beautiful, and so were the girls. It was huge, and it was crowded. We had made that trip several more times that summer.

The Transition

The pool had a sixteen-foot-deep section, which was actually a separate pool altogether. The diving platform seemed to be a mile high. I jumped off of it once, and boy, was that scary. I was quite pleased with myself, but I never did it again.

The larger section of the pool was only four feet deep. There were "no diving signs" painted everywhere. Kids still manage to hurt themselves, earning scrapes and bruises and even more serious injuries from not listening to the lifeguards, not reading the signs and trying to show off.

However, our favorite trip was the one to Coney Island. Several subway trains went there, but for us, it was the D train to the last stop. I always rode in the first subway car and stood up, looking out of the window. I found that to be fascinating because I got to see everything. I loved it.

Coney Island is located in Brooklyn, New York. My favorite ride was the cyclone. My favorite place to eat was Nathan Hot Dogs. I also loved their frog legs. My favorite game, anything. Coney Island reminded me of the county fairs back home.

The only thing missing was the livestock, grass, trees, and roasted turkey legs. I would usually win something. I enjoyed pitching dimes for glasses, plates, etc. I once won a pair of thick, tall, orange glass vases. I was so proud of them.

I brought them home and put them on our three-shelf bookcase in Castle Hill. Aunt Lou didn't mind. I think she must have liked them as well. I found them to be attractive. They were a matching pair of orange and reddish color vases. Do I dare say that they looked like they could have been hand-blown?

Sometimes we would walk the boardwalk but we never went onto the beach. Our trip to Coney Island was always the highlight of the summer.

One summer, I got a job through a city-run neighborhood organization. This organization provided summer jobs to inner-city youth. The job was in the Melrose section of the Bronx. This neighborhood was getting a new medical clinic.

Our job was to get the facility ready to be occupied. We painted, removed rubbish, washed windows, etc. It was opposite the Forest Projects on Caudwell Avenue. While working there, I met a guy named Jerry. Jerry was visiting his father who lived in a development called the Concourse Village, not too far away. Jerry lived with his mother in New Orleans and had come to the Bronx to visit his father.

He had come up this summer to stay with his father. Things just flowed between Jerry and me. We would spend afternoons together, laughing and playing. He had a very different accent. It was almost to me like a foreign language. I found it to be quite interesting.

I discovered from my World Book Encyclopedia that New Orleans is a Louisiana city on the Mississippi River, near the Gulf of Mexico. Nicknamed the "Big Easy," it's known for its round-the-clock nightlife, vibrant live-music scene and spicy, singular cuisine, reflecting its history as a melting pot of French, African and American cultures. Embodying its festive spirit is Mardi Gras, the late-winter carnival famed for raucous costumed parades and street parties.

I enjoyed listening to him talk about New Orleans. He would tell me about Mardi Gras. I had never heard of it. He would tell me about the parade. He told me about the costumes and beads. He told me what women had to do to get them. I found it all so fascinating.

It was a summer that I never forgot. I never got to meet Jerry's father. One day, Jerry was suddenly gone, just not around anymore. I never saw or heard from him again. It was such a good summer friendship. I missed him a lot and had no way of contacting him. We never saw each other again.

I graduated from P.S. 28 and went on to the neighborhood junior high school, Creston Junior High. To my surprise, this was an all-boys school with a name, not a number. This school was located on the west side of the Grand Concourse on Creston Avenue and

183rd Street. There was no uniform required, however, we did have to wear a collared shirt and neck-tie every day.

I remember two teachers from that school. One was an English teacher named Mr. Warren. The other was a Spanish teacher named Ms.Nahun. Mr. Warren was the worst teacher ever. He screamed, yelled and hollered at different students the entire class period. He never accomplished anything, including completing a lesson. Most of the students had no respect for him.

I was not one of them. Aunt Lou did not play that, and I was not the type of kid who would disrespect an adult anyway. I wanted to make Aunt Lou proud of me. I would have been killed if it was reported to Aunt Lou that I was disrespectful to any adult. I was grateful to her for taking my sister and me into her care.

Mr. Warren was a tall, white, lanky man. He took long, awkward strides. Because of his unusual gait, he reminded me of a slinky toy. He wore glasses and had long, dark brown hair. His hair was just shy of touching his shoulders. He had no control of his class and not a clue of how to gain it. And we were the good kids! I felt sorry for him. He did not belong in the classroom.

There was this one kid in our class who carried a briefcase that looked like a suitcase. When class was over, he was always the first one out of the classroom. When the bell rang, this guy was gone. One day, the bell rang, and he took off.

The Transition

Unknowingly, I was observing this at the same time as another kid. We commented at the same time. I said, well, off to the bus station and the other guy said, well, off to the airport. I thought about what we said. I saw him going to the bus station because that had been my experience with traveling.

The other kid saw him going to the airport because that had been his experience with traveling. That was very revealing to me. If our realities are based on facts, then our perceptions can't be wrong. Perception is all relative to your life experiences. The airport was as intangible and invisible to me as was the bus station to him. I had never flown and would be willing to bet he had never traveled on a Trailway Bus.

Miss Nahun, on the other hand, was absolutely gorgeous. I never had her for Spanish. However, I'm sure that she taught it well. Whenever we changed classes, if Ms. Nahun had to go to another floor, every boy in the vicinity would rush to the staircase.

All eyes followed her beautiful legs up and up the staircase. She wore black-rim glasses and red lipstick. Is that not classic hooker material? Every boy hoped to glimpse something that no other boy had seen. We were just a bunch of stupid, horny teenagers. I think she secretly enjoyed driving our little boy minds crazy. She was never absent, and neither were we.

Then there was Spivey. Spivey's family had moved to the Bronx, and they were from Mississippi. We became friends at school. We did not have any classes together, and he did not live in my neighborhood. I befriended him probably because both of us had southern roots.

Spivey was very country and had a deep southern drawl. Unlike most of us boys, he decided to do something about his horniness other than masturbating. He told me that he went to Times Square in downtown Manhattan and got him a prostitute. I could not believe it.

He told me that she took him to a room. When his time was up, the girl tapped him on the shoulder to get up. He said that he didn't. He said that he wanted more. I could not believe what he was telling me. After refusing to get up, he said that she somehow tightened her vaginal muscles.

He said that it hurt his penis so bad that he yelled out. "That got me up," he said, "it really hurt."

We laughed the rest of the week about that. Although, he said it wasn't funny at the time and I bet it wasn't. I did not have the courage to do what he did. I lost contact with Spivey after the ninth grade.

<u>The Transition</u>

I struggled with math. Algebra was kicking my but. I needed help. Aunt Lou could not help me because she didn't know it. I was going to fail the class and the regent's exam. She came out to the school and met with my homeroom teacher, who also happened to be my math teacher. She told him of our situation and her inability to help me and asked if he would tutor me. She offered to pay him. He agreed to tutor me after school for free.

That's exactly what I needed: tutoring. I was fine once I learned the rules and how to apply them. I passed the class and the regent's exam with a score of 86%. Both he and Aunt Lou were very proud of me. I passed all of my ninth-grade regent exams.

Ninth graders were allowed to go off of school property for lunch. There was an all-girls junior high school on the east side of the Grand Concourse. We (the boys) rarely ventured over to their territory and vice versa. Lunch was only forty-five minutes. I mostly bought pizza and hung out with classmates, Glen S. and Vandy E.

Glen S. invited me once to his house for lunch. He lived around the corner on the grand concourse. One block from the school. His building had an elevator. His apartment had a sunken living room with parquet floors, and his bookshelves were built into the walls. Glen had hundreds of books and offered to give me some.

I said okay because we had several shelves that I could put on at our new place in the Castle Hill Projects. He must have given me twenty-five books or more. I was impressed. Remember, it didn't take much to impress me. His building had a superintendent and a doorman, much like Ms. Lucy's building.

I was too embarrassed to ask him what his family did if they wanted heat. I also wondered if a wooden box held his toilet water, too. His wooden floors were parquet. Wood-like linoleum covered my floors. Don't get me wrong. Coming from where I came from, I was very grateful for everything we had. I thanked God and knew that my sister and I were still in a better place.

I was beginning to discover how other folks more fortunate than me lived. I wanted a better life and believed that I could have it. Vandy E.'s family owned a Chinese laundry in the basement of one of the nearby buildings. Vandy was a big guy. He was a gentle giant. He introduced me to his entire family, which I thought was really nice.

We were all bright kids. We all got along quite well with each other. And, again, just like PS 28, there were many races in each class. I was in the brightest ninth-grade class, 9ep. I forget what the "ep" stood for, but our coursework was more challenging and we had to take the state regents exams. This was not offered to the regular ninth graders. It was me and one other black kid in a class of twenty-seven students. These guys were all intelligent and looked it. I was proud of my academic achievements.

<u>The Transition</u>

The overall school was a good one. Some of the guys were gay. No one, to my knowledge, bothered them about their preferred sexual orientation. Donald W. liked me and let it be known. He was a small guy. His fingers reminded me of those similar to a tree frog.

I befriended him because we had something in common. He could sing very well, and I was in the choir at my church. I didn't know where Donald lived. He was shy and never did join my circle of friends. We lost contact after the ninth grade.

Sports was also a big deal. I was on the basketball team only because I was tall. I sucked, to put it mildly. One guy named Alex was outstanding. Supposedly, all of the High Schools wanted him, which was understandable because he was an exceptional player.

Although I never played hooky from school I knew where the hooky parties were held. It was usually at the same apartment every day. I would only go during lunchtime. Just to show my face, trying to be cool. I remember someone in the group saying that we should take on a nickname.

They thought this would make us all seem really cool. The name that I chose for myself was Priest. It made me feel like I was still a part of the group but also still a part of Christ.

Mark Batterson states, ***"We're too Christian to enjoy sin and too sinful to enjoy Christ. We've got just enough Jesus to be informed, but not enough to be transformed."***[23]

The idea of nicknames was short-lived and soon forgotten. Those who already had them, kept them.

At the hooky parties, I saw all kinds of drugs. There were drugs and junkies all over the place. I mostly knew everyone there. One time I had gone by, and there was this green leafy stuff completely covering the kitchen table. I quickly surmised that it was marijuana.

I remember guys in the living room tying belts around their upper arms and holding one end of the belt with their teeth. This was to force a vein to appear. This enabled them to shoot the liquified drug (smack, cocaine or some other drug) directly into their veins. It was not a pleasant sight and I couldn't stand to watch them do it.

What on Earth was I doing there? There go I but for the grace of God! The devil had a trap set for me. It was only by God's grace that I did not fall into it. All that exposure never enticed me to try any of it. If anything, it turned me away; I was too afraid and too saved! Not sure who I feared most, God or Aunt Lou.

---

[23] Batterson, All In (You are one decision away from a totally different life), 25

Mark Batterson also declares, ***"Sin always overpromises and underdelivers, while righteousness pays dividends for eternity. Nothing is more illogical than sin. It's the epitome of poor judgement. It's temporary insanity with eternal consequences. And we have no alibi, save the cross of Jesus Christ. It's not worth it, and we know it. Yet we do it. We sell out for so little instead of going all in for so much."***[24]

I was amazed at how street junkies would nod and slowly dip towards the ground. Then they would slowly come back up to an almost standing position. I never saw a junkie fall onto the ground. This was not true for alcoholics. Alcoholics stayed on the ground.

The junkies that I knew took a somewhat paternalistic interest in me. They would encourage me never to get involved with drugs and to stay in school. I know that this is a rather perverted way of looking at it but it did help to motivate me not to end up like them. I was also conscious not to let that become a false sense of security.

We once hung out at Dirty Mike's apartment. Dirty Mike got his name from being just that. He was physically dirty and smelly. He lived in the building directly behind mine. His building was on

---

[24] Batterson, All In (You are one decision away from a totally different life), 149

Valentine Avenue, just on the other side of the large rocks that could be seen from Aunt Lou's bedroom window.

Dirty Mike's building was a lot nicer than mine. He did not have a doorman, but his building was much more modern. It also had an elevator. He lived with his mother.

On this particular day, we only had a half day of school, so we hung out at his place. His apartment was nicely furnished. They had an aquarium in the living room with several fish in it. It was an average-sized tank on a stand. We fried some chicken in his kitchen and made quite a mess.

We ate the chicken in his living room and tossed the bones into his fish tank. His kitchen and living room were trashed. I never went to Mike's house again. I hope he survived that. I'm sure that his mother wanted to kill him.

Dirty Mike had a nice-looking girlfriend, and I could never figure out what she saw in him. He was a slob, but you never know what attracts some people to other people.

One night, I was hanging out with some friends. We were playing inside the staircase of Dirty Mike's building. One of the kids had some drugs and asked me to try some. We stopped on a staircase landing between floors. He pulled the drugs from his pocket. It was in a small cellophane packet. He dipped the handle of a small spoon into the bag.

This white powdery substance rested on the back of the spoon. He was lifting it up to my nose. Just as I was about to snort it, the super of the building burst through the door and yelled, "What are you kids doing in here?"

We dropped everything and ran out of the building. I realized then just how close I came to being a junkie and thanked God for that not happening. I will never forget that night. You cannot tell me that was not a blessing. The devil had a trap set for me. That super was my ram in the bush. Lord, I thank you!

How does one escape an environment like this? It's just a matter of time before you succumb to the pressures of your peers. But, in my moment of weakness, God stepped in. The devil can't make us do anything; he can only suggest and tempt us. Proverbs such as these warn us. You lay down with dogs, you get up with fleas, or what can you expect from a pig but a grunt?"

John C. Maxwell writes, ***"The people you associate with will greatly determine how you think. One of the positive values of attending church is that the Christian receives encouragement from other believers there. It's possible to know the characteristics*** *of a person by knowing his or her friends. Peer pressure is often the greatest influence upon the life of an individual.*"[25]

As you go forward in your life and find obstacles in your way, it may serve you to review Hill's seven principles for Outwitting the Devil in your life:

1. **Definiteness of purpose**

2. **Mastery over self**

3. **Learning from adversity**

4. **Controlling environmental influence (associations)**

5. **Time (giving permanency to positive, rather than negative thought habits and developing wisdom)**

6. **Harmony (acting with definiteness of purpose to become the dominating influence in your own mental, spiritual, and physical environment)**

7. **Caution (thinking through your plan before you act)**

In reviewing these seven principles, you may identify and reveal what is holding you back from achieving your greatest success. Hill says, *"Your only limitations are self-imposed."*[26]

---

[25] Maxwell, John C., Think on these Things (Meditation for Leaders). (Beacon Hill Press, 1999), 16

[26] Hill, Napoleon and Lechter, Sharon. Outwitting The Devil (The Secret to Freedom and Success). (Sterling, 2011), 257

Napoleon Hill says, *"throughout nature one may find evidences that all-natural law moves in an orderly manner, through the law of harmony. Through the operation of this law nature forces everything within the range of a given environment to become harmoniously related. Understand this truth and you will catch a new and a more intriguing vision of the power of environment. You will understand why association with negative minds is fatal to those seeking self-determination. Do you mean that nature voluntarily forces human beings to harmonize with the influences of their environment. Yes, that is true. The law of hypnotic rhythm forces upon every living thing the dominating influences of the environment in which it exists. If nature forces human beings to take on the nature of the environment in which they live, what means of escape are available to people who find themselves in an environment of poverty and failure but desire to escape? They must change their environment or remain poverty-stricken. Nature permits no one to escape the influences of his environment. However, nature, in her abundance of wisdom, has given to every normal human being the privilege of establishing his own mental, spiritual, and physical environment, but once he establishes it, he must become a part of it. This is the inexorable working of the law of harmony."*[27]

What had we done to receive such grace? What had we done to merit such mercy? Mark Batterson says, *"Mercy is not getting what you deserve – the wrath of God. Grace is getting what you don't deserve – the righteousness of Christ. Everything that you've done wrong is forgiven and forgotten. And everything Christ did right – His righteousness – is transferred to your account. And then God calls it even."*[28]

Aunt Lou, Bernardette and I attended Tremont Baptist Church every Sunday. It was and still is a beautiful gray stone church that sits on a hill. It has beautifully stained-glass windows and a balcony. I only knew of one other person from my neighborhood my age who attended my church.

In the basement was a raised stage where plays and other performing arts activities took place. I remember Mrs. Furgerson convincing me to be in a talent show. She wanted me to recite the longest poem I had ever seen from memory. **The Creation by James Weldon Johnson (1871-1938).**

---

[27] Hill and Lechter, Outwitting The Devil (The Secret to Freedom and Success), 236

[28] Batterson, All In (You are one decision away from a totally different life), 25

The Transition

James Weldon Johnson, born in Florida in 1871, was a national organizer for the NAACP and an author of poetry and nonfiction. Perhaps best known for the song "Lift Every Voice and Sing," he also wrote several poetry collections and novels, often exploring racial identity and the African American folk tradition.

The Creation

And God stepped out on space, and he looked around and
said: I'm lonely—I'll make me a world. And far as the eye of God
could see, Darkness covered everything,
Blacker than a hundred midnights, down in a cypress swamp.

Then God smiled, and the light broke, and the darkness
rolled up on one side,
and the light stood shining on the other, and God said: That's
good!

Then God reached out and took the light in his hands, and
God rolled the light around in his hands, until he made the sun;
and he set that sun a-blazing in the heavens.

And the light that was left from making the sun, God
gathered it up in a shining ball, and flung it against the darkness,
spangling the night with the moon and stars. Then down between
the darkness and the light He hurled the world;
and God said: That's good!

<u>The Transition</u>

Then God himself stepped down—and the sun was on his
right hand,
and the moon was on his left; The stars were clustered about his
head,
and the earth was under his feet. And God walked, and where he
trod
His footsteps hollowed the valleys out and bulged the mountains
up.

Then he stopped and looked and saw that the earth was hot
and barren.
So God stepped over to the edge of the world and he spat out the
seven seas—
He batted his eyes, and the lightnings flashed—He clapped his
hands, and the thunders rolled—And the waters above the earth
came down,
The cooling waters came down.

Then the green grass sprouted, and the little red flowers
blossomed,
The pine tree pointed his finger to the sky, and the oak spread out
his arms,
The lakes cuddled down in the hollows of the ground, and the
rivers ran down to the sea; and God smiled again, and the rainbow

appeared,

and curled itself around his shoulder.

Then God raised his arm and he waved his hand over the

sea and over the land,

and he said: Bring forth! Bring forth! And quicker than God could

drop his hand,

fishes and fowls and beasts and birds swam the rivers and the seas,

roamed the forests and the woods, and split the air with their

wings.

and God said: That's good!

Then God walked around, and God looked around on all

that he had made.

He looked at his sun, and he looked at his moon, and he looked at

his little stars;

He looked on his world with all its living things, and God said: I'm

lonely still.

Then God sat down—on the side of a hill where he could

think;

By a deep, wide river he sat down; with his head in his hands, God

thought and thought, till he thought: I'll make me a man!

Up from the bed of the river God scooped the clay; and by

the bank of the river

He kneeled him down; and there the great God Almighty

The Transition

Who lit the sun and fixed it in the sky, who flung the stars to the most far corner of the night, who rounded the earth in the middle of his hand; this great God,
like a mammy bending over her baby, kneeled down in the dust toiling over a lump of clay till he shaped it in is his own image;

Then into it he blew the breath of life, and man became a living soul.
Amen. Amen.

By James Weldon Johnson (1871 – 1938)

Mrs. Furgerson was my coach. She encouraged me to use my arms, and she would recite - And the light that was left from making the sun, God gathered it up in a shining ball, and flung it against the darkness – turning sideways and swinging her arms wide. Show some emotions, she would tell me.

The night of the show, I was a nervous wreck. I didn't use any of the inflections at all; it was mostly monotone, and after around the fifth verse, I hesitated a lot, trying to remember my lines. I'm lucky that I wasn't booed from the stage, but would people do that to a kid in a church? Of course not. Aunt Lou, Mrs. Furgerson and Dr. Robinson loved it and thought that I did a wonderful job.

My neighborhood friends and acquaintances did not go to my church, except for Larry W. There was Charles C. who had a club foot. We nicknamed him "crow toe." There was Looney, which was his nickname. He was special needs, and I never did get to know his real name, I don't think any of us did. There was Eddie C. and his sister Zelda C. There was Cynthia and Jeana; they were sisters. Their mother demanded to know every detail of their daily lives.

So, she got the skinny on all of us. These last four people lived around the corner on Valentine Ave. They lived in private homes. Also around the corner in a private house was Tweedy. Tweedy was the bully. I later learned that he and "crow toe" had become an item. The boys all made homemade skateboards and had plenty of hills to try them out on.

Susan, another one of our friends, lived in Larry's building on the fifth floor. She was very nice but also very ugly. She was a little older than us and mostly kept to herself. I liked Susan but was embarrassed to be seen out in public with her. I felt sorry for her. People would stare at her face. She had a wonderful personality and a beautiful figure. She was such a sweet person.

Her kindness made you not focus so much on how her face looked. She was not disfigured or deformed in any way. She was just plain ugly. These were some of the folks that I hung out with in my neighborhood, not to mention the two junkies, Charles and Mack.

Except for a few homes on Valentine Avenue, all were neat and well-kept. We all hung out together at one time or another. Summertime was the best, and Susan and I would hang out on her building's rooftop, occasionally being chased off by her super.

One evening, three of us guys were coming home from some event or party in Harlem. It was suggested that we take a cab home. I said, ok and I saw no harm in it and assumed that each of us would pay our fair share. We hailed a cab, and I sat in the middle. Our destination was Dirty Mike's address in the Bronx on Valentine Avenue.

When we arrived at his building, both guys jumped out of the cab and ran. The cabbie instinctively chased after them. This left me sitting there in the back of the cab. After figuring out what had just happened, I, too, did the same thing: jumped out and ran. The cabbie then chased after me, yelling, stop, stop.

It's a good thing that there were no cops around. It was late at night. These guys had pre-planned this unbeknownst to me, and even if they had told me this was what they would do, I would not have gone along with it. Realizing that they were dangerous, I never hung out with them again.

It also taught me not to just follow along with people. I learned to choose my friends very carefully. Here again, I narrowly missed being caught up in a situation that could have easily changed the trajectory of my life forever. Lesson learned: Know your audience.

Then there was also Charles and Mack. These guys were older than us. Both of whom I suspected of being drug addicts. Charles was the scariest. He had a tongue that looked like a coral sponge, straight from the Caribbean Sea. His tongue was nasty; it was fat and swollen. It reminded me of Johnny's tongue back in Lumberton, but Johnny wasn't a junkie, and he wasn't nasty.

Charles was repulsive. His tongue wasn't smooth anywhere. When he spoke, you could not help but see it. Mack, his sidekick, wanted to be a smooth criminal. He was a fast talker, a con man. I'm sure that he was a junkie, too. These were some of my associates in the neighborhood.

I would hang out with them and the others. Sometimes, they would go to Echo Park to get high. I would never participate in the drugs but would act as the lookout for the police. I was very blessed. At the time, I didn't realize just how blessed I was. His Grace was being extended to me time and time again. I was being saved over and over again. Perhaps that's what being saved means.

Timothy Keller declares that ***"We are too fallen to save ourselves, too flawed to keep our covenant with God. There will*** *have to be an intervention of radical grace, and it can come only from God himself."*[29]

Aunt Lou called me into her bedroom one evening. As she sat on the side of her bed, she patted the space beside her, beckoning me to sit next to her. I sat beside her and she said, "Curtis, I want you to listen to me very carefully because I'm only going to say this once."

"Son," she began, "I cannot be with you all of the time. I know your friends, who you hang out with, and what they do. The drug addict I know because I have to step over them every day. I'm raising you and your sister as best I can.

If you become involved with drugs, you will no longer be welcome to live here with me. I will have you put away. Do you understand?"

"Yes," I said, "I understand."

"Okay, that's it." She never mentioned drugs to me ever, again, never.

However, there is one habit I did start, and I wish she had stopped me. It was cigarette smoking. That habit nearly killed me

---

[29] Keller, Timothy. Preaching. (Penguin, 2016), 48

and would have had I not quit. Satan will take you out in any way that he can.

Aunt Lou was a smoker. She smoked Camels with no filter. I was fourteen when I first started smoking, and at first, I did not like it. I thought it was boring and did not see what the attraction was. I did not know how to inhale and probably would have given it up.

One night, I was at a party. We all were smoking. I had a mouth full of smoke, and a girl asked me a question. Being the gentleman that I am, I did not want to blow the smoke into her face, so I swallowed it. It felt great! I had done it. I had inhaled.

I continued to practice my newly discovered skill. Little did I know, that was the beginning of my addiction. The devil had a trap set for me, and nicotine got me. She found out because I started taking her cigarettes. When Aunt Lou found out about my smoking, she did not object. She just started making me buy my own.

I think her thinking was, I'd rather see him with a cigarette in his mouth rather than a needle in his arm. If this is the only thing he will do, then I'll allow it. However, I wish she had stopped me. It nearly cost me my life, and I will explain to what extent later.

Author Norman Geisler explains it this way, *"There are no conditions for God's giving of salvation; it is wholly of grace. But there is one (and only one) condition for receiving this gift – true saving faith. There is absolutely nothing in man that is the basis for God saving him. But there was something in God (love) that is the basis for man's salvation. It was not because of any merit in man but only because of grace in God that salvation was initiated toward man. Man does not initiate salvation (Rom. 3:11), and he cannot attain it (Rom. 4:5). But he can and must receive it (John 1:12). Salvation is an unconditional act of God's election. Man's faith is not a condition for God giving salvation, but it is for man receiving it. Nonetheless, the act of faith (free choice) by which man receives salvation is not meritorious. It is the Giver who gets credit for the gift, not the receiver. Why, then, does one person go to heaven and another not? Because God willed that all who receive His grace will be saved and that all who reject it will be lost."*[30]

Echo Park was a park without a playground. It was located on a hill and was opposite our church. There were no basketball or handball courts, swing sets, or monkey bars. It only had footpaths with benches along them. Because it was hilly terrain, the footpaths were all railed in. These rails prevented a good sled ride in the snow. It was a park to feed the pigeons. My friends found it to be a good place to get high.

---

[30] Geisler, Norman, Chosen But Free. (Bethany House, 2001), 185

The Transition

Our basketball court was on Webster Avenue. We had to play sidewalk basketball. Our rim was the last rung of the fire escape next to the cleaners. That last rung served as our basketball hoop. If we got lucky, someone would secure a cardboard box to it. It was pathetic, but it was our reality.

The other popular games were Skellies and Crack Top. Both were sidewalk/street games. One involved chalk, the other a spinning top. The chalk was needed to draw boxes on the sidewalk or asphalt. Soda bottle caps were filled with hot liquid wax. After it cooled, it made them heavy. This extra weight allowed them to slide better across the concrete without flipping over and rolling away. The goal of this game was to get your bottle cap into the correct box drawn on the ground.

You had to have a spinning top with a good sharp metal point to play crack top. As the name suggests, this game's objective was to crack someone else's top. It was a horrible game when you think about it. It was a game of precision. If you were really skilled you could actually split someone else's top in half or put a serious gash into it. Either result was acceptable.

To prepare to throw down your top, you held it upside down. Then wrap your string around the tip, starting at but not including the metal point. You made sure that the string was tight. You wanted your throw to be hard and accurate. At the end of your string, you always made sure that you had a loop to put a finger through. This enabled you to control your spin. The object of the game was to hit an already spinning top. Sometimes, when someone's top was split or chipped, fights would break out.

If it was a bigger guy or a bully, guys would say they were going home to get their brother. Although I never got into any fights, I knew that I could not go home to get my brother. This made me angry. I had a brother, but he was never around.

I didn't think of Robert as being grown and living on his own. Robert was ten years older than me. He was an adult. I often wondered if my anger toward Robert was because of his not being around or because he was gay. It was probably a little of both. I had a gay friend, two of them, to be exact.

Pastor Jakes states that ***"From boyhood and particularly during the teenage years, a man is conditioned by peers, the media, and other cultural factors to want to be seen as 110 percent heterosexual, studly, and macho, the king of conquests with women. (The perception lingers that there's a direct correlation between a man's number of sexual exploits with women and his masculinity. This is not necessarily the case at all, since a man who cannot control his sexual desire often battles insecurity, fear and anxiety over his manhood.) Even though he may be totally free of any homosexual desire, interest, or tendency, that doesn't*** *mean that he doesn't have some insecurity or anxiety about being misunderstood when it comes to same sex friendships.* "[31]

Robert left home (Lumberton) when he was really young. I've been told that he was 16 years old. That would have made me 6 years old and Bernardette 2 years old at that time. Robert did things that I can never forget, but through the grace of God, I have been able to forgive. I remember one time he came home from New York and had one of his lovers at our house.

He lied to us about coming to New York and who we would be staying with. I always suspected that, at some point, he had molested Bernardette. She weakly denied it when I questioned her about it. I did not believe her denial. I remember as a little boy, maybe ten or eleven years old. Robert would be laughing and playing with Bernardette in bed and I would try to get her away from him. He would make me go away and leave the room.

Even at that age, I knew something wasn't right. I think she was trying to protect him. I never had much respect for him. He seemed to think that being gay gave him the right to behave and act in any way he wanted. He behaved as if he did not have to be held accountable for anything. It was all about him.

---

[31] Jakes, T.D., He-Motions. (G. P. Putnam Son's, 2004), 152

<u>The Transition</u>

He loved being the center of attention. When he lived with us that short while in Castle Hill, I would watch him and Bernardette dancing in the living room. I never wanted to join them. I would sit in a corner, watching them while I read a book. Bernardette idolized him. They had this special relationship. It always made me uncomfortable, but never jealous.

One time, Aunt Lou wanted to punish me once for doing something that I should not have done. She called Robert. She asked that he come over to give me a whipping. Not that she couldn't do it herself. I guess this was her attempt at keeping Robert involved in our lives.

We were still living on Webster Avenue at the time. He came over and I'm sure Aunt Lou told him what I had done. She told him to whip me in her bedroom. She gave him a belt and told me to go into her room, and he followed.

He first hit me across the back of my thighs with the belt. I felt the sting but did not cry. Then he hit me again across my back. With that, all of my hatred, resentment, dislike and disrespect towards him rose to my mouth. I yelled at him, "You better not hit me again."

Aunt Lou immediately burst into the room. She told Robert that was enough. I left the room crying. Why did she have him discipline me? If I needed a whipping, as far as I was concerned, she was the only one qualified to give it to me.

She was the one taking care of us. She was the one scraping and sacrificing to raise us, not him. I would have seriously hurt him had he hit me again, and Aunt Lou knew it. She never called him again, at least not for that.

The city eventually condemned our building. All of the families were placed in various public housing projects around the Bronx. Miss Jannie went to the Watson Avenue projects. Villitha's family was placed in the Eden Wald Projects. Miss Freida was placed in the Sound View Projects, and we were placed in the Castle Hill Projects.

I remember Robert staying with us in Castle Hill after his return from Vietnam. He had a drinking problem, and Aunt Lou told him that he had to get his own place, and he did. I remember him taking me to what I thought was his apartment on Central Park West at 108th Street. It was big and grand. When I walked into the living room, I remember saying, wow, this is so nice. I was really proud of him at that moment and somewhat surprised. I did not expect him to have such a nice place.

As I started to walk around the apartment, he called me over to a small bedroom near the front door. He said in a low voice, "Only this room we're in now is mine. I don't have the whole apartment."

I was so disappointed, and he seemed to be embarrassed.

He could only afford to rent a room, not an apartment. As I scanned the room, I saw his hot plate on the floor in a corner next to his tiny refrigerator. I assumed that he could not use the kitchen either. I felt sorry for him.

Robert was all about having a good time all of the time. He would try to attract other men in my presence. This really made me angry. I was insulted, embarrassed and disrespected. One time, he got into a fight. I think it was because he made a pass at the wrong guy. He didn't care. It was all about him.

He would brag to me about things he would do and buy for his friends. None of which he had done for me or Bernardette. Yeah, I didn't have much respect for him. He certainly didn't put us before his friends. He also shared an apartment on 106th Street near Manhattan Avenue with some guy. Robert could never quite make it on his own.

I remember the time that he and I drove to Lumberton together. We went down in my little red Volkswagen. Robert did not know how to drive a stick (manual transmission). I did all of the driving, and I didn't mind it. At some point during the trip, both of us fell asleep while I was driving.

<u>The Transition</u>

My car ran off the road. We were travelling on Interstate Highway 95 south. It was late April and a beautiful day. Where we had run off, the road was under construction. The road was being widened and they were adding another lane. All of the trees had been removed, and this section of the roadway appeared ready to be paved. It was flat but not smooth, and the dirt was red.

After falling asleep at the wheel, the car drifted to the left and off the highway. It was the bumpiness of this unpaved section that woke us up. When I opened my eyes, there was dust everywhere.

I wasn't immediately sure what was happening, and when I realized what had happened, I gradually pulled the car back onto the highway. Cars were blowing and honking their horns.

Robert and I looked at each other in disbelief. We agreed that we would take the next exit and find a room to get some sleep. Count your blessings; name them one by one. Had this happened at any other point along the way, we would have driven into a tree or down a ravine. I probably would not be here now to tell you this story.

Author Benny Hinn states, ***"The Holy Spirit is also your great defender. For example: Who do you think protects you from the attacks of Satan? It is the Holy Spirit. Who keeps you safe? It is the Holy Spirit. That is the task assigned to Him by Christ. So often we call Him Jesus, but He is actually the Spirit of Jesus.***

Again, we only separate them for discussion's sake so we can better understand them because they are really one Being. Because where the Holy Ghost is, Jesus is -- and the Father is. When the Holy Ghost talks to you, all three are talking, but the Holy Ghost is the one you hear. The Holy Ghost is the one you sense. The Holy Ghost is the one leading you in the will of the Father."[32]

We were still visiting in Lumberton on Robert's birthday, April 29th. I had arranged with my friend Clara Mae to have a little party for him at her house. Robert and I were staying at the Holiday Inn Hotel. On the morning of his birthday, I said good morning to him, but not happy birthday.

We had breakfast together, and I said nothing about it being his birthday. Now, I could see that he was getting upset. I suggested that we ride over to see Clara Mae. He half-heartedly agreed. During the ride over, he did not say one word to me. I knew he was upset with me, thinking that I had forgotten his birthday.

We got to Clara Mae's house and he refused to get out of the car. I went inside. I said to Clara, "Clara, he is hotter than a firecracker. He thinks that I've forgotten it's his birthday. He is so angry that he refuses to get out of the car."

---

[32] Hinn, Benny. Good Morning, Holy Spirit. (Thomas Nelson, 1990), 74

<u>The Transition</u>

Clara started to laugh. "Let me go get him," she said. Clara approached the car and coaxed him to come inside. Everyone had gathered in her kitchen, it was Betty Lou, Ruby and a few others. She brought him into the kitchen, and we all shouted, Happy birthday! We started singing 'Happy Birthday.' Clara had baked a beautiful chocolate cake with candles. He started to cry. It was a great day. He said to me, "I thought you forgot."

Over the years the relationship between Robert and I did get better. At some point, life got the better of him. He tried to commit suicide. He drank some antifreeze and attempted to slit both his wrists. My wife said that he could not have been too serious about taking his own life because he was still alive.

She said that he did not drink enough antifreeze and did not cut his wrists deeply enough. We visited him in the psych ward of the VA hospital on 23rd Street in Manhattan. By then, I had gotten married, and Sandy had our first daughter.

Robert recovered and, sometime after that, contracted AIDS. He lived with it for over 10 years. According to his doctor, Robert lived well beyond the life expectancy of an AIDS patient at that time.

During this time, I brought him to see our new home. We had moved into a beautiful townhouse in northwest Yonkers. I really wanted him to see it. I wanted him to see how successful his little brother had become.

He did get to see it. He loved it. It was three levels with many stairs and a partial view of the Hudson River. Sandy said, "You know gay people, they love their stairs."

He adored Jillian. I didn't like it when he held her in his arms. I never took my eyes off of him. His holding her made me very uncomfortable.

Robert lived in Harlem at 32 West 132nd Street. It was a rat-infested five-story walk-up. So was every other five-story walk-up in Harlem. He had a one-bedroom apartment on the second floor. His living room window faced the street.

His bedroom was in the rear with those ugly window guards at the fire escape. He had a small lap dog named Mikey. Mikey was a mean little dog with a nasty disposition. He was of the terrier breed. He was not friendly and bit me. I did not like him either. Robert ended up giving him away. I said, good riddance.

Not too long after his visit to our home, Robert had become incapacitated. He had lost a lot of weight. He had become very fragile. His hair on his head had become very straight. This had to be the result of his cocktail of daily medications.

<u>The Transition</u>

He would get encouraged if his T-cell count rose. T-cells are a type of white blood cell called lymphocytes. They help your immune system fight germs and protect you from disease. This count had become the barometer for how well he was doing. I began to take him to his doctor's appointments. He could no longer walk or stand on his own. I had to pick him up and carry him in my arms to my car. He had house attendants with him throughout the night. I started going by daily to see him.

This began to take a toll on my health. I wasn't getting enough sleep. It also started to affect my job performance. I sent an e-mail to my boss.

It read as follows:

Original Author: White, Curtis;

10/03/96, 19:29 hrs

Good morning,

My brother, Robert White has advanced HIV/AIDs. He is not expected to see Thanksgiving. His wishes are that he be allowed to die at home. He has been provided with 24hr home care provided that I can be with him when an attendant doesn't come. This has not been a problem in the past but will be now should I have to care for him on either shift. This will reduce the # of hours that I work, here. I will only work a few hours tonight because he was re-examined and admitted to the VA hospital on 23ʳᵈ Street (10ᵗʰ fl.) today. He will be released the latter part of next week. In effect, being sent home to die. I don't anticipate having to be totally absent from work until the time of his death at which you will be promptly notified. He is single, lives alone and I am his only family member in New York. When he does die there will be no viewing of the body and my family will hold a private funeral service.

Thanking you in advance for your understanding.

Curtis

The response was the following:

Curtis,

You have my heartfelt sympathies. I know how it feels to suffer this type of loss. Take care and keep in touch.

Mike

I needed this kind of response. My personal experiences with UPS up to this point were not empathic. This allowed me to exhale, take a deep breath and give my full attention to Robert.

One day, while giving Robert a shave, he looked up at me and said, "You have always been the big brother."

I was surprised. During this period, I learned so much about Robert. AIDS had stripped him of his pride and vanity. I learned that he was funny, witty, and grateful. He had become humble. I liked this new Robert. Who knew!

Robert knew a lot about the bible. He was no stranger to Christ. He went to a Catholic school in his early years in Lumberton. While in New York, he was Baptist, Pentecostal and eventually, Seventh-Day Adventist.

Unfortunately, through his sickness, he had learned and realized who his real friends were. He was confined to his recliner in the living room. People would come and go as they pleased. As he grew weaker, he started to give some of his possessions away and his so-called friends also started helping themselves. He was not aware of this.

They took all of his clothes. This became apparent when I had to take him to his last outpatient visit. He asked me to go into his bedroom and bring him a pair of pants and a shirt. His so-called friends had taken everything he had.

They took everything except what was on his back. And, on his back were just his pajamas. Robert loved clothes and had lots of them. He had several full-length mink coats with matching hats. I have a picture of Robert in a stunning red suit.

Robert had clothes everywhere. I wheeled him into his bedroom. Every closet, drawer and cabinet had been emptied. He said, "Curtis, they took everything." His large, sunken eyes filled with water. I really felt really bad for him.

His condition continued to worsen. He was eventually hospitalized at the VA hospital on 23rd Street. He lost his ability to communicate, feed himself and breathe on his own. At this point, his doctor warned that his death was imminent. I knew that he wanted to see Bernardette.

I told him that I was bringing her to see him. Tears rolled down his face. I flew Bernardette up from Lumberton the next day. They got to see each other hours before he passed. I'm sorry that he never got to meet his nephew. Our son Justin was born one year later, in the same month that he died.

Robert told me that he wanted a funeral, and afterwards, he wanted his body cremated. He had made all of his funeral arrangements beforehand, and all we had to do was show up. Mickey's Funeral Home was the place. They were located in Harlem on Lenox Avenue. Mickey had dubbed itself as the "Funeral Home to the Carolinas."

The address was several blocks from Robert's apartment but further downtown. Mickey was an honest man. When I met with him, he said, "Your brother Robert has taken care of everything."

The Transition

Mickey handed me a check. This is what's left from his insurance policy, he said. I was not even aware that Robert had an insurance policy. Honoring his wishes, I had Robert cremated. His ashes were scattered at our family cemetery in Lumberton.

Having to move from Webster Avenue, we were relocated to 2245 Randall Avenue in the east Bronx. The buildings here were very similar to Stephanie's and more closely resembling the buildings on Amsterdam Avenue. They were called projects.

My neighborhood High School was named Adelie E. Stevenson. It was brand new and within walking distance of my building. I started high school in the eleventh grade. I skipped the tenth grade because I had gone to school all summer taking extra courses. This was to make up for the grade taken away from me at P.S. 28. I said that I would do it, and I did it. It felt wonderful.

I remember taking an advanced English class at Roosevelt High School on Fordham Road that summer. I wrote a short story about a swimming incident that had taken place in my hometown. It was about a day of swimming at one of our spots called the sand-hole but with a tragic ending. The teacher was so moved by it. She asked me if it was real and was relieved to find out it wasn't. I got an A in her class, and she encouraged me to continue writing.

Although we had moved away from Webster, we continued to attend Tremont Baptist Church. It was a forty-minute ride across town on the number 36 bus. I always preferred to ride in the back. A young lady would get on the bus every Sunday morning with her three children.

I always admired her. It was just she and her three children going to church. I used to fantasize about being her husband and helping her with the kids. I've always liked older women. I always wanted to get married and have children of my own.

High school was uneventful. As stated earlier, it was a new school. Everything was new. I enjoyed history the most. My teacher, Mrs. Porter, was amazing. Band was great, also. I wanted to play the saxophone. The band teacher asked me to play the baritone instead, and I did. It was me and one other person. He was a small guy. He was terrific. I learned a lot from him.

I fell in love with a clarinet player named Sabrina C. She was beautiful. I used to carry her books home. She had a Siamese cat and warned me that it was not friendly. I didn't listen and got a good scratch on my wrist. That scratch was visible for years. The school's automotive shop was also very impressive. They worked on real cars.

Maureen was another love interest. She was an Irish girl with long red hair and glasses. She was nice and more interested in me than I was in her. She gave me her phone number. I would call her house, and her little sister would always answer the phone.

<u>The Transition</u>

She would say, "Maureen, it's Cuuurrrrrtis."

She lived in the Bronx, somewhere on Pelham Parkway. She had to take two buses to get to school. We kissed each other once after school, in the lunchroom. I lost touch with both her and Sabrina.

Bernardette was attending JHS 113, a junior high school. She was not doing well. She started hanging out with the wrong crowd. Started playing hooky and was giving Aunt Lou a tough time. She would tell Aunt Lou that she was not her mother and tell me that I was not her father.

None of us could talk to her. Aunt Lou's reins on her were tight. No tighter than the ones that she had on me. Robert was nowhere to be found, and Bernardette didn't like being told what to do. She wanted to go back to Lumberton. There she knew that she would have the freedom that she wanted. She tried talking me into going back with her. I reminded her there was nothing to go back for and nothing to return to.

Bill was an alcoholic. He couldn't take care of us. Here in New York, we had an opportunity to go to college for free. I told her, "We will never have this opportunity again."

She wasn't hearing me and began to insist that Aunt Lou let her go back home. Aunt Lou reluctantly gave in. I remember her saying to Bernardette, "You are right. I am not your mother. If you want to leave, you can go."

I refused to go. I kept my eye on the prize, which, for me, was a free college education. I think her leaving to go back to Lumberton was one of Bernardette's biggest mistakes. I think that Aunt Lou has always regretted letting Bernardette leave her care. Maybe she should have fought her a little longer. But who's to say? Aunt Lou certainly had nothing to be ashamed of or sorry for. The devil had Bernardette, and Bernardette wasn't resisting.

I didn't attend my high school graduation because I just wasn't interested. I was asked to autograph the picture of someone in our yearbook. I don't remember exactly who it was, but I do remember writing, "Greater is he that is in you, than he that is in the world."

I was most interested in the going to college. The New York City University system was free to all NYC residents. Just the thought of going to college was a dream for me. I got accepted to Hunter College. I could have gotten all kinds of financial aid because of my situation – deceased parents, Aunt Lou being a single female head of household and low income.

Aunt Lou refused to complete any of the financial aid applications. She said the government didn't need to know all of her business. Little did she know that the government already knew everything they wanted to know about her. I never received any financial aid and was probably among the most qualified students to get it!

An opportunity to go to college for free! Realizing the possibilities that lay before me, I renewed my commitment to myself to be no trouble at all to Aunt Lou. I believed getting a college degree would be my ticket out of the projects. I wanted a much better life for myself than what I had been exposed to.

I just wanted so much more out of life. I wanted to live, not just exist. Some of my friends accused me of thinking I was better than everyone else in the projects. I corrected him and said, "No, that's not true. I just want more out of life than they do."

I would not allow myself to get comfortable in the projects.

This was not going to be my resting place, as was the case for so many others. They were looking to take over the apartment from their parents. How sad, I thought. Once a month, we would stand in line to receive boxes of "government" cheese, sugar, butter, flour and canned meat. Yes, this was a good thing for those who needed it, and we were one of them.

John C. Maxwell states that *"some people become more satisfied with their positions than their growth. There are certain levels of nesting upon the mountain of life that appealingly say,*

"Stop here, settle down, and be satisfied." I used to watch with great interest as climbers would look up toward the top of the mountain and then decide to climb no higher. They felt content to sit and wait while their friends continued to stay and camp. Instead of receiving strength to go higher, they rested on what they have achieved and settled into the "sparrow's nest." An eagle does not roost in a sparrow's nest, says English preacher Joseph Parker." [33]

This was much-needed help for those less fortunate. The projects were supposed to be a stepping stone out of poverty, so many people made it their solid rock. They rested on what their parents had achieved. I refused to allow myself to become content and complacent in those surroundings. For me, it was very humiliating. I knew and believed that God had something better for me. I was not meant to be poor.

However, my college education was free. I remember feeling panicky about making it to graduation. I wasn't sure about how long this tuition-free college education program would last. The city called it open admissions. My fear was that this program would end before I could graduate.

If that happened, I thought that I would never get my degree. So, I took a lot of courses each semester. I carried 18 to 21 credits

---

[33] Maxwell, Think on these Things (Meditation for Leaders), 67-69

per semester while working. My goal was to get my degree as quickly as possible. It was free, and I was not sure how much longer it would remain free.

I remember telling myself that partying and having a good time could wait. I realized all that fun stuff would still be there when I graduated. I was serious.

Hunter College does not have a campus. There are no trees, grass, etc. It is all concrete. I got my four-year degree in three and a half years and did it while working. I was the first and only one in my family to obtain a college degree. My degree is in Sociology.

I did not attend this graduation either. I picked up my degree from the bursar's office in September, in the fall of 1977. Aunt Lou was very proud of me and had my degree mounted and laminated on a plaque.

A year after Bernardette went back to stay with Bill, Aunt Lou and I drove to Lumberton to visit her. We found her, Bill and Alice living in a house just off of 5th Street. The outside appearance looked horrible. There was garbage all over the yard and porch and children's toys scattered about. My initial thought was, did Bernardette have a baby? She had not.

We knocked on the door and were told to come in. As we entered the house, we stepped into the living room. A man was sitting on a couch smoking a cigarette. Someone else was sitting in a rocking chair diagonally across from him. There was a space heater going full blast between them.

We asked for Bernardette. The man on the couch looked up at me and quickly put his head down again. He pointed to a closed door and said, "She's in the back. You can go on back there."

I opened the door, and to the left was the kitchen. I looked down and I was actually looking at the ground. Some of the floorboards were missing. To the right was a bedroom with bunk beds in it. Bernardette was standing there, seemingly happy to see us. I wanted to cry.

We walk back into the living room. To my amazement, the man sitting on the couch was actually Bill. I didn't even recognize him when we first came in. He was so small and so frail and shriveled-up. I supposed that the other person was Alice. I could not believe my eyes. The house was literally about to fall down around them. I remember thinking, and this is what she wanted to come back to? Aunt Lou and I said our goodbyes and left in disbelief.

They were like Nomads. Year after year, we never found them in the same house. One year, I had come home and found them across town near the Armory. This was one of their better homes but it was very close to some railroad tracks, literally within spitting distance. I was staying with them for a few days and asked if trains still ran on those tracks. No, I was told. Trains don't run on them anymore.

I slept in the living room on the couch, and everything was fine. Early that Saturday morning, I was awakened by the couch bouncing around on the floor. This low rumble and a vibration rippled through the entire house. I rushed over to the window to see what was causing the ground to tremble. There was a gigantic locomotive slowly passing right beside the house.

Looking straight ahead, all I could see through the window was black wall of metal slowly passing by. I stuck my head out of the window, allowing my eyes to follow this wall of metal upward. Sitting atop this moving mountain of steel was the train's engineer. He looked down at me, smiled and waved.

I honestly thought that I was dreaming. This was all natural to them. Bill said it only happened once a week, and it was just a single locomotive, not a train. I didn't know whether to laugh or cry, so I thanked God for Aunt Lou.

Bill was a very heavy smoker for as long as I had known him. He died from lung cancer a short time after our visit. Bernardette informed me of the arrangements, but I did not go to his funeral. In my subconscious mind, I still held him responsible for the death of my mother. I thought of his death as his just desserts, and I still wasn't sure if he had ever molested Bernardette.

Aunt Lou was a tough woman. She didn't take any mess from anybody. She was not afraid of confrontation. She could also be somewhat of a bully. I did my very best to stay out of trouble. She had her opinion about things, and that was it. She was a hard worker. She worked at an ink pen factory in Brooklyn. She worked at Macy's department store on 34th Street in Manhattan. There, she worked in their wig department.

She also had an entrepreneurial spirit. While in Castle Hill, she opened her own beauty salon. She named it after us, all of us. It was named Curloudette Beauty Salon – **Cur**/tis, **Lou**/ise and Bernar/**dette.** It was a combination of our three names. It was her business, and she was the sole operator. She did not have it very long. I'm sure the overhead was too high, with her being the only operator. But, as she would say, nothing beats a failure but a try.

Aunt Lou had fallen in love with a New York minister.

Frederick J. Eikerenkoetter II (June 1, 1935 – July 28, 2009), better known as Reverend Ike, was an American minister and evangelist based in New York City. He was known for the slogan "You can't lose with the stuff I use!" Though his preaching is considered a form of prosperity theology, Reverend Ike diverged from traditional Christian theology and taught what he called "Science of Living."

<u>The Transition</u>

His church was located in the area of Manhattan called Washington Heights, on Broadway and West 175th Street. It was a large old movie theater called the Palace. It held hundreds of people. We always sat on the balcony but this was by choice.

Aunt Lou would drag me with her to see him. Women swooned over him because of his good looks. He would promise his followers a life of prosperity. He sold prayer cloths

and laminated palm cards with his picture on it. The place would be packed. His lifestyle was very flamboyant and that is what he promised you if you followed his teachings. I knew this guy was a conman.

Aunt Lou believed in him until she didn't. I'm not sure what happened but I'm sure something did. And then it's on to the next flavor of the month. People can be so gullible, if it sounds good, then it must be good.

And there go I, if not for the grace of God.

It is a sad State of Affairs

When Ministry becomes Performance,

Then the Sanctuary becomes a Theater,

The Congregation becomes an Audience,

Worship becomes Entertainment,

And Man's Applause and Approval

Become The Measure of Success!

(Posted on Facebook by William "Bill" Baker)

Aunt Lou was also a very proud woman. She believed in working for everything she got. She never applied for welfare. Her circumstances made her eligible for a lot of assistance. She did not take it. Her applying for and receiving assistance was not because she was lazy. The assistance was to complement what little she already had. Refusing it, I feel was to the detriment of us all.

Things really didn't have to be as hard as they were, but as hard as they were, it was still better than being in Lumberton. After losing Curloudette, she rented a booth in a salon on Castle Hill Avenue. She seemed happy and was doing ok.

Her boyfriend, CJ Brown, would come around occasionally. I remember him from Webster. We called him Uncle CJ. He, too, loved his liquor. Aunt Lou tolerated his drinking. I knew little about him except that he worked for General Motors. He painted cars for them. According to Aunt Lou, he made "good" money. He got a new car every other year. He was a nice man who lived in Teaneck, New Jersey, with his other family.

CJ loved sports and took me to a Yankee game once. It was the Yankees vs Orioles. He offered to buy me a banner. We were sitting in the middle of the row, down on the first tier between home plate and first base. I suppose we had good seats. I raised my hand.

"What banner do you want, kid?" yelled the attendant.

"Give me the Mets," I yelled back. Uncle CJ cringed and covered his head. The crowd laughed. This was my first pro game ever. The guys selling banners seemed to have hundreds of them, so I thought you could buy a banner for whatever team you wanted. You don't know, what you don't know.

One night, he decided to take me out to practice my driving. His car was a beautiful blue Buick Electra 225. In the "hood," it was called a deuce and a quarter. I was driving up Castle Hill Avenue on the inside lane. I went to switch lanes and nearly side-swiped another car. The other driver flashed a badge and told me to pull over. I pulled over.

CJ has got his hands on his forehead. The guy said, "Do you realize that you almost hit me?"

"Yes, sir," I said.

He showed me his badge again and told us he was some kind of federal officer.

<u>The Transition</u>

"You're lucky that there are no cops around," he said. He got back into his car and left. CJ drove back to Castle Hill. He never offered to take me out driving again.

We were relocated to Castle Hill projects sometime in 1971. I finished my ninth year at Creston Junior High School. Castle Hill was a nice area. It was near the water (The East River) and near both the Throggs Neck and Whitestone bridges. It was also surrounded by private houses. Jamie Towers, a condominium complex with 4 or 5 buildings was also on one side.

At the end of Castle Hill Avenue, there was the Castle Hill Beach Club. This had no affiliation with the Castle Hill projects. The Castle Hill Beach Club was a private club. It was seemingly understood in the neighborhood that blacks need not apply. For the years that we lived there, I never ventured to the end of Castle Hill Avenue. There was a new high school and still plenty of undeveloped land.

We were a far cry from Webster, in more ways than one. Wow, we could live like Stephanie, so I thought. Minus the scented soaps, stuffed animals and shag carpeting. We had large patches of grass. Stephanie's complex didn't have any grass and very few trees. We had plenty of both.

We were given apartment 5H. It was front-facing. Looking down on Randall Avenue. From my bedroom window, I could see both bridges. No cats or dogs were allowed. However, many people violated this rule, including Aunt Lou, who got a cat after I moved out. You also could not own an air conditioner, dishwasher, washing machine or clothes dryer. We could not afford any of those items anyway.

There was a strip mall around the corner on Castle Hill Avenue. In it, there was a supermarket, a five and dime, a deli, a candy store, a laundromat and a pharmacy. I got a job at the McCory's department store. I was the stockboy. The manager was a Mr. Michaelette. His wife would come around nearly every day. She had more pills than the pharmacy. Mrs. Weaver worked in the fabric department and Fran ran the soda fountain island.

In the world of business, whoever performed the least best for the quarter had to take and keep the company mascot for a week. The mascot was a real live skunk. One quarter, my store got this coveted privilege. His scent glands had been removed, thank God. Whenever you approached him, he would turn around to spray you.

Looking back over his shoulder, he was confused as to why you were still standing there. He was very confused, the skunk, that is. Of course, he was kept in the basement, which made him my responsibility. I wanted to know what would happen if the skunk died under your care. I never got an answer, but he lived.

The Transition

As a stockboy I received all incoming deliveries. I had to mop the front of the store every evening. I found that a little embarrassing, especially when my friends saw me. That's ok, I thought. It's honest work and everything that I own, I got legally.

I realized that those folks living in the fast lane also did not live for long. They were robbed, dispossessed and strung out, always wondering when the rug was going to be snatched out from under them. That was no way to live. I had nothing to be ashamed of.

The UPS delivery driver and I had developed a friendly repour. One day, he said, "Curtis, UPS is hiring. I think you would do good there. You are a hard worker, and you come to work every day. I know this because I work every day and I see you every day. You should apply, he said. It pays $2.15 an hour."

I was making $1.15 an hour.

It was a no-brainer. I took the information and applied within days. Within a week, I was hired as a part-time employee for United Parcel Service of America. I doubled my money. I was loading and unloading packages from trucks. UPS did not call them trucks. They were called package cars.

Going home to Lumberton was becoming less and less frequent because of my growing responsibilities. I had started a new part-time job with UPS and was about to start college full-time. I would not be eligible for a vacation for a year, and my summers would be dedicated to summer school. My primary goal was to get my college degree as quickly as possible. I was on a mission.

I started working for UPS on June 15, 1973. I was hired as a part-time employee and worked as such throughout my college years. I received my BA degree in Sociology on September 1, 1977, from Hunter College City University of New York. Mission accomplished! I started working full-time for UPS the same month I received my degree.

I wanted to have my own personal car. I would sit at our kitchen window in Castle Hill and visualize myself parking my car in any vacant space that I could find. I believed that if I could conceive it, then I could achieve it.

After becoming a union member, I was encouraged to join the company's thrift plan. It was a company-sponsored profit-sharing savings plan. The maximum amount anyone could contribute was $6.00 per week. I joined and contributed the max. I continued to work, and I continued to visualize myself parking my car.

In 1975, one UPS driver told me he was retiring and moving to Florida. He said he could not take all his cars with him and was looking to sell his 1973 Volkswagen Super Beetle. His asking price was $1400. I only had $1200 in my thrift plan account.

He said, I'll take it. What a blessing! The car was in mint condition. I kept it for six or seven years and ended up giving it away to a family in Brooklyn. The guy came to our house in the Bronx and drove it back to Brooklyn.

Kids can be mean and cruel. My perception of Stephanie's neighborhood changed. I quickly learned that living in the projects was no badge of honor. Private homes, condos and co-ops surrounded the Castle Hill Projects. If you lived in the projects, the kids from those homes were not eager to hang out with you. As time went on, I realized why.

I knew we were poor but did not know that the projects were built primarily for the poor. Besides, I never thought of Stephanie and her parents as being poor. Or that living where they lived was indicative of being poor.

Napoleon Hills writes, ***"For individuals who made the personal choice to succeed in life, who resisted the temptations and weaknesses of irreligion and sought, instead, the help of God (called by various names in the book), there was no limit to how far they might go. Limits were self-imposed, or imposed by the negative outside force of evil, personified by the Devil."***[34]

---

[34] Hill and Lechter, Outwitting The Devil (The Secret to Freedom and Success), 256

The Transition

I didn't know it then, but Castle Hill was going through a transition of its own. The transition was called white flight. Castle Hill was predominately white and remained that way until Co-op City appeared. What was the draw of Co-op City? This is the information that I recently discovered from google.

Co-op City is a New York State Mitchell-Lama housing cooperative in the northeast Bronx with 15,372 residential units in 35 high-rise buildings and seven (7) townhouse clusters consisting of garden and duplex apartments. It is the largest single residential development in the United States, with a population of approximately 50,000 residents and its own zip code, 10475. Built on 320 acres of property, only 20 percent of the land is developed, leaving a majority of the community's natural beauty undisturbed and lots of green spaces in a serene, park-like environment.

Life in Co-op City revolves around cooperative living. The development has many conveniences on-site for shareholders. There are shopping centers, community centers with meeting rooms, parking garages, playgrounds, professional offices, shopping and dining options, senior services, a public library, a firehouse and an education park with a nursery through high school levels, most within walking distance.

Co-op City has its own tri-generation power plant, providing the development's electricity, heat, hot water and air conditioning,

209

amenities included in owners' monthly maintenance changes, and garbage pick-up.

Co-op City is accessible to all points of the city by public transportation, including an express bus to Manhattan. A Metro-North railroad station is also planned for Co-op City pending completion of the Penn Station Access Project. It is truly a city unto itself.

The color of Castle Hill quickly changed. More and more whites fled to Co-op City, while more and more black and brown people moved into Castle Hill. I would imagine that these newcomers were from neighborhoods much like the one we left. But, many of them did not appreciate their better surroundings. They walked on the grass. Threw garbage out of the windows, peed in the elevators and played in the hallways. It was embarrassing. I hated the projects.

The proliferation of drugs quickly followed. One mother witnessed her teenage son's murder. He had a new car and jewelry and wore flashy clothes. Everybody knew what he was into. He reminded me of my cousin D'Andre, and we know how that story ended.

Those smart enough also knew that his lifestyle would be short-lived. When you mentioned the projects, some people would cringe. Now, I knew why. I made very few friends. Bernardette had a boyfriend who looked like the local hoodlums. I told him never to come to our house again. Of course, she hated me for doing that. I did not like him, nor did I want to know him. He appeared to be a crack-head to me. She always seemed attracted to guys who were just up to no good.

My next-door neighbor, Darryl S. and I became friends. By all human traits Darryl was a handsome guy. Girls were easily attracted to him. He stood about 5 feet, eight inches tall which is not exactly tall for a man. He wore a big afro that was meticulously cared for and you would never find him without his trusted afro-pic. He was cloaked with an almond complexion and enjoyed looking at himself in whatever medium that reflected his Adonis-like looks.

He had a younger sister. I rarely saw his sister or his mother. Darryl S. was at our house all the time. He knew everything going on in the neighborhood. He was also a woman beater. He would beat his girlfriend, Julie, often.

He would slap, punch and kick her. I never knew why she took the abuse. She had several brothers and was a big girl. She was taller than him and weighed a lot more than him. I said to her one day, that she should leave him alone. She just shrugged her shoulders. My friendship with him did not last long. He was not someone that I could continue to befriend.

<u>The Transition</u>

Ricardo A. was a Puerto Rican friend living in the Castle Hill Projects. His mother tried teaching me Spanish. Whenever I would come over, she would always be cooking something. She would not allow me to speak English in her house. I quickly learned foods such as pastilles, yucca, arroz con habichuelas, etc. Somehow, Ricardo and I lost track of each other after high school.

My girlfriend at the time also lived in the projects. She, too, was going to a CUNY school – a two-year college. She was a modern dance major at Bronx Community College. Only 4'11" in height, very strong, super flexible and very talented. I went to see her perform there once. She performed a solo dance to the song, Nights in White Satin by the Moody Blues. She did a wonderful job. A performance that I will never forget.

We used to go see a lot of modern dance performances. At one Alvin Alley performance, the theater seemed full, and there was only standing room. The house lights were still up, and we were standing up in the back. A guy stood up in the middle row, turned around and offered his seat. I motioned to Angela to take it.

As she started to walk toward him, he stopped her and said, "No, not you, I mean you," pointing to me. The crowd quietly gasped and went, whoa. I openly declined his offer and felt embarrassed for Angela, my girlfriend. Why make a grand, publicly embarrassing and most insulting display like that? I did not appreciate the attention at all. And it's for reasons like this that I have very little tolerance for faggots.

Gilbert S. and I also became friends, but I seem to forget how we met. Gil lived in Jamie Towers. That was a very nice co-op between Castle Hill Projects and the high school. Gil's parents had a beautiful apartment. Every floor was carpeted. Mahogany cabinets in the kitchen. They had a terrace, and there was a swimming pool in the center of the complex.

The walkways were clean. All of the grassy areas were manicured. Now, this is how I wanted to live! I aspired to get a college degree and not live in the projects. Gil went to Pace University. In high school, the most successful person that I saw in my building was the maintenance guy who worked for NYCHA (New York City Housing Authority). That's who I wanted to be. To me, he was the most successful person in my world. I called myself, trying to be realistic. Now, how sad is that?

Church was still a very big part of my life. Aunt Lou's law was we would go to church every Sunday. Gil and I would go to the clubs every weekend. No matter what time I came home Saturday night, I knew that I was going to church that Sunday morning.

Gil and I went to all kinds of parties, house parties, block parties; it did not matter. Gil found them all. What I liked most about him was that he was smart and not into any drugs. I thought of myself the same way. We made a good friendship that is still intact to this day. We travelled the East Coast together – from Boston, Mass. to Columbia, SC and all points in between.

That changed around the beginning of my senior year in college. My major was sociology, and my minor was African Studies. I took a course with a very popular black professor, Dr. Yosef A.A. ben-Jochannan.

He had authored a book titled 'Black Man of the Nile and His Family.' In his book, he describes a being who supposedly lived thousands of years before Christ. This being, according to him, performed miracles greater than Jesus. This really shook my faith. So much so that I used this as an excuse to stop going to church.

In my last semester at Hunter College, I took an independent study course in public housing. It was with the Featherbed Lane Neighborhood Improvement Association. Their entire existence was to protect people from slum lords. They would represent tenants in court and sue landlords for not providing basic services. I believe this course offered six college credits. I did a lot of walking and interviewed hundreds of tenants.

Our office was on the ground floor of this renovated townhouse. The head of the Association was a lady named Betty. She was a tall, not-so-pretty woman with heavy black-rimmed glasses. Her right-hand man was a Puerto Rican guy named Steve.

The Transition

Steve was a Puerto Rican hippie. He may have been a lawyer. He was extremely knowledgeable in housing law. He also seemed to be extremely bright. He was about half Betty's size. They appeared awkward together. They were truly the odd couple.

While working there, the office secretary took a liking to me. I pretty much ignored her. One day, she plopped herself down in front of my desk and asked, "Why don't you ever say hello to me? My name is Lois."

I didn't know what to say. Of course, I had taken notice of her.

She was a good ten years older than me. She was nice and attractive, and I did like older women. From that moment forward, we talked daily. She had two children whose father did not live with them. She said that he was a correctional officer out at Riker's Island.

Rikers Island is a 413-acre island in the East River in the Bronx that contains New York City's largest jail. The island is the site of one of the world's largest correctional institutions and mental institutions and has been described as New York's best-known jail.

I remember one time Lois had a house party. She wanted me there. I went, but I was uncomfortable. I was obviously the youngest thing there. She made sure that she introduced me to all of her girlfriends. I was her prized stallion. She had offered me to move in with her and the kids. I declined and told her I was trying to get my own apartment.

"Actually," I said, "I have a place, but I am short three hundred dollars for the security and first month's rent."

When she realized she could not persuade me to move in with her and the kids, she said, "Let me lend you the money."

I accepted her offer.

I moved into my apartment. As time went on, I began to see less and less of Lois. She did not like this. She demanded her three hundred dollars back and that I pay her immediately. She was no longer that nice, sweet lady. I paid her back without delay.

At the end of my semester, Betty asked me to stay on with the Featherbed Lane Neighborhood Improvement Association. She wanted me to join her salaried full-time staff. They worked long hours. If this were to happen, I would have to give up my part-time job at UPS. I asked, what was the salary? The figure she quoted me was less than what I was making working part-time for UPS. She increased her offer by two thousand dollars and it was still less. I had to respectfully decline.

She was surprised that UPS paid that well. And part-time at that! She said that she understood. My semester ended, but I continued working for her that summer. By the fall, I was working full-time with UPS and had stopped seeing Lois altogether. Not seeing Lois anymore made me feel like I had dodged a bullet. I was glad that chapter of my dating life was over.

The last time I was in Lumberton, I went to a club in the country. I parked on the side of the road. When I stepped out of the car and looked up into the night sky, the heavens seemed to unfold. I had never seen anything so beautiful. Trees lined both sides of the roadway like two black walls covered by a canopy of stars.

I jumped onto the hood of my car and leaned back against the windshield to get a better view. I gazed into the heavens with awe. As I gazed, I noticed three red dots, each smaller than a pinhead. They moved and danced around each other with incredible speed. Their movements seemed to be deliberate but confined to a definite space. They appeared to bounce off of invisible walls as if they were in some kind of box. It was strange but not alarming, only because they were a million miles away. I watched them move until they eventually disappeared from my sight.

Unlike being the stockboy at McCory's department store this new job that I found with UPS was unionized and paid twice as much an hour. UPS (United Parcel Service) was a package delivery company that paid well. The guys that I worked with were all package handlers, but we did not deliver any packages.

Any employee who handled packages had to become a union member. Even part-time employees such as myself. But first, you had to complete a thirty-day training period satisfactorily. Upon successful completion of that, here in New York, you had to become a member of the Teamster Local 804 International Brotherhood of Teamsters (I.B.T.) union.

As a part-time employee, I worked in the Local Sort area and became a teamster during the summer of 1973. The local language in our union book at that time defined all part-time employees "as employees not otherwise gainfully employed who, when reporting to work as scheduled, shall be granted a minimum of three hours. Should any part-time employee work beyond the fifth hour, he shall be guaranteed eight hours of work or pay." (Agreement between Local 804 I.B.T. and United Parcel Service (New York) Article 7).

And you know that if you got paid for eight hours, you worked for eight hours. Ideally, you would work between three and five hours daily, Monday through Friday. We usually started work at around 6 pm and were on our way home by 10 pm.

It was the perfect job for a student, and that was the primary pre-requisite: you had to be in school. My first assignment was that of a package auditor. My auditing job ended after several weeks, and I became a loader/unloader. It was physically a tough job – loading and unloading trailers filled with packages weighing up to fifty pounds each. This weight restriction was later raised to not more than seventy pounds per package.

The group that I worked with was small; there were only six of us. We all attended various colleges throughout the city and suburbs. We were quite an eclectic group. We did not view ourselves as making United Parcel Service a career. We were there for the short haul. Time enough to obtain our degrees and then move on. We didn't want to be truck drivers for the rest of our lives. At least, that's how we saw things.

One day, while unloading a package car, I came across a wad of money left on the top shelf inside the package car. It wasn't just a few dollars; it may have been as much as one hundred dollars. I didn't count it all. It was just lying there on the top shelf. No wallet, no nothing, just cash with no one around. I took the money immediately to the payroll clerk, John. I told him where I found the money and gave him the package car number.

He thanked me and said that if no one claimed the money, I would be allowed to keep it. Several days later, he handed me eighty dollars. He said no one claimed the money, so it was mine. I thanked him, and I thanked God for my honesty.

I also knew that I had just passed some kind of test. No one had prepared me for this test but God. A test that would govern my attitude for the rest of my life. I would always strive to tell the truth and be honest in my dealings with others.

Mark Batterson says, ***"God tests us for two primary reasons. First, it's an opportunity for God to prove Himself to us. Second, it's an opportunity for us to prove ourselves to God."***[35]

I often wondered if I was the only person in my group who was tested that way. None of the other guys talked about finding money or what to do with it if you did. I never shared that experience with any of them, somehow thinking I wasn't supposed to. As far as I knew, none of us were thieves.

However, as the work increased, we did have a thief join our group. He stole record albums, and he was prolific at it. He would put boxes of record albums into his book bag. I did not know if any of the other guys were aware of this guy or not. As a loader or unloader, oftentimes you worked alone. It made me nervous working around him. I decided that I would not rat him out, but if questioned, I would not lie.

One day, he was no longer at work. He just never came back. No one seemed to know what happened to him. I never saw him again. Perhaps they caught him. I was happy that he was gone. We

---

[35] Batterson, All In (You are one decision away from a totally different life), 42

were a hardworking, great bunch of guys. We loved listening to music as we worked: The Rolling Stones, Doobie Brothers, Lenny Kravitz, etc., some great songs. However, Trans-Europe Express by Kraftwerk was our most favorite song.

Early in my college years, I had several girlfriends, and we were all sexually active. Because I was still living with Aunt Lou, my sexual promiscuity was limited to motels or the back seat of a car. Everybody claimed to be safe and clean and birth controlled. Sex was almost as casual as getting a drink of water and was always unprotected. We were all playing Russian roulette with contracting a sexually transmitted disease (STD). It was not smart behavior, and the inevitability of this happening, happened.

My ability to urinate became very, very painful. I knew something was wrong and that I had to do something about it. It just so happens that the girlfriend that I contracted this STD from lived in Brooklyn. To visit her, I often crossed the Manhattan bridge, which connects to the Flatbush Extension in downtown Brooklyn. I noticed that there was a public health clinic on the extension and decided to go there. I went alone. The interior reminded me of the jailhouse in Lumberton due to the various gates and locks and the security.

My suspicions were that I had contracted syphilis or gonorrhea. The "clap" as we called it. I was asked to fill out a form, and blood was taken from me. It was confirmed that I had syphilis, and I was told that penicillin would take care of it. I was to abstain from having sex for a week and follow-up with my doctor. I was asked if I knew who I had gotten the disease from, and I gave them her information. When I told her about this, she denied having it, but I knew better. I insisted that she get treatment and took her there. Of course, our relationship ended, and I had one other person to notify. This person was my main girlfriend, and it really bothered me to have to tell her of my unfaithfulness and that I had given her an STD.

I picked her up that evening from a modern dance class in Harlem. We were driving across 125th when I told her. She was saddened and began to cry. I apologized and asked her if she had anyone that she needed to notify, and she said yes. I nearly lost control of my car. I was shocked. She had been unfaithful, too. I was surprised that I did not pick up on that. I remember feeling self-assured that if my girlfriend was fooling around, I would definitely know it. I remember standing around with the fellows in the park, listening to them brag that they would definitely know if their girl was cheating. I didn't have a clue and nor would they. I realized then that if a woman decides to have an affair, you will only know about it if she wants you to know about it. Our relationship did not recover from this, but I was humbled.

The Transition

Although I was accepted to Hunter College, my acceptance letter arrived too late to make the 1973 fall registration deadline. I started classes in the spring of 1974. I was so excited. This is what I had been waiting for. Now, all I needed was to get my degree as quickly as possible.

I wasn't sure how long the Open Admissions policy was going to last. I believed that getting a degree would be my ticket to get out of the projects and out of poverty. I had been poor all of my life and was still poor and did not like it.

I knew that fast money was not the way to go. The guys in the projects with flashy clothes and sports cars also had short lives. One particular guy that we knew had his brains blown out while his mother watched him walking to his car.

That kind of life never influenced or impressed me. I knew I could have those finer things in life if I got an education, worked hard, trusted God and was willing to wait. I believed that God had so much more in store for me.

Looking over my shoulder all the time, to me, it was not living. It was surviving in fear; you might as well be dead, as far as I'm concerned. I realized this while living on Webster Avenue. I was living amongst the walking dead. The things I would acquire in life had to be obtained legally, honorably and honestly. I wanted to live comfortably and peacefully.

Philip Yancey declares that **"Fear, like pain, serves as a warning system, only with the added benefit of functioning in advance of harm."**[36]

How was I going to accomplish this? Through education and hard work. That was my plan. No, I did not like living in a drug-infested neighborhood, no, I did not like living in the projects, and no, I did not like having to stand in line to receive government cheese. I just knew that God had something so much better for me.

After completing my college placement exams, I was placed into a remedial math class. This both surprised and upset me. I was pretty good in math; remember, I passed my algebra regents. Nevertheless, I had to take the class. It was really easy.

I volunteered to help fellow classmates, and I tutored others. My professor knew this. My final grade was a "C." I questioned the professor about it. He said that I had several uncompleted homework assignments. I could not believe it.

I did not get off to a happy start, but I refused to let this hold me back or dampen my enthusiasm. This was my opportunity of a life time. I was getting a New York City college education for

---

[36] Yancey, Philip. Where Is God When It Hurts? (Zondervan, 1990), 55

The Transition

FREE! This is what I had been trying to explain to my sister. To me, this opportunity was priceless.

The following three paragraphs are excerpts from an essay based on ***Austerity Blues: Fighting for the Soul of Public Higher Education,*** **by Stephen Brier and Michael Fabricant, October 2016**. Although written nearly forty years after I graduated from Hunter College, this article underscores my sense of urgency to graduate.

"The demographic impact of CUNY's new Open Admissions policy was immediate: in Fall 1970, the entering class was 75 percent larger than the previous year's; one year later Black and Puerto Rican student enrollment in CUNY's senior colleges increased to 24 percent of the total as contrasted to half that number a year earlier. White, working-class students, many of them of Italian and Irish descent also benefitted from CUNY's new Open Admissions policy."

"By 1975, CUNY had created a more racially and ethnically diverse pool of 253,000 matriculating undergraduates (a 55 percent increase in total enrollment since 1969). While 78 percent of first-year students entering CUNY in 1969 had been white, by 1975, that percentage was now 30."

"Despite these demonstrated successes, opposition to Open Admissions took many forms. They ranged from traditional CUNY

225

faculty lamenting Open Admissions while nostalgically recalling CCNY's "high standards" and reputation as the "poor man's Harvard," to conservative politicians and business leaders in New York and across the country, opposing expanded use of public funds. In June 1976, with CUNY's budget in tatters, the Board of Higher Education broke down and imposed tuition on CUNY students…"

I earned my Bachelors of Art degree in Sociology from Hunter College in the fall of 1977, not having paid one cent for it. Hallelujah!

I was working and still living at home in Castle Hill. One of the things I wanted was a rabbit fur coat. A full-length rabbit coat. I thought that they were so cool. I had saved up enough money to buy one. So, I bought it.

It was popular at the time. It was your typical rabbit brown and white fur. Owning one, I thought, would make me feel good. I felt accomplished but not complete. I was ghetto fabulous but not proud of it. I had only worn it a few times. I decided to wear it to school one day. It was a very cold day. I was headed to Hunter College, 68th Street between Lexington and Park Avenues.

Things were fine until I stepped onto the #6 train at the elevated Castle Hill Avenue station. The subway car was heated and a ceiling fan blew warm air above me. Shortly after entering the subway car, I noticed puffs of rabbit fur in the air. More and more fur began to fill the air. People started to wave their hands to keep the fur out of their faces.

I was so embarrassed. I moved to get away from the overhead fan. My fur coat was disintegrating before my eyes. Patches of fur were missing. Needless to say, I never wore that coat again and learned that a rabbit coat was not a real "fur" coat. Lesson learned! But, something more deep-seated was missing. I was not fulfilled, not content. I was not satisfied.

Craig Groeschel says, "*Suddenly, we could buy things that earlier were barely even a dream. Don't miss the subtlety of what happened. When we had limited resources, God was our source. He was all we needed. Then when we had access to those things that were once far off, they slowly, and wrongly, became the answers to our problems. Without realizing it, our team started to think, if we don't have it, we can work for it, buy it, or create it. In the meantime, we started to forget about the one that it was all about. At the start, God was it. He was everything we needed. Now, we thought we needed certain things to grow. To us, it wasn't as much about God. It was about everything else. And we started to lose it. Why? Because when you start to trust outward and physical*

resources instead of the inward and spiritual truth, you'll always lose it."[37]

My first official full-time job interview occurred in a skyscraper in some part of midtown Manhattan. I forget what the job was but I do remember what I wore to the interview. I wore a tan suit. I looked like I may have been going on a safari. I had no idea that I was dressed inappropriately. I thought my interview went well, but I was never called back.

It wasn't until years later, thanks to UPS, that I learned the term business attire and how one should dress for job interviews. A dark color suit, preferably navy blue, white shirt and dark tie. Shoes should be polished and either black or brown, worn with dark color socks. I was the complete opposite, but you don't know what you don't know.

If I had still been living with Aunt Lou at that time, she would not have allowed me to make that mistake. After all, she taught me how to read the New York Times newspaper on the subway. She practiced with me at home so I would not make a fool of myself on the train. It was all about knowing how to fold it.

---

[37] Groeschel, Craig. it (How Churches and Leaders Can Get it and Keep it). (Zondervan, 2008), 165

She understood that these nuances, both big and small, often made the difference in how smoothly one moved on in life. Do I get the job, or will I get the promotion, or do I get the girl? It all depended upon knowing how to present yourself. What were the nuances I needed to know about being a man, a father, a husband and a Christian?

About Being a Man

T.D. Jakes best answers this question. *"God desires for you to come to Him not with lofty words that express theological and historical facts about what He has done, but with a heart that is dependent upon who He is and what He does and will do in order for you to take your next breath. He wants you to come with a desire to know Him, and with a willingness to lay your entire life bare before Him so He can heal you and restore you and create in you the likeness of His Son, Jesus Christ."*[38]

Philip Yancey says, **"… the Christian virtues described in the Bible develop when we choose God and his ways in spite of temptation or impulses to do otherwise."**[39]

T. D. Jakes goes on to say that, **"There are many ways to praise the Lord. A person might dance, walk, stand with his**

---

[38] Jakes, So You Call Yourself A Man?, 78
[39] Yancey, Philip. Where Is God When It Hurts? (Zondervan, 1990), 90

arms raised, fall on his knees, lie flat on his face before God. He might sing, shout, talk, cry, laugh. What's important is that a man find a way to open up and express himself to the Lord. There's no "right" form of expression for praise – the only thing that must be right before God is a man's heart, humbled to praise Him from the depths of his emotions."[40]

Mark Batterson reminds us that, *"Man's chief end is to glorify God, and to enjoy Him forever. We exist for one reason and one reason alone: to glorify God, and to enjoy Him forever. It's not about you at all. It's all about Him. It's about glorifying God in whatever circumstance you find yourself in. Anyway. Anywhere. Anyhow. Whenever. Wherever. Whatever. There is no circumstance in which you cannot glorify God."*[41]

About Being a Father

Pastor Jakes goes on to say, **"It has become so easy for fathers to run from the responsibilities of their calling at the first provocation. But they must be willing to face their fears and insecurities and stand their ground. They must persevere regardless of their confusion or uncertainty, and if all they can**

---

[40] Jakes, So You Call Yourself A Man? (The Introduction)
[41] Batterson, All In (You are one decision away from a totally different life)

do is simply be present, they will have gone a long way toward breaking the cycle of pain."[42]

The great missionary Hudson Taylor said, **"All God's giants were weak people."** Moses' weakness was his temper. It caused him to murder an Egyptian, strike the rock he was supposed to speak to, and break the tablets to the Ten Commandments. Yet God transformed Moses into "the humblest man on earth." Gideon's weakness was low self-esteem and deep insecurities, but God transformed him into a "mighty man of valor." Abraham's weakness was fear. Not once, but twice, he claimed his wife was his sister to protect himself. But God transformed Abraham into "the father of those who have faith." Impulsive, weak-willed Peter became "a rock," the adulterer David became "a man after my own heart," and John, one of the arrogant "Sons of Thunder," became the "Apostle of Love."[43]

About Being a Husband

T.D. Jake declares, **"Or we give up. We just quit. It is easy for us to walk away. But if you want to stay, you have to learn how to encourage yourself if you are not blessed with a woman who knows how. What do you do when you need encouragement and you're not getting it at home like you should. Before you go**

---

[42] Jakes, He-Motions, 30
[43] Warren, Rick. The Purpose Driven Life. (Zondervan, 2022), 275

out and get some surrogate encouragement from some illicit source, you may have to do what David did in a dark place in his own life. The Bible says that David "encouraged himself in the Lord." So many women base their responses to their husband and their understanding of the dynamics of the relationship on what they observed from their own parents' marriage. For many African-American women in our matriarchal culture, they view the way their mothers dominated their fathers and consequently vow to be more flexible, more responsive, and often more dependent on a man. In other households, where the mothers were controlled and dominated by their husbands, their daughters grow up and want to make sure that they are not run over like their mommas."[44]

About Being a Christian

Mark Batterson, "**We're too Christian to enjoy sin and too sinful to enjoy Christ. We've got just enough Jesus to be informed, but not enough to be transformed.**"[45]

Leslie Copeland states, "**Embodying the fruit of the Spirit and leading as a Christian is impossible without the Holy Spirit working in and through us. As the third person of the Trinity,**

---

[44] Jakes, He-Motions, 217

[45] Batterson, All In (You are one decision away from a totally different life), 25

the Holy Spirit is integral to how Christians are empowered to lead. The Holy Spirit guides, corrects, convicts, settles, grounds, strengthens, and empowers us to do the work God calls us to do."[46]

The nineteenth century Scottish preacher Robert Murray M'Cheyne says, **"A Christian is more flawed and sinful than you'd ever dare believe and yet more loved and accepted than you'd ever dare hope – at the same moment."[47]**

J. Oswald Sanders adds, **"All Christians need more teaching in the art of prayer, and the Holy Spirit is the master teacher. The Spirit's help in prayer is mentioned in the Bible more frequently than any other help He gives us. True prayer rises in the spirit of the Christian from the Spirit who indwells us. Between God and the devil stands the Christian at prayer. Jesus was not so much concerned over wicked people and their deeds as with the forces of evil that caused those people to sin."[48]**

Pastor Rick Warren declares that, **"A saved heart is one that wants to serve. … but God says, every member of his family is a minister. In the Bible, the words servant and minister are**

---

[46] Copeland, Leslie. Christ-like Leadership. (Judson Press, 2022), 20
[47] Keller, Timothy. Preaching. (Penguin, 2016), 105
[48] Sanders, J. Oswald. Spiritual Leadership (Principles of Excellence for Every Believer). (Moody, 2007), 87-88

synonyms, as are service and ministry. If you are a Christian, you are a minister, and when you're serving, you're ministering."[49]

To reiterate, it is important for a man to find a way to open up and express himself to the Lord. Fathers if you want to stay in the household, you have to learn how to encourage yourself if you are not blessed with a woman who knows how. Husbands, the Holy Spirit's help in prayer is mentioned in the Bible more frequently than any other help He gives.

Being a man should develop certain qualities, as does being a father or a husband. Often times these titles exist in silos which prevent the knowledge of each from bleeding into the other. However, following the teachings of our Lord and Savior Jesus Christ promises eternal life.

Nuances should be slight or delicate. What I needed to know about manhood, fatherhood, being a husband and becoming a Christian had not been delicate at all. As I had cried out, Father, does it have to be this hard. It really doesn't if you allow yourself to be open to and believe in the teachings of Jesus.

Father, Son, Holy Spirit = the Trinity = God.

---

[49] Warren, The Purpose Driven Life, 228-229

Father, Man, husband = a trinity = each of which offers an opportunity to become a child of God.

Author Norman Geisler says, ***"One of the great motivating factors in the Christian life is the assurance of salvation. Thank God, the Bible assures us that we can know that we have eternal life (John 5:24; 1 John 5:13). And nothing can separate us from the love of Christ (Rom. 8:36-39). Even if we are faithless, God remains faithful (2 Tim. 2:13). These and numerous other passages of Scripture inform us that true believers are eternally secure."*** [50]

---

[50] Geisler, Chosen But Free, 148

PART 3

NOTHING BUT THE BLOOD

(LEARNING TO TRUST GOD)

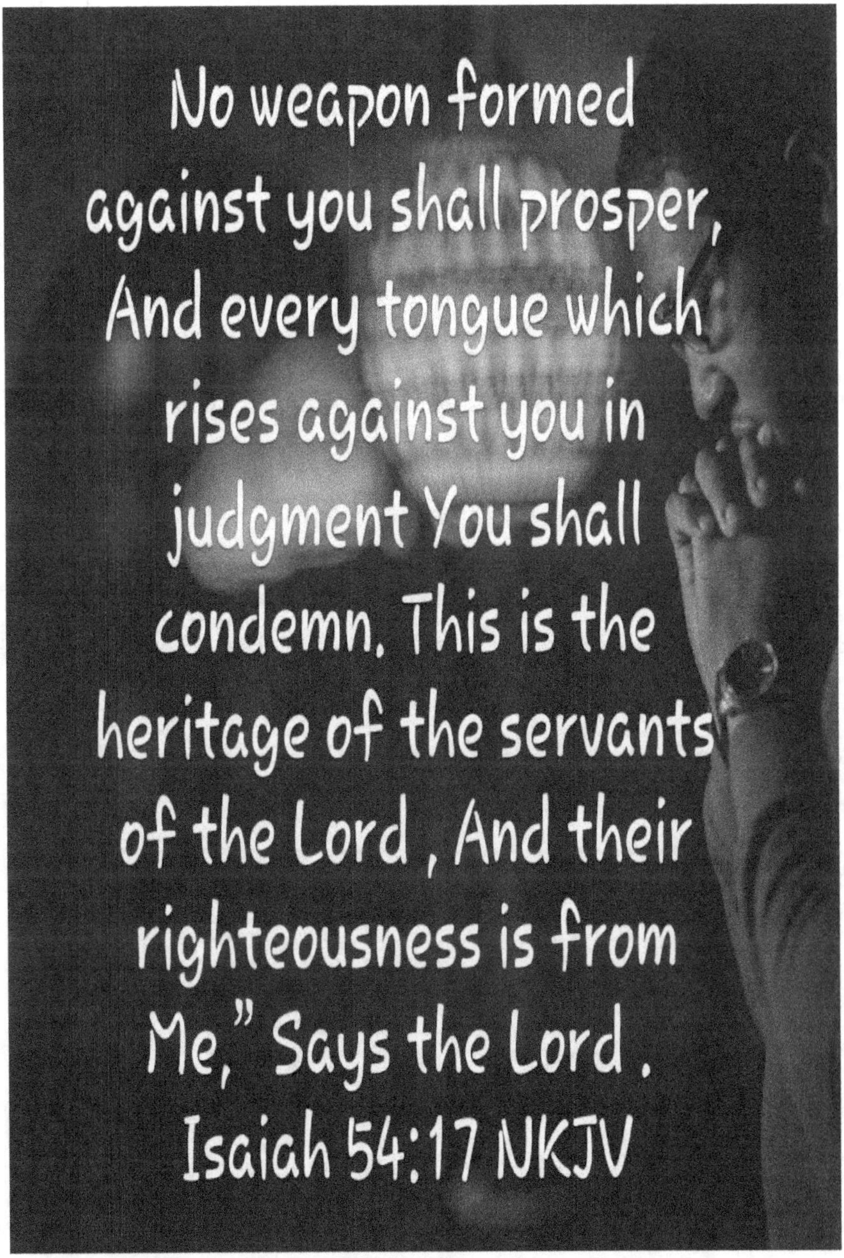

No weapon formed
against you shall prosper,
And every tongue which
rises against you in
judgment You shall
condemn. This is the
heritage of the servants
of the Lord , And their
righteousness is from
Me," Says the Lord .
Isaiah 54:17 NKJV

Ponder this, author Napoleon Hill writes,_"The Devil's word is not worth much among you earthbound sinners. Neither is God's word. You fear the Devil and refuse to trust your God."[51]

The New York Post newspaper published an article written by Brad Hamilton on June 3, 2017. It started as follows: *When a flash of lightning zapped the city on July 13, 1977, panic hit New York. Already gripped by economic collapse and the Son of Sam terror, the city was plunged into total darkness. During the now-notorious 25-hour blackout, which affected all five boroughs, some 1,000 fires were set and 1,600 stores looted.*

According to Wikipedia, (**David Richard Berkowitz** (born **Richard David Falco**, June 1, 1953), also known as **the Son of Sam** and **the .44 Caliber Killer**, is an American serial killer who pled guilty to perpetrating eight shootings in New York City between July 1976 and July 1977, which resulted in six fatalities.

Berkowitz grew up in New York City and served in the United States Army. Using a .44 Special caliber Bulldog revolver, he killed six people and wounded seven others by July 1977, terrorizing New Yorkers. Berkowitz eluded the biggest police manhunt in the city's history while leaving letters that mocked the

---

[51] Hill, Napoleon and Lechter, Sharon. Outwitting The Devil (The Secret to Freedom and Success). (Sterling, 2011), 140

police and promised further crimes, which were highly publicized by the press. He confessed to all of them, and initially claimed to have been obeying the orders of a demon manifested in the form of a black dog belonging to his neighbor, "Sam." He subsequently admitted that the dog-and-devil story was a hoax.

Although the blackout of 1965 was not as far-reaching geographically as that of 1977, it was just as devastating. I had been working for UPS for nearly four years at this point. One of my co-workers lived in Harlem. Harlem was just a ten-minute walk away from the job. Once he crossed over the 138th Street bridge (a.k.a. Madison Avenue bridge), he was home. He lived in the projects on 135th and Madison Avenue.

He was excited about the blackout and wanted to be with his friends. He knew that they would be looting stores, and he wanted to be a part of that action. Two-days later, he returned to work with a cast on his right ankle up to his knee. He explained that he and some friends started looting stores the night of the blackout, as he had predicted. His ankle was broken when a police officer's night stick struck it. He never returned to work after that, and we never saw Eddie again.

Working nights had its advantages but it could be and often was dangerous. They were also the least favorable hours for most people to work. The building we worked out of was isolated and located in a non-residential area surrounded by other commercial establishments – a diner, a carwash, and a coal yard.

At UPS, payday was on Thursday, and the stick-up artist in the area knew it. They also knew that UPS employees would have cash on them. On payday, you could cash your paycheck in the building. The subway was only three blocks away, but at 11 pm, you were usually all alone. Several guys quit because they were held up walking to the subway on payday. I usually got a ride home, especially on payday.

September of 1977 is also the year that I received my degree from Hunter College. I started working full-time for UPS shortly after that. To obtain a permanent full-time or part-time position within UPS, you have to work thirty days within a sixty-day period. This was an agreement between the company and the union.

Although I was already a part-time union employee, it made no difference. Going for the full-time position, I was still treated like a brand-new employee. As a package driver, I knew that I had to meet the same criteria and maintain certain production indices like everyone else.

I was told I needed to pick up my pace during my first job performance review. I asked specifically what I needed to do. Your SPORH (stops per on-road hour) is currently at 12.6. You need to be at 13.5 or higher.

<u>Nothing but the Blood</u>

I was told that if I had not reached these goals by my next review, I would have to return to my part-time job. From that day forward, my production numbers never dropped below 13.0, often exceeding 13.5.

One of the tricks to help my numbers look better was to work through my lunch hour and punch out as soon as I returned to the building. Turning in my cash-on-delivery (C.O.D's) monies and my delivery sheets could be time-consuming. So, I contemplated doing this task on my own time - off the clock.

I did not realize it at the time, but in taking this shortcut, I was also setting myself up for trouble. Either I would have to get better and faster at delivering or continue to work through my lunches and turn in my paperwork and monies on my own time, forever. I later thought better of that idea and decided I needed to work faster, smarter and harder.

I had never worked so hard before in all of my life. Part of my delivery area was Webster Avenue, the area where I grew up. I remember delivering packages to Smitty's Barber Shop and how proud he was of my accomplishment. It reminded me of how we all reacted when Villittha got her job down on Wall Street.

I remember delivering to a building on La Fountain Avenue, apartment 3B. I knocked on the door. Who is it? was the response.

UPS, I said. Just a minute was the response, so I waited. The door never opened. I knock again. Who is it? UPS, I yelled. Just a minute.

I hear some kids whispering and giggling behind a door in another apartment behind me. So, I wait some more. No one opened the door. I bang on the door again, this time with a closed fist. Who is it? UPS, I shouted. Once again, just a minute was the response.

A guy was coming up the stairs behind me. He stopped and said, "You know you are talking to a parrot, right?"

"You gotta be kidding me," I said. The kids behind the door really started laughing. I was out done!

I remember literally running to complete my deliveries faster. My feet were killing me. They were bad feet anyway. One time, I stopped and said with tears in my eyes, Jesus, does it have to be this hard? I met with my immediate manager and his boss again at my next and final review.

They insisted that I had not reached my targeted production goals. I said you told me that I needed to be at 13.5 or higher. He said I did not tell you that. I said, yes, you did. His boss said, are you calling me a liar? I said, are you denying that you told me 13.5 or higher?

He said yes. Then, I'm calling you a liar, I shot back. He turned beet red. He was a big man. He rose from behind his desk and yelled to my manager, throw him the "f"- out of my building. I said that I had met their criteria but, in all likelihood, I probably had not due to my ailing feet. He was insinuating that I was a liar. I may not have made the targeted production numbers, but a liar, I was not.

I was escorted to the exit. I was already a union member but only part-time. That they could not take away from me. So, I returned to my part-time job. Not getting the driving job was one thing. To blatantly lie to my face was another. I lost all respect for both of them.

Mark Batterson put it this way, ***"Failure is not the enemy of success. It's the greatest and closet ally! We treat failure and success like they're antonyms. Failure is part of every success story. Think of it as the prologue. You have to choose a dictator. You can let fear dictate your decisions, or you can let faith dictate your decisions."***[52]

This was an issue that I was sure my union officials would support me on. As part-timers, our union dues were half the amount of the full-time union employees. Not knowing where to start, I wanted to get the union involved, so I started at the very bottom. I did not want to step on any union official toes.

---

[52] Batterson, Mark. All In (You are one decision away from a totally different life). (Zondervan, 2013), 89

So, I started with my immediate shop steward, who quickly said, sorry, kid, there isn't anything I can do for you. So, I went to the next level, the union business agent. He, too, was quick to say, sorry, kid, there isn't anything I can do for you. The only person higher now in my local was the union president. He seemed to be a very powerful man. He had authorized a few strikes and was extremely popular with the employees.

I made an appointment to meet with him. I did not think that I would get it because everyone told me that he would not meet with me for two reasons – the first was because I was a part-time employee, and secondly, because I was black.

It was no secret that less than a decade earlier, UPS only hired blacks as janitors and porters. Blacks were not hired as package delivery drivers and certainly not promoted at that time to supervisors or managers within those ranks.

Black or White, the money is the same and any union worth its salt would want to have as many employees under its umbrella as possible. If he did not see me, I was prepared to take my fight in another direction. Minorities were steered to the menial jobs and night work because those were the least desirable jobs.

In 1973, most of the full-time driving positions at UPS were held by white males. However, a short decade earlier, UPS didn't hire blacks as package drivers. The Civil Rights Act of 1964 changed all of that. In 1964, Congress passed Public Law 88-352 (78 Stat. 241). The Civil Rights Act of 1964 prohibits discrimination on the basis of race, color, religion, sex or national origin.

As stated earlier, provisions of this civil rights act forbade discrimination on the basis of sex, as well as race, in hiring, promoting, and firing. I was surprised at the degree of prejudice that still existed. It was prevalent. UPS is a heavily unionized job.

As part-time employees, we also had to join the union. Our union dues were half of what the full-time employees had to pay. We were teamsters, members of local 804. UPS seemed to favor ex-military people. At that time, nearly all full-time employees seemed to have some type of military experience.

We were taught that UPS drivers do not drive "trucks." They drive "package cars." It was a great marketing strategy. Businesses and individual retail customers liked the idea of their merchandise being delivered to them from "package cars" rather than trucks.

I finally received news that I had an appointment with the local 804 union president. My appointment disproved both suspicions that it would never happen. I was elated. To my surprise, a lot of my co-workers were impressed not with me but with the union president. The fact that he thought I was important enough to have some of his direct time.

Nothing but the Blood

Initially, the union did not like the company hiring part-time workers. Part-time employees were perceived as a threat to future full-time job positions. Only two paragraphs pertained to part-time workers in the union book of nearly one hundred pages at that time.

The word spread that I had a meeting with the union president. His office was located in Long Island City, Queens, N.Y. I remember walking up a long flight of metal stairs. The stairs were attached to the back outside of the building.

A large grey metal door led to his office at the top of the stairs. When I stepped into his office, there he sat, a small man behind this big, gigantic redwood polished desk. It was very impressive and somewhat intimidating. He looked powerful. I believed that I would finally get some satisfaction.

He listened attentively as I explained my situation. I was surprised that I never saw anyone else in or around his office during my entire visit. He never interrupted me and listened to my entire story. However, he also never asked me any questions.

After I finished, he leaned forward, resting both elbows on top of his desk. He clasped his hands together, interlacing his fingers. Then, resting his chin on his two thumbs, he leaned in further and said, well, kid, there isn't anything that I can do for you.

Quite frankly, I was shocked. It was as if they all had rehearsed the same response because all three union representatives said the exact same thing, "Sorry, kid, there isn't anything that I can do for you."

Wow. He didn't even offer to look into it for me or say, let me see what I can do. Not even to say, give me a few days, let me find out what's going on. I was so very disappointed. What a letdown. It was a gut punch.

Now, I took it personally. Perhaps it was me. I thanked him for his time. I left his office knowing then, that I was not on the winning team. I knew then that I would either go into management or quit. I no longer wanted to be a part of the union.

But before making any decision, I decided to go to the Department of Labor to file a discrimination complaint. I filed a complaint with the EEOC (Equal Employment Opportunity Commission). The EEOC is responsible for protecting you from one type of discrimination - employment discrimination because of your race, color, religion, sex (including pregnancy, gender identity, and sexual orientation), national origin, disability, age (age 40 or older), or genetic information. I believed that those managers intentionally lied to and misled me. It wasn't right, and I was determined to do all I could to make it right.

Author John C. Maxwell writes, ***"The key that unlocks the door to success is the key of commitment. Without that key, the door will never open. No amount of genius, talent, finesse, or "right connections" will ever bring the fruit of success without a real commitment. Most frustrated quitters never achieve their potential, not because of bad breaks or unusual problems, but because of a failure to commit themselves to their goal regardless of obstacles. The level of your determination to accomplish your work is measured by what it takes to make you quit."***[53]

Shortly thereafter, UPS called me to meet with the Human Resources manager. He asked me if I had filed an EEOC complaint. He asked what was the nature of the complaint and who was involved. I told him all that had transpired.

Several weeks after that meeting, I was told that I would be given a full-time job. Not as a package delivery driver but as a full-time pre-loader. I would have to work nights. This was fine with me. As far as I was concerned, I had earned a full-time job and got it.

Through it all, I was being blessed. The Holy Spirit knew that a driver's job was not suited for me physically. I was given a

---

[53] Maxwell, John C., Think on these Things (Meditation for Leaders). (Beacon Hill Press, 1999), 90

full-time job on the inside that perfectly matched my physical capabilities. A job that I did not know existed.

Norman Geisler states that **"… it makes a world of difference what we believe. Belief affects behavior, and so ideas have consequences. Good ideas lead to good consequences, and bad ideas have bad consequences. A person who believes the railroad crossing signal is stuck when, in truth, a train is coming, may soon be dead! Anyone who believes the ice on the lake is solid when, in fact, it is thin, may be about to drown! Likewise, false doctrine will lead to false deeds. To repeat the limerick, "Johnny was a good boy, but Johnny is no more. For what he thought was H2O was H2SO4.(sulfuric acid)!"**[54]

It was a job at night loading the package cars for the delivery drivers. It meant I would become a full-time union employee and accepted it. I also realized where the real seat of power existed, and I wanted to be a part of that winning team.

I was twenty-three years old now and living on my own. I had real responsibilities and adult obligations. I was excited and somewhat apprehensive about my future. The devil was successful in getting me out of the church but not getting the church out of me.

---

[54] Geisler, Norman. Chosen But Free. (Bethany House, 2001), 136

One snowy night, a co-worker convinced me to go into a corner bar with him to have a quick beer. We were both union employees, and of course, consuming alcohol while on the clock was not allowed. We go into the bar. It's roughly 2 am in the morning.

The bar had the typical L-shaped counter. At the short end of the bar was a full window that looked out onto the Avenue. Opposite the long side of the bar was the wall facing the street. On this wall were two narrow windows about five feet high and five feet apart.

Looking out onto the street, you could see that it was snowing and see the heads of people walking by. I see two guys walk by very quickly. The first guy comes into the bar and marches down immediately to the far end of it. The second guy enters and stops at the door. They were both wearing long leather trench coats.

They open their coats and swing out sawed-off shotguns. They ordered everybody to get down onto the floor. One guy remained seated at the bar, refusing to move. I assume that he was a cop. The 40th police precinct was just a block and a half away. Cops from that precinct, I'm told, frequented this bar all the time.

The robber at the far end of the bar walked over to him, yelling for him to get down onto the floor. He placed both barrels of his gun against this man's temple. I closed my eyes because I thought he was going to blow this guy's brains out. The guy finally complied.

Then they tell us all to get up, and we were herded into the bathroom at the back of the bar. There were approximately ten of us, and we were packed in there like sardines. One of my legs started to shake uncontrollably.

Now, I prayed that no one entered the bar from the outside because this could frighten these clowns, and they might start shooting. The robbers ordered us to stay in the bathroom and not to come out. After several minutes of silence, we began to slowly come out. The cash register was left open and empty. The barmaid was also gone.

She was very attractive, and for some reason, we believed that she was in on the hold-up. I was thankful that they did not rob any of us. It was payday for my co-worker and me. We had over five hundred dollars cash between us. We never entered that or any other bar in the area again. Well, I know that I never did.

The men I worked with at night were much older than me. I hung out with them and occasionally was taken to one club. The things that went on in this place are unspeakable. I wanted to vomit. I had to leave and didn't get to see it all.

Pastor T.D. Jakes tells us, *"... but when you are really a child of God, there should be an uncomfortability with sin that makes you cry out to God for His cleansing and grace. God knows how to get you to the right place without taking a wrong turn. Trust Him. Don't stop talking to God about the parts of your life that are in contradiction."*[55]

The name of the club was Sin City, and that is just what it was. Just the name alone was foreboding to me. I waited for them outside, and I remember thinking that God destroyed Sodom and Gomorrah for this very same thing.

I felt as repulsed as I did when I witnessed the rape of that girl in Lumberton. Be careful of who you follow and hang out with. Let the Holy Spirit lead you. I knew better and felt so convicted.

J.D. Greear states *"While God is the one who changes our desires, we are the ones who make the choice to submit. Many people feel the pull of God on their hearts and resist it, and Jesus places the blame for that squarely upon their shoulders."*[56]

One time, I went into a gas station. I was standing in line with three or four other people to make my purchase. I looked down, and on the floor in front of me was a twenty-dollar bill. There wasn't

---

[55] Jakes, T.D., He-Motions. (G. P. Putnam Son's, 2004), 256
[56] Greear, J. D. Stop Asking Jesus Into Your Heart. B & H, 2013

anyone behind me. I put my foot over the bill before anyone else spotted it, then picked it up and put it into my pocket.

After leaving the gas station, I felt horrible. I knew that bill had to belong to someone on that line. I should have done the right thing and asked who it belonged to, but I didn't. I felt awful, was not happy and could not enjoy it. That was the Holy Spirit convicting me. Letting me know that I had done something wrong. I would never do that again.

Benny Hill declares, ***"You should never doubt the leading of the Holy Spirit. At a time when your "inner man" is troubled, don't move. If you attempt to be your own guide, you'll literally collapse. Listen to His voice as He speaks to your very soul."***[57]

In the spring of the following year, the two managers who threw me out of the building asked me to become a supervisor. They said, "We like the way you handle yourself, and we think you will make a good supervisor." They approached me, imagine that!

However, all kinds of red flags went up in my head. I knew what my plan was, and they made it a lot easier for me. Everyone told me not to go into management. They said that I was being set

---

[57] Hinn, Benny. Good Morning, Holy Spirit. (Thomas Nelson, 1990), 76

up. I would have no protection from the union, they said. I laughed at that thought.

They want to fire you because you embarrassed them, because you filed an EEOC complaint, because, because, because. I refused to listen to all of the "naysayers" and accepted their offer. They warned me that it was a trap.

I knew that staying in the union was not for me. I wanted to be on the winning team; from my experience, the winning team was not the union. The union told me repeatedly that there was nothing they could do for me, and I finally believed them.

The options that I chose for myself were still the same. I would either become a supervisor, and I was not really sure if that was an option for me, or I would quit.

But, according to author Napoleon Hill, ***"The urge to continue was stronger than the desire to quit." Remember that time when you wanted to quit, but something drove you to keep going? It may have been your "other self."***[58]

Here was my opportunity to become a full-time supervisor. It was being handed to me on a silver platter. I was an honest, hard-working kid from the projects. I was never interviewed by anyone

---

[58] Hill and Lechter. Outwitting The Devil (The Secret to Freedom and Success), 14

except the two managers who threw me out of the building eight months earlier.

During our meeting, when the subject of my starting salary arose, a figure was written down on a piece of paper. It was folded over and pushed across the desk to me. I picked it up, opened it and smiled. I immediately agree with the figure. I wasn't sure of what else to do.

I did not know this was my invitation to negotiate my starting salary. I did not negotiate because I did not know that I could, I did not know that I was expected to, and I did not know how to negotiate. There, I sat with a college degree, years of job knowledge, and experience, and I had no idea of the bargaining power that I held.

I could have easily negotiated hundreds of dollars more per month for myself. I did not know my self-worth, so they took advantage of me. Years later, I would discover that I was one of the lowest-paid supervisors in the district. It would be years later still before I would catch up to the average supervisor's pay.

However, I was not so naive as to believe that those two managers did not have some ulterior motive for promoting me. The Holy Spirit had my guard up. I was promoted to a full-time night preload supervisor.

I was an hourly employee one day and a supervisor the next. No training, no orientation. I knew the job because I had been doing it for nearly a year. I knew nothing about managing a business. My degree was in Sociology, not Business, and my attitude was that if I didn't like being a supervisor, I'd quit.

I knew that I had my work cut out for me. They made me a supervisor over the same guys that I was working beside the night before. The same guys that took me to Sin City. The same guy that I was with during the bar holdup.

It was very uncomfortable for me and for them. It was only by the grace of God that I survived. Not only did I survive, I thrived. My degree was in "people." I knew how to motivate and draw the best out of people. I was fair, honest, humble and perhaps a little modest.

John C. Maxwell writes, ***"One of the greatest days of your life will be the day when you discover your potential. You and your talents are not an accident. You're not a number in a lineup. You're not a statistic lost in the shuffle of mass humanity. You are special in God's eyes. You have distinct gifts and talents. You have shoes to fill that no one else can wear. Inside you is enormous potential just waiting to be developed and put to use. It is no accident that as your self-image changes, your performance changes. Your actions are a direct result of how you see yourself.***

Those who think little of themselves produce little. A person who pictures himself or herself as a failure will be a failure. If you believe that you have little to offer the world, you'll sit and contribute nothing. But when you begin to feel good about yourself, you'll begin to feel good towards others. As you feel worthwhile, you'll become worthwhile. The better your self-image becomes, the greater the development of your potential."[59]

Within a couple of years, both of the managers who had promoted me were moved on. One morning, my new manager called me into his office. He motioned for me to sit down. As I sat opposite him, he reached into his desk drawer and withdrew a yellow sheet of paper folded over several times. He pushed it across his desk to me. He said, I want you to read this. It was a note from his former boss, the one who promoted me.

This was written six months after I had been promoted. It read, and I quote, "Curtis has been here long enough now. It's time to find his replacement." I didn't want to believe it, but I was not surprised. I asked him. So, why didn't you fire me?

Because I am my own man, he said. I've been watching you, and you are a darn good supervisor. Keep up the good work. May I keep this? Yes, he said. Oh, my God! Our God tells the faithful that

---

[59] Maxwell, Think on these Things (Meditation for Leaders), 77

he will let no weapon formed against you prosper. This was their plan all along. To promote me and then fire me.

At this point, I had been in New York for a little over 10 years. I had gotten baptized, lost my southern accent, got my college degree and was now a full-time supervisor for United Parcel Service of America.

Rick Warren reminds us that ***"The Spirit of God uses the Word of God to make us like the Son of God. God's Word generates life, creates faith, produces change, frightens the Devil, causes miracles, heal hurts, builds character, transforms circumstances, imparts joy, overcomes adversity, defeats temptation, infuses hope, releases power, cleanses our minds, brings things into being, and guarantees our future forever!"***[60]

I continued to work nights, and after several years, I was sent to SBTS (Supervisor Basic Training School), a UPS management orientation school. At this point, it appeared to me that I had decided to stay with UPS, and UPS had decided to invest further in me.

I was taught the company's history, philosophy, methods, etc. Jim Casey, one of the founding fathers of UPS, was an extraordinary man. I found myself most taken by his management

---

[60] Warren, Rick. The Purpose Driven Life. (Zondervan, 2022), 186

philosophy. He addressed groups of management people throughout his life.

One of his more popular talks was **<u>"A Talk with Joe"</u>** in 1956. Jim expounds, "Even so, there will be times when you will get deeply discouraged. You will have family and other problems that you cannot share with others. You'll not always be free of financial worries. You'll find yourself blocked on some of your plans. You'll become physically and mentally tied. Adversities will detract from the effectiveness of your work. You'll feel your progress is not fast enough. You'll want more money and you won't see when or how you are going to get it. You'll see others advanced to positions you thought should have been given to you. There will be times when you'll feel like quitting and you'll say to yourself: "I'm all done. No more of this for me."

Pastor Rick Warren says, ***"At some point in your life, you must decide whether you want to impress people or influence people. You can impress people from a distance, but you must get close to influence them, and when you do that, they will be able to see your flaws. That's okay. The most essential quality for leadership is not perfection, but credibility. People must be able to***

trust you, or they won't follow you. How do you build credibility? Not by pretending to be perfect, but by being honest.[61]

Jim goes on to say, "But, Joe, you are made of stout stuff and you'll snap out of your mental depression. When you try to figure out what you would do if you left the company, you'll decide that you are in a pretty good business after all. Your negative thoughts will be superseded by positive action. You'll re-examine the questions that bother you and you'll see new light. You'll find a compromise between the perfect situation that you hoped for and the imperfect situation that really is. And soon you will be surprised to see that the middle ground of little promise turned out even better than you had originally hoped. Things will work out favorably for you, Joe, because impulsiveness will give way to patience. You will have learned from experience that progress is nearly always made one hard step at a time."

I felt as though he was talking directly to me, which I'm sure was his objective. However, he was not. It wasn't until 1957 that the first African American package driver was hired. His name is Ken Jarvis and just as I've never met Jim Casey, neither have I met Ken Jarvis.

---

[61] Warren, The Purpose Driven Life, 277

<u>Nothing but the Blood</u>

Remembering Ken Jarvis: A Pillar of Opportunity and Excellence at UPS (**06-17-2024**).

A message from Darrell Ford:

The UPS community mourns the loss and celebrates the incredible life of Ken Jarvis, a true trailblazer for our company. Ken joined UPS in 1957 as our first African American package car driver. His dedication and pursuit of excellence enabled him to advance through the ranks, culminating in his retirement as vice president of Human Resources after 37 years of service.

Ken's story is one of resilience and triumph. After serving in the Korean War, he came home to a country that didn't recognize his potential. He faced discrimination, even losing a promised job with a state highway patrol because of his race. However, through the National Urban League – a civil rights organization that advocates for economic empowerment even today – Ken found a position at UPS as a driver.

Later, as vice president of Human Resources, Ken shaped our company's policies to be more inclusive and helped create a culture where everyone could succeed. He served as an inspiration to his colleagues and paved the way for countless others – there's no doubt the legacy he leaves will benefit our business and our people for generations to come. His impact may be best summarized in his own words: "I was promoted into management and had the opportunity to develop managers who looked like me. To me, that was the greatest achievement – that I was able to participate in the total integration of UPS."

Ken accomplished so much in his career, but what is perhaps most remarkable was his dedication to giving back. After retiring, he co-founded The MARCH Foundation (Mutual Alliance Restoring Community Hope), an organization that supports the education of African American youth. The foundation has awarded over $1 million in scholarships to more than 1,000 African American students attending Historically Black Colleges and Universities.

As we think about our company's purpose today – moving our world forward by delivering what matters – let us be reminded that *Ken truly delivered what matters for UPS, the logistics industry, and society.*

Our thoughts are with Ken's family and loved ones during this difficult time. We are deeply grateful for the path he forged and the legacy he leaves behind — one that will inspire future generations to value dedication, excellence, and inclusion. UPS'ers can contribute to his lasting legacy by donating to the MARCH Foundation here.

At this juncture I would like to acknowledge the minority department heads, trailblazers if you will, that I knew and worked with personally throughout my thirty-seven-year history with UPS. They are: **Artie Lucien, Moises Huntt, Dennis Skinner, Irv Winston, Kim Van Utrecht, Henry Beards, Janice Jackson, Gary Wright, Rhonda Atherley-Ward, Lisa Robinson, Aurora Ritter, Justin Laporte, Beverly Riddick, Brent Cudjoe, Laura James, Valerie Annette Santiago, Juan Vicente, Maurice Pazmino, Diva Sandrasagra, Shunda Fussell Clark**, and **Ulysses Gary**.

When talking about Jim Casey's leadership skills they were remarkable, as were also illustrated in his "Determined Men…" and Inspired Management collection of speeches.

In one of his 1947 talks, Jim Casey writes, "Within each of us there is a mysterious innate force that drives us onward. It wants us to do better and be better. Call that force conscience, ambition, determination, power of will, or whatever you chose, it constantly whispers in our ears words of advice, stimulation and encouragement. If you will but heed the voice and utilize that inner power to the limit of its potentialities, nothing on earth can stop your progress."

That inner voice for me has always been the voice of the Holy Spirit.

John C. Maxwell states that ***"One of the prime responsibilities of a leader is to encourage others. Many times,*** *people with problems become slaves to their situation because they can see nothing but problems. Nothing will more quickly and effectively shrivel a bad situation into proper perspective than focusing attention upon the positive elements of a problem. Every person has hidden potential. You give the person confidence. You change the atmosphere in which people live.*"[62]

I met my wife in my senior year at Hunter College. At that time, I was still living at home – in the Castle Hill Projects. Aunt Lou was really arguing with me a lot. She was always berating me about one thing or another.

She called all of my female friends whores, and I really didn't know what that was all about. It really bothered me as she continued to nitpick.

Perhaps this was her way of telling me that it was time for me to leave the nest. I did not like living under her roof anymore. She had become unnecessarily mean and petty. I did not know why. Was it me?

Had I changed and made her become this way? She had become a different person. I had seen this spirit once before when she ended her long-time friendship with Stephanie's mom.

---

[62] Maxwell, Think on these Things (Meditation for Leaders), 56-57

Dr. James T. Jefferson says, ***"In spite of that there are two forces at work. The first one that should be pointed out is the negative one, the influence of Satan and sin. Satan, in his opposition to God and what God stands for is constantly opposing God by doing everything he can to dissuade people from having any interest in wanting to live a descent and wholesome life. Satan, as an opponent of God, seeks to misinform and mislead all he can to prevent them from becoming followers of Jesus. Satan goes to church himself to distract as many people as he can from hearing about the love of God and God's willingness to accept all who come to Him in faith for forgiveness and salvation."*** [63]

I chose to ignore her behavior and continued to treat her as I always had. I believe, that had I not done so, she would have severed our relationship. She had done too much good for both me and Bernardette to allow that to happen. I continued to love her. I was 23 years old.

I vowed to myself that whenever I did leave, I would never come back. I would not give her the satisfaction of seeing me fail. I was determined not to fail.

---

[63] Jefferson, James T., One Night In Bethlehem. (It Is Written, 2023), 18

When I moved out from Aunt Lou, I was angry because I felt that I did not deserve that type of treatment from her. I was a good kid. I didn't give her any trouble at all.

So, why was she treating me this way? I even went through the dirty clothes in the bathroom hamper to make sure that I had everything that belonged to me. I didn't want to have to return for any reason.

I didn't tell her I was looking for a place until I found one. I wasn't sure she would have allowed me to stay until I found a place. Don't get me wrong, I was eternally grateful for her raising me and always will be, but it was time for me to go.

She had prepared me to live on my own. She taught me how to be responsible, how to cook, clean, iron, shop, etc. She taught me how to manage money even though she nor I had any of it.

The process of looking for an apartment was frustrating. The "real estate agency" I used would give anybody a list of supposedly available apartments for a fee. You had to set up your own appointments with the owners or landlords to see the apartment.

I remember wanting to rent a basement apartment in a private house in the Eastchester section of the Bronx. I called and spoke with the owner. We had a lovely conversation. A date for me to see the place was established. I showed up on the day and time of the appointment.

As I approached the front door, I saw someone part the venetian blinds to see who was coming up the driveway. So, I knew someone was at home. They saw me and were not pleased. No one ever answered the door. I was not what they were hoping for and unfortunately for them, they were unable to determine that from our phone conversation.

This incident reminded me of a trip to my hometown. I drove my VW Beetle to North Carolina. While waiting at a stop light, an elderly white man literally let his car roll into the back of my car. Being that Volkswagen Beetle engines are in the rear of the vehicle, the weight of his car jammed my engine cover against my fan belt.

My car had to be towed away. A police report was completed. My car was repaired, and I later returned to New York.

When I returned to my apartment, I called the man listed on the police report and pretended to be an insurance agent. I just wanted to have some fun. Hello sir. My name is Johnnie Rocket, and I am the insurance agent investigating the accident that took place between you and one of our clients last week. Will you please tell me in your own words, sir, how this accident happened?

He said, "That nigger came down here in that little red foreign car. We was waiting at the light, and when the light turned green, that nigger put his car in reverse and backed up into me. You know that nigger, he didn't know how to drive that foreign car."

Well, sir, I said, it just so happens that you are talking to a nigger, and there is no further need for this conversation. "Oh, my Lord," he screams. "Lord, I'm sorry, I didn't know it," and I hung up the phone as he continued to apologize. I guess I sounded like one of the good old boys to him.

My UPS supervisor/friend thought perhaps he and I could share the rent for a private home. I didn't like that idea. I also discovered that I wanted my apartment in a building, not a private home. This gave me more autonomy and privacy. Besides, I wanted something that I could call all my own.

I finally found a place in an apartment building in the North Bronx. A studio apartment on Decatur Avenue, apartment 4A, in the last building on the block. It was at the southern base of the infamous Woodlawn Cemetery. This was the apartment that Louis had loaned me the three hundred dollars to secure.

She never got to see it, the apartment, that is. The building had a nice lobby and was also elevatored. There was also an attached garage with car spaces available. I got a parking space. The neighborhood was nice. It wasn't the projects, and it certainly wasn't 1700 Grand Concourse.

The building superintendent was a soft-spoken southern man. He was one of the nicest people I had ever met. Montefiore Hospital was nearby, as was the Bronx River Parkway and two elevated subways, the #2 train on White Plains Road and the #4 train on Jerome Avenue.

My apartment building was situated between the two. My rent was $198 a month plus $35 a month for an indoor parking space. I was in heaven.

Now, I could tell Aunt Lou that I was moving out. She was very surprised. Later, she said, you even took your dirty clothes with you. She seemed to have been hurt by that and said, I would have washed them for you.

During this time, I had also stopped going to church. This resulted from a Black History course I had taken during my last semester at Hunter College. Dr. ben-Jochannan was the professor, and his book, Black Man In The Nile, was required reading.

According to Dr. ben-Jochannan, "others" had done what Jesus did, thousands of years before His appearance. My rationalization was, maybe this Jesus thing isn't all it's made out to be. So, there's nothing so special about Jesus.

Satan had tricked me, and I used this as an excuse to stop going to church. Although I had forsaken God, I would learn that he had never and never would forsake me.

Rick Warren states that ***"Satan loves detached believers, unplugged from the life of the Body, isolated from God's family, and unaccountable to spiritual leaders, because he knows they are defenseless and powerless against his tactics."***[64]

I got along well with my fellow supervisors at work, most of whom were white. I had one white supervisor tell me that we all should get promoted at some point, but he had better get his promotion before me. He had a real sense of entitlement, and I believe they all probably felt that way.

Having come from the South, I certainly knew what it was like to be discriminated against. If anyone had a reason to be prejudiced, it could have easily been me.

From my first day at P.S 28, my heart welcomed all people. In the South, you were told to your face where you stood, but here in New York, you had to read between the lines.

---

[64] Warren, The Purpose Driven Life, 136

John C. Maxwell says, ***"What enters our mind and occupies our thought process will somewhere, sometime come out of our mouth."***[65]

I learned the job by watching the other supervisors, some of whom were absolute idiots. I gleaned what was good and let the rest go. I quickly realized that I could not say or behave like my white colleagues and have it be perceived or received the same way.

Don't get me wrong, it was not a yes sir, no sir environment, but the subtleties were always there of perceived racial superiority on their part.

For example, if they were being assertive and I behaved the same way, I was perceived as being threatening or insubordinate. If they raised their voice to make a point, they were being outspoken, and if I did the same, the response would be, who do you think you're talking to?

This was a white-male-dominated industry, and to gain favorable credibility, you had to have "balls," but if you were non-white, you had to have permission to use them. If not, you were almost immediately emasculated and told that you didn't follow the chain of command, or you were reprimanded and chastised.

---

[65] Maxwell, Think on these Things (Meditation for Leaders), 14

Learning the labor aspect of the job was probably the most challenging. I was firm but fair, and my word was my mantle. Honesty was always the best policy but did not always yield the desired results. I was where I wanted to be.

The Teamster's Union was a tough outfit; they danced around certain issues very gingerly, and I had to learn the steps to the dance. There was always bigger fish to fry.

I had to grow up fast. I was running with the big dogs. Just because you were "right" did not necessarily mean that you "won." I learned that in this business, the grease was always hot, and if there were bigger fish to fry, then whatever you had going on could easily become toast – less important.

I had an employee on the brink of termination, and deservedly so. He was a mean and nasty individual, which made my job easier. Harry was both an attendance problem and a performance problem. I had done my homework on him for months, made sure that all of my tees were crossed and I's dotted.

The week he was to be terminated, my boss decided to make a deal with the union for something that was more important. Harry's termination was put on hold. I felt defeated and that all of my hard work was for nothing.

My boss encouraged me to continue to do what I was doing and not to get discouraged. You have done nothing wrong, he said. We simply had bigger fish to fry.

You had to be tough to be a union official and even tougher to be a supervisor.

Once, all four of my car tires were slashed, and UPS replaced all four tires without hesitation. Fear and intimidation did not prevent me from doing the right thing.

Mark Batterson goes on to say, *"When we compromise our integrity, we don't leave room for divine intervention. When we take matters into our own hands, we take God out of the equation. When we try to manipulate a situation, we miss out on the miracle."*[66]

I had one manager who would always try to make me look weak and incompetent. He would undermine whatever I did. Whatever I negotiated with the shop steward, he would override or strike it down.

I realized quickly that he did this to make himself look important and to gain favor with the union. I continued to do the

---

[66] Batterson, All In (You are one decision away from a totally different life), 139

right thing. His incompetence was finally exposed, and he was demoted.

I worked hard and played hard. My apartment building sat on a hill and overlooked Webster Avenue, Metro North train tracks and the Bronx River Parkway. You could see the #2 subway Gun Hill Road stop off in the distance.

Also, in the distance on a clear day, you could see Co-op City. I had absolutely little to no furniture – one bed and a desk – that was it. If you wanted to sit down you had to sit on the bed. One female friend said, you don't leave a girl much of a choice, do you? This is how I began my bachelorhood.

At this point in my life, my wife and I had been dating on and off for a few years. I thought of her often and how we first met. I was a senior at Hunter, and she was a freshman.

I was immediately attracted to her. I noticed her at school one day as she walked by. I peeled away from a bunch of guys that I was talking to. I began walking beside her, trying to guess her name.

She just looked at me, smiled and kept walking. Satisfied that I had made a complete fool of myself, she finally relented and said, Sandy. I did not think that she liked me.

<u>Nothing but the Blood</u>

She showed very little interest. I would follow her and her girlfriend after class, hoping to get to talk to her. I know that sounds a bit creepy.

I discovered that she worked on the tenth floor in the periodicals department. Remember, Hunter College, much like Baruch College, is mostly a vertical institution. Located in the core of Manhattan, they don't have rolling green campuses.

I would study in the periodicals room, hoping to get a glimpse of her, and I'm sure they knew it. I would look up from my books and see her and her girlfriend quietly leaving, walking down the hallway to the elevator.

I would quickly gather my things to follow them as they giggled amongst themselves. I was smitten.

One day, I asked her if I could drive her home. To my surprise, she said yes. I had a red 1973 Volkswagen rabbit. It was a little beat-up. A piece of cardboard suppressed some springs in the front passenger seat.

I found Sandy to be beautiful. She was tall, shapely and soft-spoken. I thought the condition of my car would be the deal breaker. To my surprise, she sat in it like it was a royal coach. That was the moment that I fell in love with her.

She lived in Hollis Queens, wherever that was. I was a Bronx boy. She directed me to her house. I could not believe it. It was a large two-story colonial-style home on 192nd Street off of Hillside Avenue. I had never been in any house like it before. Nor did I know anyone who lived in such a majestic home.

How will she react when she finds out that I lived in the projects? Now, I thought this would be the real deal breaker. I hated where I lived and was embarrassed by it. To spare myself that embarrassment, I was working really hard to get my own place somewhere else, anywhere else, outside of the projects.

Sandy had become my reason for living, for the weekend, that is. We never saw each other during the week. She was still in school, and I was way too busy with work. Besides, our clocks were opposite each other.

She was in school all day, and I worked all night. We dated on and off over the next few years. I had grown to love her dearly. Sex was not a part of our relationship. Sandy had resisted that for years.

Then it happened, and it wasn't immaculate. I got her pregnant the very first time. We got married immediately. That was something that I would have done anyway. It was the right thing to do, and it was something that I wanted to do.

I always believed in the sanctity of marriage and wanted to have children and a family of my own. We had a small celebration at her house. Aunt Lou attended.

The official nuptials took place at the Bronx County Courthouse. I didn't consult with anyone or ask for any advice. My friend Terrence and his wife were our witnesses.

So, it was done. We were married, and she moved into my studio apartment.

We had one bed and one desk. Our first dinner together as a married couple was by candlelight. The candle was placed on top of her blue suitcase as we sat on the floor in the middle of our big, empty room. Her pregnancy was beginning to show.

I was a young adult now. Living on my own. Aunt Lou reported to the NYC Housing Authority that she no longer had anyone living with her. They told her that she had to take a smaller 1-bedroom apartment, which she expected.

A year or two later, she was placed in a senior citizen building one block from the Castle Hill subway station. She liked her new location better than Castle Hill, and so did I.

It was a single building and she was only one block from the subway, not that she needed to be that close.

Aunt Lou was too proud to say, that she missed Bernardette or worried about her. However, her actions let me know that she did. Whenever we traveled to Lumberton, the first place she wanted to visit was Bernardette's house.

I would drop her off there and she would spend the entire day with her. She gave her cat, Tinker, to her because her new location did not allow any pets. Bernardette kept Tinker for many, many years.

We continued to travel south almost every year. A cousin in Maryland started travelling with us. She and Aunt Lou grew-up together. I call her Auntie. By her own admission she was no push-over. If you did not bother her, she did not bother you but was not afraid of a fight.

She has had a rough life. At one point, she was married to a drug dealer and briefly moved to New York with him. Literally fearing for her life, she was able to leave him with the help of her landlord. By the grace of God, she returned safely to Maryland. There has been such tragedy in her life.

Her oldest daughter was murdered by her boyfriend. They had two little boys, one of whom died two months after the mother. Her next child was a boy who drowned at the age of thirteen in some kind of swimming accident.

Her second oldest daughter was just mean and selfish. I remember visiting a cousin in Baltimore with my wife and our only daughter at that time. My wife and I wanted to show a video of our daughter's gymnastics competition. Naturally, we were very proud of her and wanted to show the video to the family.

This daughter took her two children out of the house and refused to let them watch the video. I never understood why she would do something so mean and cruel. According to her mother she was also very bossy and disrespectful to her boss and co-workers. She worked for a law firm, had a great salary and benefits. She had a very nice apartment and had been working for the firm for over fifteen years. She was a very proud and arrogant women.

Leslie Copeland reminds us that, ***"Proverbs 16:18 says, "Pride goes before destruction, and a haughty spirit before a fall." And, James 4:6 reminds us that "God opposes the proud, but gives grace to the humble." Pride doesn't just show up in overly confident Christian leaders. It also makes an appearance when we overestimate our own ability to resist the enticements that befall others. Obviously, not everyone is tempted by the same things, but everyone is tempted by something."***[67]

---

[67] Copeland, Leslie. Christ-like Leadership. (Judson Press, 2022), 129

Several years after this point one of her daughters went to a party in another town. Her mother let her drive her car. After the

party she called her mother and said that she was tired and wanted to stay over and driver back home in the morning.

Her mother said, no and insisted that she bring back her car that night. She didn't feel like driving but did so anyway fearing the wrath of her mother. Enroute home that evening it appears that she may have fallen asleep at the wheel, run off the road and died from her injuries. One can only imagine the guilt and remorse her mother had.

Her job had given her time off and encouraged her to seek medical help. The burden was too heavy and she was unable to recover. She lost all that she had and due to the stress that she was under was admitted to a hospital.

Upon her release her oldest daughter agreed to be her caretaker. Shortly after being in the care of this daughter, her health begins to deteriorate. Immediately, family members blamed her for her weight loss and her inability to properly care for her. Some thought that one of the reasons that she treated her so poorly was because she blamed the mother for the death of her sister.

Custody was taken away from her daughter and given to her older sister. She was placed in a nursing facility near her and she is doing much, much better.

Mark Batterson says, ***"The lesson of Lucifer's fall is this: whatever you don't turn into praise turns into pride. Instead of deflecting praise to God. Lucifer let it feed his ego. It was the sinful desire to be lifted up that led to Lucifer's downfall."***[68]

Auntie says, that she treated all of her children the same. She believes this to be true but from what I observed in those early years, I would disagree. Her oldest surviving daughter, the one with custody is doing fine. This is the one who has been the favored child all along.

Unfortunately, I believe that unknowingly her favoritism toward this one daughter was to the social detriment of her other children. The other sisters dare not compare themselves to her. They were not as successful and not as educated, not as pretty, not nearly as popular and graceful. By local standards she had married into a prominent family. She and her husband embraced Christ at an early age and are doing extremely well.

---

[68] Batterson, All In (You are one decision away from a totally different life), 44

Auntie's youngest daughter is doing fine. She is divorced and has two daughters. She is retired. Auntie's son is well. He was discharged from the service and has always worked in the food industry.

Auntie has been a devout Christian now for many years. Under the circumstances she believes that she did the best she could and I'm sure that she did. She did not have an easy life and realized that what little she did have was only by the grace of God.

Now, at her age she seems to be a woman full of regrets. However, bemoaning in the dawn of this her eleventh hour, she realizes that she cannot correct or redirect the past. She begs for more of God's grace and mercy in the twilight of her life in hopes of making things right, for herself. She, Aunt Lou and I continued to travel south together for many years.

The Cutlar Moore Bridge proved to be an even more interesting place as I got older. One summer, while visiting home, I went fishing there. It was late afternoon, and I was the only one on the river bank. I was fishing very close to the bridge but not underneath it.

The area that I was fishing in offered the most direct sunlight because I wasn't under any trees. As I'm fishing, a woman appears seemingly out of nowhere. She actually startled me because I did not hear her approaching. I see her walking towards me, alone.

Although you could not see the vehicles above travelling back and forth across the bridge, you could clearly hear them. I did not hear any vehicle stop or any car door open or close. Where did this woman come from?

She looked maybe twenty-five or thirty years old, slim, and somewhat attractive. I would say that her nationality was Native American. She had on a thin, pink, A-line straight dress that was lightly flowered and fell several inches below her knees.

She stopped walking at a good, safe distance from me. She was empty-handed and carried no kind of bag or pocketbook, and she certainly did not have a fishing pole. She was completely empty-handed.

She squatted down facing me, and the fabric from her dress fell between her legs, as did her arms. The length of her dress still allowed the fabric to cover her knees. She started talking to me.

She was very friendly. I was the only person fishing; the sun was going down, and it was getting dark.

While watching her, I'm still trying to figure out where she came from. The nearest house was a quarter of a mile away. Had she come from there, perhaps?

Ironically, it was the very same house that I ran to as a frightened little boy, leaving Ms. Mamie due to that sudden thunder storm. Now, here I stand in the same place as an adult man, all alone to face a very different kind of storm.

I started to pack up my gear. She kept her distance, and I kept my eyes on her. She never advanced any closer toward me. She continues to make small talk. I was uncomfortable but did not feel threatened.

I was all packed up and ready to go but I couldn't just leave her there, so I offered her a ride. Is there any place that I can drop you off, I asked. Yes, she replied. I will show you where.

We get into my car. She sits in the passenger seat up front, caddy-corner facing me. She was staring at me the whole time. There was something eerily, unsettling and unnerving about her.

She possessed a certain boldness and confidence, yet she was not aggressive. She stared at me emotionless, then says, we can do something if you like. The hairs on the back of my neck stood straight up.

Pastor Rick Warren states that ***"On the path to spiritual maturity, even temptation becomes a stepping-stone rather than a stumbling block when you realize that it is just as much an occasion to do the right thing as it is to do the wrong thing. Temptation simply provides the choice. While temptation is Satan's primary weapon to destroy you, God wants to use it to***

develop you. Every time you choose to do good instead of sin, you are growing in the character of Christ."[69]

The Holy Spirit let me know right then that I was having a conversation with Satan himself. There was no doubt in my mind about that.

She directed me to a location, but I refused her offer. She laughed and then asked me for a few dollars, which I gave her.

She then directs me to a house near Coot's canal. I drive there. She gets out in front of a small, shabby, run-down house. It just so happens to be the last house on Front Street.

If you remember, Front Street is where my life's story began. I drive off praising and thanking God for giving me the strength to rebuke Satan, yet again.

Never in a million years would I have expected to be propositioned in such a way and at such a location. This is how Satan operates. He appears when you least expect him.

Thank you, Holy Spirit, for allowing me to recognize him for who he is.

We must remain vigilant at all times. Once I recognized him, I realized that he had no power over me. I realized that Satan can

---

[69] Warren, The Purpose Driven Life, 201

tempt you and make suggestions to you, but he does not have the power to force you to do anything. The choice is ours.

Pastor Rick Warren reminds us that, ***"You won't be able to say no to the Devil unless you've said yes to Christ. If you are a believer, Satan cannot force you to do anything. He can only suggest. There is power in God's Word, and Satan fears it. Don't ever try to argue with the Devil. He's better at arguing than you are, having had thousands of years to practice. You can't bluff Satan with logic or your opinion, but you can use the weapon that makes him tremble – the truth of God. This is why memorizing Scripture is absolutely essential to defeating temptation."***[70]

Satan approaches us in many different ways and forms. If we are not careful, he also entices us through loved ones, family members and friends. But he is powerless as long as we keep Jesus in front of us.

Author Bobbie Jefferson, reminds us that **"Satan is already a defeated foe. All we have to do is rebuke him and command him in Jesus' name and he will flee (run). So, believers need not be afraid of Satan. We have been given power over him. Jesus defeated him for us."**[71]

---

[70] Warren, The Purpose Driven Life, 214-215

[71] Jefferson, Bobbie. Elusive, Omni book, 2018, 27

The key is being able to recognize and resist him. He is much, much smarter than we are, and that's why we need the guidance and protection of the Holy Spirit.

Things at UPS were hectic. Due to the circumstances surrounding my promotion, I was constantly looking over my shoulder, waiting for the other shoe to drop. I kept my head up and my nose clean.

I had to remind myself that if things did not work out, I was going to quit. I was not getting fired. It was a healthy fear, I suppose.

I was never absent or late. It was seven years before my first unscheduled absence. I learned my assignments well. If they were going to fire me, I wasn't giving them any reasons. I had developed a very good rapport with my employees.

I had gained their respect. I managed people well, very well. My production numbers were among the best in the district. This, unfortunately, had an adverse effect on my career.

Remember, this was my personal social experiment. I wanted to experience all that UPS had to offer me before I left. Being a union employee for the rest of my career was out. What could management offer me that the union could not? After all, management was the winning team, or was it?

<u>Nothing but the Blood</u>

I've learned that you don't have to fight your battles alone, but it will make all the difference in the world if you know who is on your side. I was getting to know who was on my side and whom shall, I fear – it was the Father, Son and Holy Spirit. That Holy Trinity had now become my winning team.

I was only travelling to Lumberton once or twice a year now. Clara Mae and I had not reconnected since Bernardette, and I had left Lumberton. Her spirit was resonating within me. I began asking people about her. I wanted to find her, I wanted to see her, I wanted to hug her.

I was told where she lived, and I knocked on her door early one Saturday morning. She answered the door and screamed when she realized that it was me. We embraced and cried together for what seemed like hours. She wiped away my tears and took a good look at me again. She said, Curtis, I've been praying for this day.

Through the years, we remained in touch. Ruby, her daughter, had gotten married and had two little boys. As the years waned, we all became more immersed in the Christian faith. We began to visit each other. On Clara's first visit to New York, she said the buildings were taller than a Ferris wheel. We all became very close, and I began to help economically wherever possible.

Ruby started her own ministry and then, something happened. She divorced her husband, and Satan had driven a wedge between our relationship. She stopped communicating with me. She had changed, so much so that it prompted me to write the following poems. Now, I prefer to call it an Ode to Ruby:

A Friendship Poem (An Ode to Ruby)

Here it is;

I'm left again, to wonder;

where our friendship stands.

After all; this is how the argument began.

Is it something that I said? or perhaps she's fallen;

bumped her head. I know, I'll call her on her cell; oh, what the hell;

I don't want to leave; another message.

Did she receive; the Xmas package that I sent?

she only acknowledged a certain percent. Perhaps the rest;

she just considered mess. I know school is out; she can't be that busy;

but who am I to decide. I would really like to talk to her;

to see how things are going; if there is a need; I hope that I'm not boring.

This friendship you see; means a lot to me.

It started; when she was; just a little girl. Back then we both;

were in the world. Providing gifts; was something that I did;

but I only provided gifts to a few. As time went on;

she felt left out; ignored, forgotten, perhaps never to count.

These gifts are for boys; not for girls; besides, how would it look,

if I provided for you? But she was right; there was no good reason;

why I should ignore her, in my good season.

So, the gifts began; began with pleasure; and as God would have it;

became gifts of pleasure. Driven by a force unknown;

I knew; that what I was doing; really wasn't wrong.

<u>Nothing but the Blood</u>

He let me know; that, through this one, thousands and thousands
of souls;

would be won. I thought our friendship; would last forever;

as I'm reminded to say; never say never.

Has it all been just a sham? all this time, our friendship fragile;

as fragile as a lamb. I've only seen you; once in 3 years;

our conversations pass; pass like light years;

What am I really, guilty of? God only knows;

it is not because; we haven't made love. I am profoundly sorry;

for anything; I may have said; I'm profoundly sorry; for anything;

I may have done; I'm profoundly sorry; for any intent; you see my
friend;

this friendship was meant. You bring joy to my life; because of
what;

you have done. I am so pleased; that I was the chosen one.

<u>Nothing but the Blood</u>

You may think that I; really don't get it; but I really do.

It's time to move on; our relationship is through. Through your silence;

you have made it abundantly clear; please remember;

that relationship and friendship are two different things.

What is it that I could have possibly done? to bring such wrath,

resentment and indignation; It has been; your pursuit of happiness;

that has intrigued me the most; And I am deeply hurt;

that you would think; that I would boast; of my love for you.

Out of respect, honor and adoration; I will no longer attempt,

to communicate;

And pray; that you come to realize; that I am not;

the enemy.

Love, Curtis

After she responded and blamed me for everything and nothing, I wrote again:

A Friendship Poem (Part 2 | An Ode to Ruby)

I'm not sure;

of where your anger comes from;

it seems to be; so deep seated.

Perhaps you think; it best to direct it at the one;

who can best receive it.

But I refuse to be; your whipping tree;

to pay for the miss deeds of others. Because we know;

as quite as kept;

that most of it is aimed at;

our mothers.

Our secrets and lies; will all come to pass.

How can I cause; so much harm;

yet be so far away?

<u>Nothing but the Blood</u>

When the only thing; that stands between;

is the Holy word as we pray.

Our Father; lead us not into temptation.

So; as I step aside; and scream inside;

this battle is not yours.

I hear; peace be still; silent night;

and grab my pillow tight.

I try really hard; with all my might; to separate;

day from night; I hear; the Demons; as they scream;

to back away; from the light. But I have heard;

that in this Word;

is all the power; we need.

I don't have time;

to leave behind; all of the wonderful things; you have done.

We can't live; in the past; all our lives;

<u>Nothing but the Blood</u>

our days are surely; numbered.

So is this a poem; I'm really not sure;

Are your antics; only semantics; Don't we all need help?

So please dispense; with all the suspense

And tell me; what is really;

bothering you.

Love, Curtis

In her pursuit of happiness, I believe Ruby has allowed herself to be consumed by many demons. Self-righteousness has enabled her to become bitter with life and to suffer from delusions of grandeur.

"There is nothing more tragic than people who don't have an anointing trying to produce it. They try to force it, but the touch of the Lord is just not there,"[72] says Benny Hinn.

Simply by closing your eyes and turning your head, will not solve the problem. Pastor Ellie Baker of the True Believers Church

---

[72] Hinn, Good Morning Holy Spirit, 129

in Lumberton, N.C. says, "Sometimes to change a situation, you must talk directly to the situation."

Pastor Rick Warren states, ***"…people become disillusioned with the church for many understandable reasons. The list could be quite long: conflict, hurt, hypocrisy, neglect, pettiness, legalism, and other sins. Rather than being shocked and surprised, we must remember that the church is made up of real sinners, including ourselves. Because we're sinners, we hurt each other, sometimes intentionally and sometimes unintentionally. The sooner we give up the illusion that a church must be perfect in order to love it, the sooner we quit pretending and start admitting we're all imperfect and need grace."***[73]

Never getting a response from her, I continue to pray that our friendship will be mended. One of her favorite gospel songs is Can You Reach My Friend by Helen Baylor. It is so fitting right now. As for Clara Mae and I, our friendship remains as strong as ever.

During this time, Bernardette married a soldier who was shortly thereafter deployed to Germany. The military was definitely ingrained into the family. Our father was a soldier, and so were our brother, uncle, and stepfather.

---

[73] Warren, The Purpose Driven Life, 162-163

<u>Nothing but the Blood</u>

My best friend joined the Army, and so did his brother. Between Fort Bragg and Camp Lejeune, the US military was the area's largest employer. Those southern girls loved to marry soldiers. It meant security, an opportunity to travel and a monthly check.

Bernardette and Alvin came to New York for their honeymoon. They stayed with Aunt Lou, and we got to meet her fiancée, and I liked him. He seemed to be a nice, quiet man. His name was Alvin, and he was from a small town near Lumberton. She enjoyed travelling with him.

They first went to San Francisco, California and then on to Frankford, Germany. She kept in touch and seemed to be doing well. She said his next deployment would possibly be to Japan, and she was excited.

That did not happen, and after several years, they returned to Fort Bragg, N.C. Alvin was voluntarily discharged with a total tenure of twenty years. The next thing I heard from Bernardette was that she had divorced him. I suspect that for her, the fun was over, and she had no more use for him.

Having married Alvin, she got to see some of the world on Uncle Sam's dime, and that was all she wanted. I believe that she would have stayed with him as long as he stayed in the Army.

No longer married, she needed to find a job. She had expressed an interest in baking or becoming a hairdresser. I sent her a professional kitchen aide mixer set and from time to time asked her if she was using it. She became defensive and upset with me during one of these calls. "Why do you keep asking me about what I'm doing with that blender, she said? If I don't want to use it or do anything with it, that's my business. Y'all keep trying to make me do something. I don't have to do anything." Her attack really made my blood boil. My response was, Bernardette you are right. I was just trying to help. I could care less if you ever use that blender because what you eat does not make me fat. I never mentioned it again. Years later, upon her death I found that blender, unused in its original box on her kitchen floor.

Living Vicariously

If the people that you love,

Believe in your dream,

Are hard at work toward your goal.

If they are working harder than you.

Then it is no longer your dream,

But their Goal!

By Curtis White

After working nights for five years, I finally got a day job. I really enjoyed it and so did my family. I was learning the delivery side of the business, which would have prepared me to become a package center manager.

However, each time I was moved to learn a new area of the business, I'd be yanked back to nights. My replacements could not wrap the job up on time.

Drivers were being dispatched late, every day. I would work two months on days and then four weeks on nights.

Then back to days for six weeks and put back on nights for two weeks.

I didn't like working nights any more than the next guy. The white supervisors, many of whom I had trained and several of whom were supposed to have been my replacement, worked nights for one maybe two years and then were moved on to other daytime assignments.

However, each time something went wrong on nights I would be snatched back to supervise my old area or to cover a vacation. I was told that it was for the needs of the business but I was the only supervisor being moved around this way.

The back and forth was killing my family life, not to mention what it was doing to me physically. My sleep was very erratic, and I wasn't getting enough rest. It was beginning to take a toll on my overall health.

These interruptions prevented me from getting to know and understand how to manage our full-time package delivery drivers.

After the third time of moving me within an eight-month period, I complained to Human Resources. I had come to realize that my bosses would continue to treat me this way as long as I allowed it. They did not care about me or my family.

As bosses, they were self-serving, narcissistic and vindictive. I had to take care of myself, and in doing so, I knew that I would make some enemies along the way.

Author Mark Batterson tells us, ***"Praying is picking a fight with the Enemy. It's spiritual warfare. Intercession transports us*** *from the sidelines to the front lines without going anywhere. And that is where the battle is won or lost. Prayer is the difference between us fighting for God and God fighting for us. But we can't just hit our knees. We also have to take a step, take a stand. And when we do, we never know what God will do next."*[74]

The Human Resources manager, after hearing my concern, came to my work location. Upon reviewing my situation, she agreed with me and said the only way to resolve this issue was to remove me from the building altogether. My bosses were unhappy with that decision, but there wasn't anything they could do about it.

My HR manager went on to say that if I were not so readily available, it would force them to do without me, and they would have to develop another "Curtis," she said. She then asked, how would you like to come to work for me in Human Resources. Wonderful, I said. I became a district safety training supervisor for the Metro New York district.

A year or so later, I developed a medical issue. A pilonidal cyst had formed at the base of my spine. Those of us in management had an excellent medical plan. We also had an in-house medical

---

[74] Batterson, All In (You are one decision away from a totally different life), 87

department located on the sixth floor of the main building. I deferred to them first.

The head doctor there, Dr. G., thought it was just a boil. If that were the case, I wondered if he would suggest that I sit in a tub of hot water to get it to burst. That thought was eerily reminiscent of the boil on my leg as a child. However, thinking it was just a boil, he lanced it there in his office.

Unfortunately, over a short period of time, the cavity filled again with blood and pus, becoming even more painful. After further research and analysis, it was discovered that it was a cyst, not a boil. It had to be surgically removed, which meant a hospital visit and stay.

I didn't fear doctors while growing-up in the south, they just were not made available to me.

We were dirt poor and living in an economically depressed area certainly made matters worse.

Medical services were used only as a last resort. I'm sure by that time it was too late to remedy the situation with the best outcome. Now, having world class medical care at my fingertips, I balked at using it. My wife to be, quickly changed that mindset. God stopped my spiritual hemorrhaging and chose to use doctors as instruments to restore my health.

This was the summer of 1979 or 1980, I forget which. This would be my first major operation, one of many. I had the operation at the hospital near my house. I remember being wheeled into the operating room.

It was very cold, and I was placed on a rather large steel folding table, much like a ping pong table. I was draped across the top of it with my behind up in the air. How embarrassing is that?

The core of this cyst, I'm told, was deep. I was left with a good-sized divot on the upper right-hand side of my left buttock. It was stuffed with gauze because it had to heal from the inside out, which I was told would take some time.

I was recuperating at home for weeks. I was very bored and decided to paint my refrigerator red. I spray-painted it, and then I got the brilliant idea of painting the wall tiles in the kitchen. I alternated between black and white.

I was very satisfied with my finished product. My visitors were amazed.

The owner of the building was also amazed.

He was so amazed that he made me pay to have it all put back to its original form. I was bored out of my mind. I would lie in bed and gaze out of my large, unclothed windows for hours. I had no curtains because none were needed. I had an unobstructed view of the northeast Bronx that stretched as far as the eye could see.

One afternoon, while gazing, I noticed a pattern of descending airplanes headed toward La Guardia airport. La Guardia airport was southwest of me, and although it was located in another borough (Queens) and on the other side of the East River, it was not very far away.

Observing planes approaching the airport wasn't anything unusual because I remember watching flights that would pass overhead between the Castle Hill Projects and the Whitestone Bridge. Now, I had a bird's eye view of their landing approach.

So, as they continued to drop from the sky, I started timing them. This day, it was mid to late afternoon, and the skies were crystal clear. I could see the headlights of each aircraft as they descended from the heavens, aligning their approach.

It was so synchronized. Every 5 to 8 seconds, a pair of headlights would appear in the distant sky.

This pattern continued for nearly thirty minutes. I was amazed at the precision. Then, all of a sudden, the planes stopped appearing. For the next few minutes, no planes appeared at all. It was very strange, almost eerie.

<u>Nothing but the Blood</u>

It was a beautiful afternoon, not a cloud in the sky. Visibility was great. I could see beyond Co-Op City, which was directly east of my location.

As I searched the skies for any aircraft at all, I observed a huge round metallic disc off to my left. Remember, my apartment building was located on top of a hill, and I lived on the fourth floor. My apartment was also located at the back of the building. There wasn't anything obstructing my view.

The object that I observed was really big and low in the sky. It was a quarter of a mile away, at most. The only thing between that object and me was air space. Terrestrially, there was Webster Avenue, the Metro North rail system and the Bronx River Parkway.

It seemed to float through the air but not randomly. It was definitely being powered, how, I don't know. It moved extremely slowly but with deliberation. There was a single band of white lights that moved around the circumference.

This band of light seemed to be broken up into sections of equal lengths. The light rapidly moved from section to section in a counterclockwise motion. It was also very close to my building. So close, in fact, I tried to see if I could see any movement behind the white lights.

I opened my window to see if I could hear any kind of motor or noise coming from it. There was absolutely nothing, not a sound, dead silence. It also had a red pulsating exterior dome light. The overall craft had a smooth dark gray metallic skin.

It came to a complete stop over an apartment building in the distance. My guess was it was over the building on either Bronx Blvd or Olinville Avenue. It was the tallest building in the area, which could not have been more than 10 or 15 stories tall, max.

This object was now between me and the elevated Gun Hill/White Plains Road subway station. I could not believe it. What was it, and where did it come from? It had to have passed over the Woodlawn cemetery.

That was the only thing to my left. It began to move again. I saw a subway train approaching the station at Gun Hill Road on the downtown side.

The train conductor had to have seen it. At one point, the train slowed down to almost a complete stop before reaching the station. He had to see it. It was extremely low and would have crossed his direct line of sight.

How could he not have seen it? There were people on the train platform. I could not have been the only person observing this.

It continued to drift ever so slowly east, parallel to Gun Hill Road, towards Co-op City. I called a friend who lived in Co-Op City. I asked her to look out of her living room window toward Gun Hill Road. She said she was looking.

I asked her if she saw anything in the sky. She said no. Nothing, I said. What am I looking for? She asked. Anything in the sky, I said. She said no.

I hung up and dialed 911. I told the operator that I wanted to report a UFO sighting. I gave her all of my personal and logistical information. I described to her what I saw.

She said yes, a few other calls had come in. She said that it was a plane advertising some product. I said, lady, this was no plane and hung up. I watched the object until it disappeared from my sight. I could not believe what I had just witnessed.

After a few more minutes, planes started approaching the airport again. It was unreal. It was as if nothing ever happened. I watch the skies for a long time after that. It was unnerving. I didn't have any proof of what I had seen.

No camera and no witnesses, none that I was aware of. But the 911 operator did say to me that a few other calls had come in. I suppose her statement will have to be my only confirmation.

One other thing I do remember. For the entire time that I was home recuperating, not one of my colleagues from work called to see how I was doing. Not one.

I will never forget that, and I vowed never to let that happen to anyone who has ever worked with or for me. I was deeply disappointed. Unfortunately, I went back to work with a different attitude toward them.

One night, while at work, I heard a faint cry of a kitten. This was before the job started. I was doing my job set-up routine and was the only one in the area. I started searching for this kitten. I found it on the back of one of the package cars.

It had gotten itself stuck in the springs. I freed it, put her in a box, and placed it in my office. Some sadistic person took her out of the box and placed her in the very narrow lap desk drawer.

She survived that, and I took her home in my knapsack that morning. I wasn't sure if my wife would allow it in the house or not. I asked her if we could keep it. She said, okay. Within a few weeks, we noticed that it was a Siamese kitten.

We named her Tang. She lived with us for 14 years. She had become blind, started falling from ledges and was no longer able to get around safely. I took her to the ASPCA on 92nd Street in Manhattan to be put down. I cried all the way home.

Nothing but the Blood

When I started to work full-time, I noticed that there was very little diplomacy used to settle differences at work. It was like the wild wild west. A lot of yelling, cursing, threats and sometimes even fist fights to settle differences. I looked forward to coming to work just to see what was going to take place that day.

A lot of the drivers, supervisors and managers were alcoholics. A lot of guys at all levels were divorced. It was said at that time, that the UPS divorce rate was higher than that of the New York City Police Department. That wasn't anything to brag about. However, if you were in management, particularly operations, everybody worked long hours. If your home life was in shambles, you usually didn't perform well at work, either.

The educational requirements to become a full-time management employee were minimal at best. We had one division manager who did not have a high school diploma.

So, there was a minimally educated workforce supervised by a poorly educated management staff. In that respect, they were equal. At that time, it was extremely difficult for a minority to get a full-time job with UPS.

Due to mechanization, better engineering, and efficiency gains, many full-time non-driving positions became part-time positions. With that, the floodgates opened for minorities and females – half the benefits and half the pay. The education requirements remained the same: you had to be a student.

I was a sociology major at Hunter College. These social dynamics I found myself living through at work were fascinating. It was a clash of two cultures. Here, you have a college-educated part-time workforce that is managed by a poorly educated full-time management group.

I remember being repeatedly told by Operation Managers that my college degree didn't mean anything. You have to know how to instill fear in the workers, I was told. Really, I thought.

I vividly remember being trained to supervise an unloading area. The full-time supervisor training me had been doing this job for quite some time. Each night, he would wait for his least-best employee to show up for work. It was always the same guy. The employee would punch in and report to his designated trailer to unload packages.

The supervisor, equipped with a stopwatch and clipboard, would stand inside the trailer with him. The employee would start to unload the packages, and this supervisor would proceed to yell obscenities at this employee.

Come on, go faster, you fat piece of excrement. I'm telling you that it's just a matter of time before I fire your fat behind.

<u>Nothing but the Blood</u>

The supervisor would be yelling, bust it out, bust it out, come on, come on. The employee never increased his speed and nor did he seem to be phased at all by the antics of the supervisor. This went on night after night with no better result. I found it to be laughable, and I'm sure it was anything but that for the employee.

The other side of this coin was that a lot of people quit. These students were not used to being treated this way, and many refused to allow themselves to be subjected to this kind of treatment.

Also, it was back-breaking work. They would work a day or two or sometimes a week or two, then never return to work.

The management team was so used to managing by fear and intimidation. They knew no other way to manage. This new part-time college-educated workforce did not respond positively to that draconian way of supervision.

At that time, management was not concerned with how many people were leaving the company. They were not concerned because so many people wanted to work for UPS because of the superior pay, benefits and union.

When we were hiring, lines of people would form, sometimes three people deep and circle the building. When that many people appeared, it would be all hands on deck. All available HR supervisors would be asked to assist with interviewing.

I remember being called on to help one afternoon. We had to pull the applications from the bottom of the stack because those applicants had been waiting the longest.

The process was completely random as to who interviewed whom. I pulled several applications from the bottom of the tray and pulled the bottom application from that group. You could not get any more random than that.

Now, with all of that randomness going on and ten of us interviewing, I was the only black person interviewing.

I looked at my first application, and it's a male-white from South Africa. Just think of what the odds would have been for me to have picked this guy's application! The look on his face when I called his name was priceless.

He was not hired because of improper work authorization. I thanked him for coming in and encouraged him to reapply when he got the proper paperwork.

I can't help but think that there was a lesson somewhere in our exchange for one, if not both of us.

Certainly, poor management was not the only reason people were quitting. The nature of the work also had a lot to do with it as well. Although it paid very well, UPS was a tough job physically.

Within operations, the work was all manual labor. You are constantly moving, bending, twisting, lifting, pushing and pulling.

If you worked on the inside, you were under constant supervision. If you worked as a driver, your production would be under daily scrutiny. UPS had a measurement for every activity and every activity UPS measured. There was constant pressure to perform at a certain level or better.

As drivers, we were instructed to place our pinky finger through the key ring of the vehicle and hold the keys in the palm of our hands at all times. This method ensured that your keys were ready so as not to lose precious seconds searching for them in your pockets.

Production was sovereign, and pieces per hour (PPH) was king. There was a lot of intimidation through yelling, cursing and threats. The only thing that mattered was how many packages you were delivering each hour. I believed in effective communication and treating people with dignity and respect. I was quiet but effective, stern yet respectful.

However, my management tactics were not popular with my colleagues, even though my production indices were met. As a result, my bosses took advantage of me. I was left in positions much longer than others due to my higher effectiveness. In my case, being effective was not rewarded. It was used as a reason not to move or promote me. I had to fight my way out of those positions.

Each year, we were asked to fill out career development plans. I wanted a job that allowed me to teach classes and, in doing so, encourage and uplift people. As far as I was concerned, a good teacher uses the same talents as a good preacher.

Author Timothy Keller says, **"I concluded that the difference between a bad sermon and a good sermon is largely located in the preachers – in their gifts and skills and in their preparation for any particular message. Understanding the biblical text, distilling a clear outline and theme, developing a persuasive argument, enriching it with poignant illustrations, metaphors, and practical examples, incisively analyzing heart motives and cultural assumptions, making specific application to real life – all of this takes extensive labor. To prepare a sermon like this requires hours of work, and to be able to craft and present it skillfully takes years of practice. However, while the difference between a bad sermon and a good sermon is mainly the responsibility of the preacher, the difference between good preaching and great preaching lies mainly in the work of the Holy Spirit in the heart of the listener as well as the preacher."**[75]

---

[75] Keller, Timothy. Preaching. (Penguin, 2016), 10-11

I concur with Timothy Keller and concluded that the difference between a bad supervisor and a good supervisor is largely located in the Manager – their gifts and skills and their preparation for any particular message. Understanding the objective, distilling a clear outline and theme, developing a persuasive argument, enriching it with poignant illustrations, metaphors, and practical examples, incisively analyzing heart motives and cultural assumptions, and making specific applications to real life takes extensive labor.

Preparing a training session like this requires hours of work, and crafting and presenting it skillfully takes years of experience. However, while the difference between a bad supervisor and a good supervisor is mainly the manager's responsibility, the difference between good managing and great managing lies mainly in the work of the Holy Spirit in the heart of the Manager and the supervisor.

I saw this training manager position as me essentially imploring the same techniques as a preacher would. I wanted to be the next hub training manager. This was my prayer. I was told that the position had not existed in the district for over a decade. I was encouraged to list it anyway, and I did.

I would always share with Clara Mae what was going on with me at work. She would say, Curtis that job is your ministry. God has you there for a reason.

Rick Warren says, ***"It may seem easier to be holy when no one else is around to frustrate your preferences, but that is a false, untested holiness. Isolation breeds deceitfulness; it is easy to fool ourselves into thinking we are mature if there is no one to challenge us. Real maturity shows up in relationships. We need more than the Bible in order to grow; we need other believers. We grow faster and stronger by learning from each other and being accountable to each other. When others share what God is teaching them, I learn and grow, too. The body of Christ needs you. God has a unique role for you to play in his family. This is called your "ministry," and God has gifted you for this assignment: "A spiritual gift is given to each of us as a means of helping the entire church."***[76]

One summer, I went to visit a friend in London, England. She was a close friend to one of my friends here in the States. This was a really, really big deal for me.

I had never, ever flown before. Friends took care of getting my ticket. They booked me on Air Iran, a 747. At that time, the 747 was the largest commercial airplane in the world. Once on board and seated, I ordered a rum and coke. I was politely told that Air Iran was a non-alcoholic airline.

---

[76] Warren, The Purpose Driven Life, 134

I noticed that the window shades had tassels hanging from them and that the wallpaper, I assumed, was printed in some kind of Iranian penmanship. I felt like I was sitting in someone's living room.

My seat was the middle seat of three near the window. As we started taxiing down the runway, I leaned to my left to look out the window. I was mesmerized.

My head was almost in my neighbor's lap. He politely cleared his throat to get my attention. I bolted upright straight in my seat and apologized for invading his personal space.

He then politely asked, is this your first time flying? I was really embarrassed as I confirmed his suspicions. Seven hours later, we landed at Heathrow Airport in London, England.

As we soared above the clouds, I began to hum in my head the hymnal, **"How Great Thou Art" written by Carl Boberg**:

Oh Lord, my God
When I, in awesome wonder
Consider all the worlds Thy hands have made
I see the stars, I hear the rolling thunder
Thy power throughout the universe displayed

Then sings my soul, my Savior God to Thee
How great Thou art, how great Thou art

Then sings my soul, my Savior God to Thee
How great Thou art, how great Thou art

I settled in and hugged myself while marveling at God's work. I joyfully closed my eyes as He gently allowed me to go to sleep.

As we approached the British coastline, I saw the greenest grass I've ever seen. Black and white spotted cows dotted the landscape as whitecap waves crashed against the black rock shoreline. The view was simply breathtaking.

As I exited the terminal, I was met by friends and taken to a house in Catford, England, a suburb of London. It was a nice townhouse on a tree-lined street with funny-looking cars and a funny name. She lived on Inch Mary Street.

It was a street lined with aphyllous trees that had recently been pruned. Her family owned a cat named Puss. It was jet black with yellow eyes. Two teeth were visible on either side of its mouth when closed, and it had the biggest head I'd ever seen on a domestic cat. It was also the ugliest cat I had ever seen.

I had a really good time during my stay. I had an invitation to go to Paris for the weekend but turned it down for no good reason. My thinking was, I can do that my next time here. Of course, that "next time" never came. One of our friends who was a telephone engineer there was also a DJ on weekends. We partied a lot during my stay there.

The clubs would be packed with people on the dance floor, but no one seemed to be moving. It was more of a gentle sway. I had a bird's eye view of the crowd from the DJ's booth. Nothing like the floor movement in a New York club.

At one of his clubs, I met a young lady from the States who was attending New York University (NYU). Her family lived in Maryland. She was on a "class trip." We exchanged information and I did manage to see her again at her dorm back in New York.

My friends set up my return trip back to New York on standby. I had no idea of what that meant. They said, that's how you get the cheapest flights. It meant showing up to the airport a few hours before the day's first flight. Passengers are placed on the standby list on a first-come, first-served basis.

Going to the airport without a ticket and trying to get a discounted seat on an undersold flight sounded very risky to me. It meant hours of waiting at the reservations desk.

We started this process on the second Thursday of my two-week stay. I was due back to work that coming Monday. I did not like this process and did not secure a flight back to New York until

Saturday. If you had a job you cared about, this was not the way to travel.

Not being airport savvy, I nearly missed my flight. Had that happened, I would have been in a lot of trouble at work. I finally got a flight out on TWA. Once inside the airport, I was on my own.

Looking at the departure board, I realized that my flight was on the other side of the airport. I only had a few minutes to get to my gate.

I literally had to sprint to the correct gate. I was the very last person to board my flight, whew! That was too close for comfort. The doors to the plane literally closed after I entered. I would never fly standby again. It was totally nerve-wracking.

Having been gone for two weeks, I was happy to be back home. I entered my apartment and had to go to the bathroom. Upon entering, I saw two pieces of what appeared to be human-sized excrement in my bathtub. This, of course, alarmed me.

I call 911 to report a possible break-in. The police came. When I opened my door, the first officer said, wow, they really cleaned you out. I started laughing and stopped when he put his hand on his gun. I explained that I had no furniture to begin with.

So why did you call us? I showed them the feces in my bathtub. They looked around and asked me if the window at the fire escape was left cracked while I was gone. I said yes. They quickly surmised that it was some kind of animal, probably a cat.

He said that it was probably on the fire escape, came in through my window, saw my nice clean tub and decided to take a dump. Then it left the same way it came in. It sounded logical to me. With everyone in agreement, they left. I felt kind of silly.

I had managed to get my own apartment shortly after meeting Sandy. Sandy and her family were very accepting of me and welcomed me to their home. She and her family were very much rooted in Christ. Her family was living a life that I could only dream of at that time. It was a life that I wanted, too.

I was a bachelor, had my own place, car, and a job that paid very well. With all of that, I was also unhappy and in a lot of debt. I was unfulfilled. Something was missing, and I knew it.

Timothy Keller states, **"What you passionately seek is there, and your desires can be fulfilled if you enter into a reconciled relationship with the one who created you and who governs the universe."**[77]

Sandy and I went out on dates a lot. I would take her to very nice restaurants such as Victor's Café, Maxwell's Plum and

---

[77] Keller, Preaching, 98

Windows on the World, not to mention the amusement parks, movies and plays.

I wasn't trying to impress her, but I fell in love with her. I had the money and did not mind spending it on her. When we went out, I had to have her back home by midnight, and I did not have a problem with that.

I took her to Hershey Amusement Park in Hershey, Pennsylvania. We had a great time. I bought three hand puppets for her three youngest siblings, Richie, Carolyn and Kenny. She was very surprised by my generosity.

Discos, she did not get to experience with me. Although, once, I got to take her to Studio 54, and we had a lot of fun.

One night, I left Sandy's home during a rain storm. It was raining cats and dogs. The gas gauge in my car was broken, but I knew that I needed to refuel. So, I guessed that I had enough fuel to make it to a Shell service station that I liked in the Bronx. After all, I was driving a Volkswagen Beetle, and they never ran out of gas.

I reached the middle of the Whitestone Bridge and my car stopped running. What on earth could it be? Had I run out of gas? I was driving in the far-righthand lane, Bronx bound. I put my four-way flashers on.

<u>Nothing but the Blood</u>

My initial intent was to remain in my car until I was spotted by either the police or some other emergency vehicle. Or perhaps someone would alert one of the toll collectors. The rain was coming down in sheets. It was after midnight on a Sunday night, so the traffic was really light.

Looking around, I spotted an emergency telephone on the middle divide separating the Queens-bound traffic from the Bronx-bound traffic. I get out of my car and run across two lanes to the phone. To my surprise, someone answered it when I picked up. They wanted to know what the emergency was and which side of the bridge I was on.

I told them that I was midspan on the Bronx bound side. They told me to return to my car but not wait inside it. I was told to wait outside of the vehicle behind the railing.

Because of the heavy rain, I could not do that. I sat inside my car and watched through my rearview mirror as approaching cars slowed down and switched lanes to avoid hitting me. (God protects who? Babies and fools) I was no baby, but I was certainly foolish to have remained in my car.)

After fifteen minutes or so, I see this huge yellow truck come up behind me. I get out of my car and walk with the driver to the back of his truck. There was a very large flashing lighted arrow on the back of his truck. The flashing light was bright white, and you could see it, I'm sure, from a mile away.

The driver and I are standing on the roadway at the back of his truck. He is getting some tools from a compartment; he is on the left side of his truck, and I'm on the right. Suddenly, he shoved me into the railing to my right and jumped into the middle lane to his left.

A car plows right into the back of his truck. From that impact, I could feel the broken glass from the vehicle's bursting headlights hit the back of my head and neck. We were that close to being hit and pinned to the back of his truck.

The driver of the car never slowed down or hit his brakes. I never saw or heard his car coming. He was either drunk or had fallen asleep at the wheel.

The driver of that truck saved both our lives that night. Unfortunately, he said this happens often. It is a very dangerous job, but I know what to look for. I thanked him profusely and thanked God even more.

Author Benny Hinn declares this, ***"Who keeps you safe? It is the Holy Spirit. That is the task assigned to Him by Christ. So often we call Him Jesus, but He is actually the Spirit of Jesus."***[78]

I had witnessed other horrific auto accidents while either going to or coming from work.

It was a bright, sunny day. Not a cloud in the sky. I was travelling south on the elevated Bruckner Expressway in the Bronx. I was following a white van in the far-left hand lane. In the distance, I could see a stopped car against the median divide – half off the road and half on.

The emergency blinkers of the abandoned vehicle were on. I began to slow down, and the white van continued at the same rate of speed in the same lane. The driver of the van only had to move over a few feet to the right, and he would have missed hitting the disabled car all together.

He never slowed down, he never moved over. He plowed right into the back of that car, and the van flipped over. The back doors flung open, and two women and a great Dane dog were now thrown onto the highway.

----

[78] Hinn, Good Morning Holy Spirit, 74

The women were screaming, bleeding and in shock. I was the first one on the scene. I helped the women get to the side of the roadway. The driver was still in the van. I don't know why he never saw that disabled car.

On another occasion after work, I was heading home from Manhattan. I was travelling north on the Westside Highway in the far-left lane. There was another vehicle ahead of me travelling in the far-right lane.

In the distance, I see a pair of headlights in the far-right lane. I'm not sure if the headlights are moving or if they are stationary. I slowed down and hoped one of them would realize something was wrong and switch lanes.

As I'm watching, all of a sudden, the headlights disappear. They had collided. I was the first person on the scene. The driver who was travelling north in front of me was unconscious behind the wheel, and the other car had two occupants in it, one of which had gotten out and was walking around aimlessly, in a daze.

He was bleeding from his head and surely would have wandered out onto the highway. I sat him down on the grass, and he passed out. The driver of that vehicle was unconscious behind the wheel. I drove to the 96th Street exit which was close by, and called 911 from a pay phone. I then drove back around and saw that the police were on the scene.

<u>Nothing but the Blood</u>

Equally as tragic is when I witnessed a young Asian man leap to his death from the George Washington Bridge. I was driving on the upper roadway in the far-right lane next to the pedestrian walkway. The traffic was moving very slowly. I was headed toward New York and was just about mid-span.

The person had on a black jacket and was wearing a black backpack. He was walking toward New Jersey, which meant that he was facing me. He never fully stopped. I just saw him place both of his hands on the railing and leap over it without any hesitation.

I did not want to believe what I thought I had just witnessed. Was that a suicide? Initially, I thought that it could have been some kind of prank, but this person was all alone.

No one rushed over to see where he had disappeared, perhaps I was his only witness. Why did he leap in front of me? As I exited the bridge, I called 911 and reported what I had just seen.

A day or two later, a police detective called me to say that a black backpack had washed ashore near 125th Street. She said that she was with an Asian couple who were missing their son and believed this backpack to be his.

She told me they requested to speak with me to see if I could give them any more details about the person they believe to be their son.

She said that I was under no obligation to speak with them and that it was completely up to me. I agreed to talk with them. They asked me to describe him, what he was wearing and the color of his backpack. They were very grateful, and I never heard any more about it.

Dr. Norman Geisler says "However, the power of moral free choice entails the ability either to choose the good God designed for us or to reject it. The latter is called evil. It is good to be free, but freedom makes evil possible. Free will is good in itself, but entailed in that good is the ability to choose the opposite of good, which then makes evil possible."[79]

Equally interesting was an experience that I had with a street beggar. Leaving work one evening and travelling my usual route home, I decided not to pay the toll that I usually pay and to take a different route. I exited the highway at the last exit before the toll. It was snowing quite heavily, but the roads were passable.

The time was roughly 3 am or 4 am. At the end of this exit was a stop light located at the edge of a small park. It looked like an open lot. There were no trees, no buildings, just a small clearing. This area was the upper part of Manhattan. The main street was

---

[79] Geisler, Chosen But Free, 22.

Broadway, and across the street were apartment buildings, stores and a McDonald's that appeared to be open.

Where I sat waiting for the light to change, I could see 360 degrees all around me. There were no people, no cars, and no trees; it was only falling snow. I was the only one waiting for the light.

Suddenly, there is a tap on my window. There stands a man shivering with his hand held out for anything I could give him. He was wearing a badly tattered green coat. I lowered my window to give him enough money to perhaps get something to eat or something hot from the McDonald's across the street.

He never said a word. I lowered my window enough to place the money into his hand. When I looked up into his eyes, I saw what seemed to me to be the entire universe. His eyes were so beautiful and crystal, crystal clear. His eyes sparkled.

I was looking into an abyss like nothing that I'd ever seen before. There was such a deep feeling of peace and tranquility emanating from him. I gave him the money, staring into his eyes as I rolled up my window.

As the light changed, I slowly pulled away. I looked back to see in what direction he had gone. I didn't see anything at all, and it had only been a few seconds. There was nothing around me, and there was no sign of him at all.

How could he have disappeared so quickly? I've come to conclude that is exactly what happened: he disappeared. Had I lost my mind, certainly not. I happen to realize that I just had an encounter with an angel.

Going to nightclubs alone was common for me, partly because I would go on Sunday nights. My work schedule was Monday night through Friday night. My friends had either school or work on Monday morning, so hanging out on Sunday nights was not working for them.

I enjoyed dancing, and I danced a lot. This particular evening, I was alone at this club and having a good time. I sat down to rest. I was sitting alone when the Holy Spirit whispered in my ear, "You've danced and had a good time. Why don't you get up, get your coat and go home."

Author Napoleon Hill best describes it. ***"Then my nerves became quiet, my muscles relaxed, and a great calmness came over me. The atmosphere began to clear, and as it did so, I received a command from within which came in the form of a thought, as near as I can describe it. The command was so clear and distinct*** *that I could not misunderstand it. My "other self" had awakened."*[80]

It was as if He (the Holy Spirit) was sitting right there on my shoulder. I thought about what he said and agreed. I stood up, got my coat and went home.

This club was located in the basement of a building in midtown Manhattan. As far as I knew, there was only one way in and one way out. I leave, go home and go to bed. I woke up later that morning to the news via the radio that the club that I was in earlier that evening had been shot up.

Three people had been shot. Thank you, Holy Spirit! What a blessing having been led out of that situation. Author Benny Hinn asks, ***"How are you led by the Spirit? You become familiar with His voice. You recognize it. You respond to it. And the more you fellowship with Him, the deeper the relationship becomes."***[81]

The first time that I entered Sandy's home was very special to me. She lived on a tree-lined street, with each home having a beautiful lawn. There were no fences, and the homes were very large. It wasn't like anything that I had ever experienced before.

---

[80] Hill and Lechter, Outwitting The Devil (The Secret to Freedom and Success), 12

[81] Hinn, Good Morning Holy Spirit, 65

As I entered their home, I saw oriental rugs everywhere, a grand piano (the one with a stick in it), and a separate study room with hundreds of books. I saw chandeliers, velvet wallpaper, crystal vases and glasses, a formal dining room with ornate chairs, gold-plated flatware, and real china.

There was a spiral staircase in the middle of the home that I was sure led straight to heaven. Wow! I found it hard to believe I had a girlfriend who lived like this. Until now, all of my girlfriends lived in the projects or in apartment buildings. This was a new experience for me.

Here I was, this poor kid from the Bronx, living in the projects and a cigarette smoker. Secretly, I yearned for the opportunity to prove that I was good enough to have a girl like Sandy. I was intimidated and humbled at the same time.

She introduced me to her family. Her mother was very warm and inviting. Her father was the same. Then I met her siblings. Each one nicer than the next. She was the second oldest out of seven kids, five girls and two boys. Everybody was just so nice. This was the kind of life that I wanted.

For me, the myth of having to be a sports figure or a drug dealer to live like this was shattered. At that moment I realized that some black people really do live like this. For me, this was a page right out of the Crosby's even though her parents were not doctors or lawyers. Everything that the Jeffersons did reinforced my belief in Christ and that following Him, I too could live like this.

Mr. Jefferson was a professional house painter and a very successful one at that. He worked in very exclusive neighborhoods of Long Island, New York. Mrs. Jefferson was a homemaker. She was an excellent seamstress and made nearly all of the cloth items in the house, the coats, dresses, sweaters, drapes, tablecloths, etc. They had a beautiful home.

Pastor James T. Jefferson states "Every single appropriate opportunity each of us who are believers gets to testify and witness in the presence of others, is an opportunity to spread the good news of the gospel; how God has made His love, mercy and grace available, active and meaningful in our lives. In reference to being a witness for Jesus, Jesus declared, "You shall be My witnesses" (Acts 1:8). Others will see the result and effectiveness of my love, mercy and grace through your new Christ-like attitude and behavior. Jesus was saying, the person you become, and how you behave, and how you relate to others, they will notice the significant improvement and marvelous change in your character, attitude and behavior known as the fruit of the Spirit, the obvious reality of being obedient to the Holy Spirit's guidance and empowerment, (the fruit of the

Spirit, evidence of being filled with the Holy Spirit, (Galatians 5:22-23)."[82]

After Sandy and I married we continued to go to her family's church in Brooklyn. After church we all would drive back to her parents' house for Sunday dinner. The Sunday dinners were just amazing and had become a ritual.

It was absolutely wonderful and I looked forward to it each Sunday. I wanted this kind of life for myself and believed that I could have it. In the "hood" a father was someone who was always talked about but rarely ever seen. For me to actually see this kind of lifestyle was something out of a fairytale.

I had the utmost respect for Mr. Jefferson, for he was the kind of man that I wanted to become. He was a God-fearing man who did not drink, smoke, or swear. He provided for and took care of his family well beyond anything that I had ever known.

Their house in Queens also had a large detached two-car garage. I also remember a trellis attached to the right side of the house. It was covered with grapevines that yielded beautiful, sweet, black grapes. There was a manicured front and backyard where Mr. Jefferson grew rhubarb, a vegetable completely unknown to me.

---

[82] Jefferson, One Night In Bethlehem, 32

Her parents were very active in their church. Each steeped in biblical knowledge and both were Sunday school teachers. They travelled to Nigeria, Africa, annually and Mr. Jefferson helped to start a Christian school there.

Nigerian ministers often stayed with them when they had business in New York. Mr. Jefferson brought us several pieces of authentic wood carvings directly from West Africa.

Unfortunately, this marriage seemingly made in heaven did not last. After being together nearly thirty years, they divorced. Ironically, the year that they got divorced is the year that the grapevine did not yield any more grapes. Amazingly, it too had died and had become symbolic for me of their failed marriage. If it happened to them, it could happen to anyone. Sandy was thankful that she had gotten married and was no longer living at home when this all took place.

Pastor T. D. Jakes states that, ***"Every man may not struggle with adultery, homosexuality, or pornography, but be assured that every man struggles with something. Too often we have double standards for grace. For some, sin becomes anything for which we are not personally tempted! 'But every man is tempted, when he is drawn away of his own lust, and enticed. Then when lust hath***

conceived, it bringeth forth sin: and sin, when it is finished, bringeth forth death'. "[83]

Ironically, my then dear friend Ruby forwarded me this message:

----- Original Message -----

From: Beverly L Perry

Sent: 08/08/2011 04:09 PM EDT

To: Charles Dickerson

Subject: Fw: Fw:

----- Forwarded by Beverly L Perry/EP/PEP on 08/08/2011 04:09 PM -----

For all you single ladies who are in such a hurry to get married, here's a quick piece of Biblical advice:

Ruth patiently waited for her mate Boaz. While waiting on YOUR Boaz, don't settle for ANY of his relatives: Brokeaz, Poaz, Lyinaz, Cheatinaz, Dumbaz, Cheapaz, Lockedupaz, Goodfornothinaz, Lazyaz, or Marriedaz, and especially his cousin Beatinyoaz. Please, wait on your Boaz & make sure he respects Yoaz...

---

[83] Jakes, He-Motions, 159

And, although the above statement is both cute and true, you don't have to settle down with whoever shows up at your door. You need to know as best you can whom you are marrying. Are you trying to fit a square peg into a round hole? Then that's on you. However, as you avoid all of the az's above, it's equally important to realize that. ***Bishop T.D. Jakes writes "You can kill a person with your words, your attitude, your absence. You can kill a relationship without any other weapon than your tongue. You can murder an association or a relationship without exploding any bomb; you can destroy it by neglect."*** [84]

The death of anything that you hold dear is traumatic. As I neared the same age at which my mother died; I became very anxious. I began to wonder if I too would die at age thirty-eight. I remember struggling with this thought at that period in my life. It was brief but powerful. I was silently struggling with the fear of dying at the same age she had. I remember waking up the morning after my thirty-eighth birthday relieved that I was still alive and thanked God that I was.

Surprisingly, as Sandy and I approached our thirtieth year of marriage, I did so with the same trepidation. Was our marriage going to survive? I was measuring myself and our marriage against her parents, who were much more steeped in Christian living than we

---

[84] Jakes, So You Call Yourself a Man? 133

were. Would Sandy and I continue to weather the storms and pitfalls of our marriage any better than her parents had?

I was no better of a man than her father and Sandy was no better woman than her mother. What have we done that they were unwilling to do? Now, having surpassed her parent's total years married by more than a decade, I would never say that our marriage is out of the woods. Satan has not given us a pass. His mission continues to be, to steal, kill, and destroy. I pray daily for the health of our marriage and the well-being of our children, daily. God does answer prayers.

I was still a cigarette smoking, club loving fool, and had not yet resumed going back to church. It seemed to me that I would be everything that my wife wouldn't want in a man. She saw something in me that I did not see in myself. She saw potential, perhaps. Or maybe even determination? Little did we know at the time that she was my ram in the bush.

Mark Batterson asks, ***"Why do we act as though our sin disqualifies us from the grace of God? That is the only thing that qualifies us! Anything else is a self-righteous attempt to earn God's grace."***[85]

---

[85] Batterson, All In (You are one decision away from a totally different life), 65

The separation and eventual divorce of her parents bothered me a lot. They were my religious heroes. How could something like this happen to them? God has given those who believe in Him the tools to deal with all sin and He has also given us free will to use those tools or not.

Dr. Jefferson states "In spite of that there are two forces at work. The first one that should be pointed out is the negative one, the influence of Satan and sin. Satan, in his opposition to God and what God stands for is constantly opposing God by doing everything he can to dissuade people from having any interest in wanting to live a decent and wholesome life. Satan, as an opponent of God, seeks to misinform and mislead all he can to prevent them from becoming followers of Jesus. Satan goes to church himself to distract as many people as he can from hearing about the love of God and God's willingness to accept all who come to Him in faith for forgiveness and salvation."[86]

What about forgiveness - was this an option considered by either of them? Was the wife a saint and the husband a sinner, or was the husband a saint and the wife a sinner? No, they are both sinners. We all make mistakes. Did anyone provide room for the

---

[86] Dr. James T. Jefferson, One Night in Bethlehem (pg. 18)

possibility of forgiveness or did pride have the last word? No matter what we have done, God always allows a way back to Him.

Pastor Jakes writes "Or you've made a mistake in your past for which forgiveness has been denied so long that you have ceased to seek it and have become an inmate to a marriage that exists only to claim tax deductions, group discounts on travel and a little convenient sex, but not much more. Your marriage has become a mere shadow of the promise it once offered. Sometimes you wonder if it is even worth continuing on. But you have the power within yourself to overcome the icy environment that you occasionally fantasize about leaving. You can bring your marriage back to the splendor it once was. You can have a relationship that is mutually fulfilling and love giving. You just have to work a little at it. Men, repeat after me: I will not give up or give in and allow myself to be defeated until I have done everything I can to see God's grace materialize in my house. Amen."[87]

When you love someone, certain things come naturally and I think that physical touching is one of them. Showing some affection. To wrap your arms around that person to say, I love you or to give any other compliment is priceless. It helps to complete the healing process and perpetuates the existing love.

---

[87] T.D. Jakes, He-Motions (pg. 204)

Although forgiveness may not be one of those "certain things," at some point it has to be. Especially, if the relationship is desired to be salvageable. Repent and ask God for forgiveness and ask for forgiveness from the person that you have hurt. Change your behavior as proof of your sincerity and if the other person has not or refuses to forgive you, continue to pray that God will lead you both to a righteous solution.

Dr. Myles Munroe writes, "Once God cleanses you, there isn't anyone who can condemn you. If you ever find that you are wrong, just confess it, agree, ask for forgiveness, and go on with your life. Whatever you justify, you cannot repent of."[88]

I remember writing Sandy a letter saying that our relationship was never going to work because we were from two different worlds. Sometime after that I wrote her another letter telling her how much I loved her. We dated for four years before getting married. Sandy had started her first master's degree program and I was secure in my position as supervisor with United Parcel Service.

It was my senior year at Hunter College. I majored in Sociology and minored in African Studies. I had taken a black history course with Dr. Ben-Johanan entitled Black Man of The

---

[88] Dr. Myles Munroe, Prayer (pg. 135)

Nile. According to Dr. Ben-Johanan, there was a "being" thousands of years before Christ who performed greater miracles than Jesus. This was the first time in my life that I questioned the authenticity of Jesus' ministry. So much so, that I had stopped going to church.

Leslie Copeland states, *"No one is exempt from dealing with temptations or for falling into the trappings of having a measure of power and authority. The cautionary tales and warnings from others are real. If we think it would never happen to us, or we would never do this or that, we will likely miss the warning signs that we are headed for trouble. Proverbs 16:18 says, "Pride goes before destruction, and a haughty spirit before a fall." And James 4:6 reminds us that "God opposes the proud, but gives grace to the humble." Pride doesn't just show up in overly confident Christian leaders. It also makes an appearance when we overestimate our own ability to resist the enticements that befall others. Obviously, not everyone is tempted by the same things, but everyone is tempted by something."*[89]

I don't think that I ever stopped believing in God, I just thought less of Jesus. According to Dr. Ben-Johanan, Jesus wasn't anyone special. So, I put Jesus on hold. During this time, I wasn't happy and I started to accumulate a lot of debt.

---

[89] Copeland, Christ-like Leadership, 129

Rick Warren says, *"People become disillusioned with the church for many understandable reasons. The list could be quite long: conflict, hurt, hypocrisy, neglect, pettiness, legalism, and other sins. Rather than being shocked and surprised, we must remember that the church is made up of real sinners, including ourselves. Because we're sinners, we hurt each other, sometimes intentionally and sometimes unintentionally. The sooner we give up the illusion that a church must be perfect in order to love it, the sooner we quit pretending and start admitting we're all imperfect and need grace."* [90]

I began to think of my life before learning of this new creature. I was happy, I always had money and I enjoyed going to church and worshipping Christ. What had I done to myself?

Rick Warren writes, *"There are three barriers that block our total surrender to God: fear, pride, and confusion. We don't realize how much God loves us, we want to control our own lives, and we misunderstand the meaning of surrender. Surrendering is not for cowards or doormats. Surrendering is not repressing your personality. Surrendering is best demonstrated in obedience. You let go and let God work. The Bible says, "Surrender yourself to the Lord, and wait patiently for Him." This is the paradox: Victory*

---

[90] Warren, The Purpose Driven Life, 162-163

comes through surrender. Surrender doesn't weaken you; it strengthens you."[91]

Here again, Christ provided another ram in the bush for me. It was Sandy!

Mark Batterson states, **"You never know what relationship, skill, experience, or attribute God will use to bring about His eternal purposes! Or it could just be your good old-fashioned work ethic. No matter what it is, it's a gift from God that is to be used for God. Do the best you can with what you have where you are."**[92]

Sandy was just what I needed. I now realize how pivotal my faith was. With a different influence I could have easily been lost forever. I will never leave you or forsake you, Jesus said.

John MacArthur reminds us, *"Remember, Eve wasn't made out of dust like Adam, but carefully designed from living flesh and bone. Adam was refined dirt; Eve was a glorious refinement of humanity itself. She was a special gift to Adam. She was the necessary partner who finally made his existence complete and whose own existence finally signaled the completion of all*

---

[91] Warren, The Purpose Driven Life, 78-81
[92] Batterson, All In (You are one decision away from a totally different life), 109

creation. Eve, the only being ever directly created by God from the living tissue of another creature, was indeed a singular marvel."[93]

So, as our (Sandy's and I) relationship developed, I welcomed the opportunity to mend my relationship with God. Sandy, I believe, could have had any man that she wanted. She is tall, shapely, smart and beautiful.

I think even she would be hard pressed to explain how and why things worked out the way that they have for us. We make mistakes, but not God.

Pastor Dr. James T. Jefferson puts it this way, *"All through the Bible God continues to make it clear that He is aware of our humanness and our "sinfulness" because of our humanness, and has done for us what He knows needs to be done. He has acted on our behalf through Jesus, and makes it clear that all who believe and accept Jesus as their Savior shall not perish, but have everlasting life. He has graciously done for us what only He can do. God is willing to mercifully and graciously, save us, forgive all of our sins, past, present and future.*"[94]

Sandy had to tell her parents that she was pregnant. They wanted to know what I was going to do as the father. It was a huge

---

[93] MacArthur, John. Twelve Extraordinary Women. (Nelson, 2005), 1
[94] Jefferson, One Night In Bethlehem, 34

embarrassment for both her family and me. Sandy's family was highly thought of in their church. Things began to happen quietly and quickly.

We announced immediately that we were getting married. I would have married Sandy even if this had not happened. She was one month pregnant by now. It was important to her parents that we get married before she began to show. They were trying to save themselves from embarrassment.

We got married at the Bronx County Courthouse and had a small private celebration at her home. Aunt Lou attended and took it all in stride. Getting married was something that I had always looked forward to. Not quite under these circumstances but I was not opposed to getting married to her.

Sandy made it clear that we would be going to church. I welcomed that command with a smile. We started going to her family's church in Brooklyn. Then I remembered a church that I had experienced in the Bronx as a teenager. It was Trinity Baptist Church. We started going there. She liked it so much that we joined.

Mark Batterson says, ***"When we obey God, we come under the umbrella of His protective authority. He is our Advocate. And*** *it's His reputation that is at stake. If we don't give the Enemy a foothold, God won't let him touch a hair on our head."*[95]

I was happy to be back in the church. Was I the prodigal son? I had this empty void in my life that only God could fill and I knew it. When I look back over my life and I think things over. I can truly say, that I've been blessed. I've got a testimony!

Leslie Copeland tells us, **"A call is God's way of saying there is something, in us – something that God has deposited – and it is time for it to come out. Some of what has been deposited in us is needed for the upbuilding of God's kingdom. The call is something tied to who we are created to be."**[96]

Our first apartment was my big empty studio. Sandy left home with all of her worldly possessions stuffed into one large powder blue suitcase. Our first dinner alone, as a married couple took place on top of her powder blue suitcase, on the floor in the middle of our big empty studio. And, dinner was by candlelight.

Things happened so fast. I had not reached out to all of my friends to let them know that I was now, a married man. Old girlfriends were still calling me but that all ended. We soon rented a junior four room apartment in the same building. It was one

---

[95] Batterson, All In (You are one decision away from a totally different life), 140

[96] Copeland, Christ-like Leadership, 5-6

bedroom with an area large enough for a baby's crib. It was an area between the living room and the kitchen.

Sandy's parents bought us a dinette set for our wedding present. Although, marriage was something that I looked forward to I had not fully accepted my responsibilities as a husband.

Pastor T.D. Jakes says, ***"… intimacy may be sacrificed. It is important for both him and his wife to remain as sensual and affectionate as possible. Some men fail to see or perceive their wives because they only see the image they have of her – images created by our past sexual and relational experiences that now impact our current expectations. Most men bring multiple previous experiences into their marriage. Your mind is like a sponge, and it has been soaked full of experiences that become the point of reference by which you define what you are expecting from the love you now have with her. These incidents may have occurred in previous marriages, past lives before Christ, or weak moments of lustful indulgence. They may be scenes you saw in a movie or a shot from a magazine. Or they may be in the form of messages we received from our parents or friends about what a wife should be. These expectations can be positive or negative, but either way, they are dangerous to the joint mission you should have with her. Your marriage is far too personal and private to still be picking up unwanted frequencies from past impulses,*** *memories, and persons who should no longer have an influence on you.*[97]

Sandy had her master's degree in special education. After Jillian was born, she began searching for work. For this to happen, we needed a babysitter. We asked our building superintendent, Mr. Knight, if he knew of anyone. He mentioned a lady in the building who cared exclusively for her granddaughter and encouraged us to approach her. We discovered that her daughter lived one floor above her in the same building. Both were very kind. The grandmother liked us as a couple and agreed to babysit Jillian along with her grandchild. She didn't charge us much, which was a tremendous blessing. Additionally, the grandmother was a retired nurse. Hallelujah! We felt truly blessed.

Sandy had adapted well to apartment living in our relatively safe neighborhood. I would leave for work around midnight and return home before noon. One Saturday morning, I distinctly remember a knock at our door. It was a detective from the New York City Police. He informed us that a triple murder had occurred just a few doors down from our apartment. He asked if we had seen or heard anything, but we were unaware of the incident or the people involved.

---

[97] Jakes, He-Motions, 202

This unfortunate mass murder really jolted me and my wife, if not the entire building. Working the night hours as I did, I cringed each time I thought of how close I had come to having an encounter with whoever committed those murders.

That's assuming that the murders took place at night. *Who keeps you safe? It is the Holy Spirit.* We had to move.

How could we continue to feel safe there? I had to protect my family.

Within the same week of these murders, I ran into Eddie C. from the old Webster/ Valentine Avenue neighborhood.

I didn't know what had become of him and had not seen him or his sister Zelda C. in over ten years, maybe fifteen years.

He was exiting a car parked across the street from our building and was walking with another man. Our eyes met and I could tell that he recognized me but did not want to engage. Picking-up on this vibe, I knew to act as if I did not know him as we walked past each other.

He was in plain clothes wearing a sleeveless leather vest with a huge holstered gun underneath it.

The gun was easily visible but I wasn't sure if he was a good guy or a bad guy. As they walked toward my building, somehow I knew his presence had something to do with those murders.

I never saw him again.

Our only daughter at that time was enrolled in a prestigious private school, so we didn't need to ask her for any favors. I think she had a problem with that.

What a blessing, so we thought. It ended up being a total nightmare. She was the landlord from hell. There wasn't anything Christian about her.

For some reason she looked down upon us and felt that she and her family were better than we were. We were doing well, perhaps too well for her liking.

Our rent was always paid on time. My wife had stopped working because she was well into the pregnancy of our second child.

Our daughter was enrolled in a prestigious private school and we didn't need to ask her for any favors.

I think she had a problem with that.

Due to this horrific incident, I thought that a private house would be better and safer for my family. So, shortly thereafter with the assistance of our church's information board we found a place. It was located further north in the Bronx, in a private home. The home owner was also a Trinity Baptist Church member.

What a blessing, so we thought. It was a new home with three apartments located on a quiet tree lined street. We rented the middle apartment and the owner lived in the apartment above us. The owner ended-up being the landlord from hell. She nitpicked about everything. She complained that she could hear us walking, we didn't place our garbage in the right location, my wife could not sit on front porch and so on and so on.

We immediately became uncomfortable there and quickly realized that we had made a mistake. For some reason she looked down upon us and felt that she and her family were superior to us. Even her grandchildren were disrespectful. It was this behavior that spurred us on to get our own property. It was not part of God's plan for us to become comfortable there.

If she behaved this way now, we shuttered to think of how she would act with a newborn baby there. Sandy and I knew that we had to find a new place before she gave birth to our second child. We had four months or 120 days to make it happen and we did.

Shortly after Thanksgiving of that year, we bought a lovely townhouse in Northwest Yonkers. Praise God! We had become homeowners. Sandy was due in mid-December. She went into the hospital from that dreaded apartment and after being released with our new baby girl Jessica, walked into her new townhouse. What a blessing! We had been delivered twice – one from the landlord from hell and the other was our second baby girl. What a mighty God we serve.

After settling in Yonkers, I began exploring fishing spots all over Westchester County. Armed with maps, I ventured up and down the county, securing a special permit to fish in the reservoirs. These waters were pristine, strictly reserved for non-motorized boats, offering some of the best fishing spots I had ever encountered. No longer did I need to trek to Lumberton for great fishing.

As I explored, I couldn't help but admire the homes I saw. They made me dream of owning one someday. It wasn't that I wasn't grateful for what we had; I simply yearned for more. I envisioned a spacious house where we could freely move about, with expansive land, an inground swimming pool, a large front porch, and an oversized deck. I pictured a home with five bedrooms, numerous bathrooms, and plenty of extra rooms, ideally located in the neighborhoods I frequented while fishing. My dream was to live in a safe area with excellent schools, waking up to deer in my backyard each morning.

Year after year, I continued fishing in these areas, paralleling how I once visualized my parking spot in the city projects with visions of my future home in upper Westchester, close to the places where I fished.

Napoleon Hill states, ***"Do not confuse the word "belief" with the word "wish." The two are not the same. Everyone is capable of "wishing" for financial, material, or spiritual advantages, but the element of faith is the only sure power by which a wish may be translated into a belief, and a belief into reality. The mind acts upon one's dominating, or most pronounced desires."***[98]

As a child, fishing in Lumberton had become a necessity. Now, fishing had become not only my favorite but also my only hobby. After moving to Yonkers, New York, I discovered a new fishing spot: the Ramapo River in Upstate New York. I had heard that this part of the river, running through the town of Tuxedo, was stocked with trout every year.

Intrigued, I decided to give it a try. This stretch of river ran parallel to an Interstate Highway. On the opposite bank, you could hear the constant hum of passing traffic and catch glimpses through the trees of a rest stop with a gas station and a fast-food restaurant.

---

[98] Hill and Lechter, Outwitting The Devil (The Secret to Freedom and Success), 46-47

The river here was shallow and narrow, offering a different fishing experience compared to what I was used to.

I arrived at this new fishing spot early one morning, just after sunrise. I parked in an abandoned lot behind a row of vacant buildings. The area was deserted; I didn't spot anyone else around. Walking along the railroad tracks, I searched for the ideal spot to fish. In the distance, I noticed two men approaching along the tracks towards me.

As we met and exchanged nods, I observed that one was tall, well over six feet, while the other was notably shorter, perhaps around five feet. They made an odd pair, both dressed in blue jeans. Their pants were wet from the knees down, which led me to think they had recently crossed the river. They looked young, possibly high school students out for a stroll.

Continuing on their way, I eventually found a suitable spot to start fishing. Shortly after, I noticed a helicopter flying low overhead, its noise proving distracting. With no other anglers in sight and the fish showing no interest, I decided to call it a day and headed home.

By noon, I was back and asleep. A few hours later, the phone rang. I answered to hear Detective Jones from the Ramapo Police Department on the line.

"Hello Mr. White," he said, "an armed robbery occurred at the 187 rest stop this morning. Your car was parked nearby. What were you doing in that area?"

"I was fishing," I replied.

"Did you see, hear, or notice anything unusual?" he inquired.

"I did see two men walking along the railroad tracks when I arrived," I explained. "They were both white males. One was tall and skinny, the other short. Their pants were wet up to their knees, like they had crossed the river."

"You acknowledged each other as you passed?" he confirmed.

"Yes," I affirmed. "They continued along the tracks, and I went down to the river to fish. That's all."

"Thank you," the detective said, and hung up.

Reflecting on the situation, I realized how much could have gone wrong, yet everything seemed to align, perhaps guided by the Holy Spirit. Although I hadn't seen any weapons, those two men were armed and had just committed a crime. It struck me that I had been the only witness to see them right after the robbery.

This scenario certainly did not bode well for me. This reminded me of what I happened to see at the Bronx Zoo. Just as I could have been found floating in the Bronx River at the zoo, I certainly could have been found floating in the Ramapo River after this robbery. But our God is an awesome God and thanks be to God that no harm came to me at all.

Benny Hinn says, ***"The Holy Spirit is also your great defender. For example: Who do you think protects you from the attacks of Satan? It is the Holy Spirit. Who keeps you safe? It is the Holy Spirit. That is the task assigned to Him by Christ. So often we call Him Jesus, but He is actually the Spirit of Jesus. Again, we only separate them for discussion's sake so we can better understand them because they are really one Being. Because where the Holy Ghost is, Jesus is -- and the Father is. When the Holy Ghost talks to you, all three are talking, but the Holy Ghost is the one you hear. The Holy Ghost is the one you sense. The Holy Ghost is the one leading you in the will of the Father."***[99]

After my brother Robert passed away, I arranged to have all his furniture loaded into a U-Haul truck. I believed Clara Mae was the person he would have wanted to inherit his belongings. Once the truck was loaded, I drove it back to our home in Yonkers and parked it on the street. My plan was to leave later that evening at midnight to reach Lumberton by the next morning.

---

[99] Hinn, Good Morning Holy Spirit, 74

After getting some rest, I prepared to depart. It was raining heavily, and I had heard about an approaching storm along the East Coast, currently off the coast of Virginia. Despite the weather, I continued to get ready. When I was ready to go and went out to the van, it wouldn't start. There were no lights, no cranking sound—nothing at all. I was frustrated.

I called U-Haul, and they sent a mechanic—a middle-aged man who seemed knowledgeable. He attempted to start the van multiple times but had no success.

"Mr. White," he finally said, "with everything I know and all my experience, I can't find any reason why this truck shouldn't start. This is unlike anything I've seen."

"I'm afraid we'll need to tow it to the shop in the morning to investigate further. I'm sorry," he added.

At 6 am the next morning, the tow truck arrived. The driver also tried unsuccessfully to start the van before hooking it up for towing. I rode with him to the repair shop, where he backed the truck into the garage and unhitched it.

Another mechanic approached and asked, "What's wrong with it?"

"It just won't start," the driver replied.

The mechanic casually reached in through the driver's side window, turned the key, and to everyone's surprise, the van started right up.

It was unbelievable, but I knew it was a sign of divine intervention. For some reason, I wasn't meant to be on the road driving that night. Once again, the Holy Spirit had protected me.

Dr. Munroe writes, "You aren't supposed to live by what you see, but by what I told you." (See 2 Corinthians 5:7) ***"We know that in all things God works for the good of those who love him, who have been called according to His purpose. (Romans 8:28) Everything works for my good, no matter what it is, because I'm called according to God's purpose and will. It is God's will that I live confidently in the knowledge that He calls "things that are not as though they were." (Romans 4:17) If I live only by what I see, I'm living in sin. Everything that does not come from faith is sin. (Romans 14:23) Faith grows out of one thing – the word of God."***[100]

Sandy earned her first master's degree in Special Education (Deaf and Hard of Hearing). She found a teaching job at a private parochial school for the deaf in the Bronx. Her second master's

---

[100] Munroe, Myles. (Understanding the purpose and power of) PRAYER. (Whitaker, 2002), 193

came a little later in Urban Studies. She enjoyed her work but was paid very, very little.

Our accountant said, "We would do better tax wise if she did not work at all." Shortly thereafter she was hired by the New York City Board of Education and was appointed to an elementary school in Riverdale, the Bronx. She was now making more than three times as much and cut her commute time by two-thirds. God is truly, amazing.

Jillian our first born was in a private Montessori school and later Sandy became pregnant with Jessica. Jillian and her sister are six years apart, born in the same month and one day apart. Both girls were accepted to the prestigious all girls Catholic Ursuline School of New Rochelle. Upon graduation, Jillian is accepted to Columbia University at the tender age of sixteen.

Following in her footsteps, her sister Jessica is accepted to the John Jay College of Criminal Justice and earns her degree in Forensic Psychology.

Our son Justin is born. Jillian obtains her degree in Neuroscience and Behavior. We build a home in upper Westchester County in Cortlandt Manor, New York, and Justin is accepted to Mercy College in Dobbs Ferry, New York. He earned his BS degree in Music Industry and Technology.

Things at work for me were going well. I was still working in the Human Resources department. During a meeting the question of how to get more minorities promoted came up. One of my White colleague's answer to this question was to promote the Black female clerk in our office. His statement really upset me. I slammed my hand down on to the conference room table while pointing my finger at him.

I said, "This is exactly the attitude that we don't need."

The topic is minority promotions and you have clearly identified a minority who has both a mental and physical disability. You have clearly and purposefully chosen an individual with a severe disability, someone who is known to be incapable of functioning on a supervisory or managerial level.

And, that's okay with you because it's "just" a minority promotion. "Promote any minority," you would say. As far as you are concerned minorities don't have to be capable or qualified to perform the job. You should be ashamed of yourself! That's not right. I was visibly upset. Our department head at this point suggested that we take a fifteen-minute break. Unfortunately, I would learn as time went on that this was the same sentiment held by a lot of my White counterparts.

God was using me. One day, a young man entered the HR office and walked over to my desk. Normally, four supervisors were stationed in my section, but that day, I was the only one there. He asked to speak with the district nurse. I informed him that she was out of the building for the day. Sensing his urgency, I offered to see if the regional nurse could assist him. He agreed, so I called for her, only to find out she was also away, both from the building and the district.

Realizing he was in distress, he expressed his need to talk to someone. I empathized and offered myself as someone to listen. Reluctantly, he agreed. I guided him to a small conference room within the office. There, he revealed that he was afraid to return home because he feared he might harm his young son. He admitted he didn't trust himself to be alone with the child. My heart sank hearing his words.

I felt a deeper purpose in our encounter and assured him that it was no coincidence he had come to me. Sensing his vulnerability, I asked if I could pray for him. He agreed.

What should we pray for? According to Pastor Rick Warren, ***"The Bible tells us to pray for opportunities to witness, for courage to speak up, for those who will believe, for the rapid spread of the message, and for more workers. People may refuse our love or***

reject our message, but they are defenseless against our prayers."[101]

I placed my right hand on his chest and prayed fervently for God's protection over him and his son. I asked God to remove any desire he had to harm his child. As I prayed, tears streamed from my eyes, but they felt different—they were not rolling down my face, but leaping from my eyes in large, full droplets. It was an unfamiliar experience for me, yet I knew the Holy Spirit was moving through me.

I reassured the young man that our meeting was no coincidence, and that it was meant for him to hear my prayer. Throughout our time in the conference room, we were undisturbed; no one interrupted us or peered through the window. It was a profoundly moving and uninterrupted encounter.

Reflecting on the experience, I marveled at how amazing God is and how he had used me in that moment. Despite witnessing mistreatment in the workplace and doubting God's presence there, I had prayed earnestly, inviting God to witness the injustices with me. I had urged Him to intervene, convinced that such things wouldn't happen if He truly walked among us.

---

[101] Warren, The Purpose Driven Life, 301

Even though my personal circumstances had changed significantly, I continued to pray fervently for God to touch and transform the hearts of our leaders. I committed myself to being a vessel for God's work wherever I went, determined to make a positive difference.

Pastor Rick Warren says, ***"At some point in your life, you must decide whether you want to impress people or influence people. You can impress people from a distance, but you must get close to influence them, and when you do that, they will be able to see your flaws. That's okay. The most essential quality for leadership is not perfection, but credibility. People must be able to trust you, or they won't follow you. How do you build credibility? Not by pretending to be perfect, but by being honest."***[102]

I was a hard worker, detail-oriented, and driven by results. Earlier in my career as an HR supervisor, I was tasked with turning around a night operation that was performing poorly. Not only did I succeed in turning it around, but I also requested to take the lead. Despite its challenges, I was confident in my abilities. Over three months, I managed to stabilize the operation. We were on the verge of consistently meeting our production goals and performing well.

---

[102] Warren, The Purpose Driven Life, 277

In the meantime, a new division manager took charge of my area. During our first meeting, he expressed his belief that my operation should be performing better than it was. I explained to him that just ninety days earlier, hundreds of packages were being left behind daily. I outlined the progress we had made and highlighted my achievements. However, he responded dismissively, saying, "I don't think you know what you're doing."

At that moment, I realized he had already decided he wanted me out, regardless of what I said. I calmly stated, "It seems clear to me that you've already made up your mind about what you're going to do. However, I refuse to leave here feeling like a failure with my tail between my legs. I know what I've accomplished here, and every day, we are improving. So, you can make your decision." With that, I stood up and left his office.

Author Mark Batterson tells us that, ***"Praying is picking a fight with the Enemy. It's spiritual warfare. Intercession transports us from the sidelines to the front lines without going anywhere. And that is where the battle is won or lost. Prayer is the difference between us fighting for God and God fighting for us. But we can't just hit our knees. We also have to take a step, take a stand. And when we do, we never know what God will do next."***[103]

---

[103] Batterson, All In (You are one decision away from a totally different life), 87

I knew he didn't like my response, but I didn't care. The next day, I was informed of my new assignment: I was removed from that operation, and his preferred supervisor took over. Instead of being sent back to Human Resources, where I had come from, I was assigned to the most challenging operation in the district.

On my first day there, the employees asked me who I had upset. They warned me that supervisors sent to this operation either get fired or quit. I found that amusing.

Three months later, my replacement was featured on the cover of our district magazine for achieving the most improved operation. It was a significant honor, but everyone knew it was my hard work that deserved recognition. I had put in all the effort, yet this guy stepped in and received all the glory. Another three months passed, and he was promoted to manager. It was a bitter pill for me to swallow, and I began to feel depressed.

Is this what Jim Casey meant when he said, ***"But, Joe, you are made of stout stuff and you'll snap out of your mental depression. When you try to figure out what you would do if you left the company, you'll decide that you are in a pretty good business after all. Your negative thoughts will be superseded by positive action. You'll re-examine the questions that bother you and you'll see new light. You'll find a compromise between the perfect situation that you hoped for and the imperfect situation*** *that really is. And soon you will be surprised to see that the middle ground of little promise turned out even better than you had originally hoped. Things will work out favorably for you, Joe, because impulsiveness will give way to patience. You will have learned from experience that progress is nearly always made one hard step at a time."*

Remember, I mentioned that I wanted to work for the winning team? Well, it seemed like I jumped out of the frying pan and into the fire. My new boss looked like me, and I thought that would be a good thing for both of us.

Now, I was working for someone who almost made me quit. He was the worst manager I had ever worked for. This manager once told me, "Never let the employees see you smile because they will try to take advantage of you."

I felt pity for him. Here was a leader who was afraid to show his true self. He believed he always had to maintain a facade of sternness. He had no idea how to manage or motivate people. Working under him was the only time I seriously considered quitting.

Did he want me to quit? I remembered what my new employees had warned me: "You're sent here to either be fired or to make you quit." But as usual, God had a plan for me.

Unbeknownst to him, this manager started dating one of my wife's sisters. Their relationship progressed, and she spoke to him about how he was treating me. His attitude towards me changed completely and immediately. He never bothered me again. They eventually married, and he became my brother-in-law. Truly, God works in mysterious ways.

Mark Batterson states that, ***"You never know what relationship, skill, experience, or attribute God will use to bring about His eternal purposes! Or it could just be your good old-fashioned work ethic. No matter what it is, it's a gift from God that is to be used for God. Do the best you can with what you have where you are."***[104]

The atmosphere at work had become less hectic, allowing me to breathe freely again. I found myself working alongside a supervisor I had only known of before, but not personally.

One night while working the same area together, he began confiding in me about problems in his marriage. It surprised me that he would share such personal matters with someone he barely knew. I listened quietly as he shared things usually reserved for close friends.

---

[104] Batterson, All In (You are one decision away from a totally different life), 109

I felt both surprised and honored that he trusted me enough to share his deep concerns. He was troubled and needed a friend, longing for love and loyalty. I asked if he was a Christian, and he confirmed. Then I inquired if he was open to another serious relationship.

From what I discerned, I believed in his sincerity and immediately thought of one of my wife's sisters. I felt guided by the Holy Spirit that Terri, her sister, would be the right match for him. I discussed him with my wife, and we arranged a blind date for them.

We all met at a restaurant in lower Manhattan. It was almost love at first sight. Now, nearly thirty-five years later with two grown children, they are thriving. I truly felt God was using me.

Not being promoted began to weigh heavily on me. In operations, the key was production: move the numbers up, get promoted. However, that formula didn't seem to work for me.

Everything I did at work was aimed at gaining recognition from my bosses. I believed that if I did the right things, they would see my efforts and promote me. Despite doing everything right for years, it hadn't happened. Meanwhile, people around me were getting promoted—some with less time, less experience, less education, and much less color in their skin.

I spoke with a former boss, the one who was instructed to replace me shortly after I was promoted. I asked him why such injustices were tolerated. He said something I didn't fully grasp at the time, but eventually did.

He said, "UPS always takes care of its mistakes." Over the years, I found this to be true. Those who had manipulated their way into positions eventually faced consequences: they were fired, demoted, or given reduced responsibilities. This pattern held true across the organization, from part-time supervisors to District Managers and beyond.

I continued to treat people with dignity and respect. Over the years, I've exceeded expectations and improved some of the most dire situations, benefiting not only others but also myself. Despite facing unfair treatment, I refrained from complaining and instead prayed and praised God. How could God allow such unfairness to persist in this place? My depression worsened, but I kept it to myself.

One morning, I woke up so overwhelmed by depression that I could hardly get out of bed. My wife had already left for work, and our only child at the time was with the babysitter. I was alone at home. As I shuffled towards the kitchen, I collapsed against the wall, weighed down by despair. I struggled to move forward, my spirits low.

With my head hung low, I cried out, "Jesus, please help me." In that moment, I felt a lifting of the burden from my soul. It was as though someone had removed two five-hundred-pound weights from each shoulder. I felt light, almost as if I could fly. Truly, there is power in the name of Jesus!

The Holy Spirit spoke to me, revealing that my faith had been misplaced. I had put too much faith in my bosses instead of in Jesus. It was a profound revelation, and upon reflection, I knew it to be true.

Unknowingly, I had allowed my bosses to become like gods to me. Everything I did at work was aimed at gaining their favor. I immediately realigned my priorities and corrected my mistake. My allegiance was now firmly with God. I remembered the scripture, "Seek ye first the kingdom of God."

Pastor Rick Warren says, *"Instead of looking to God, we look to others to make us happy and then get angry when they fail us. God says, "Why don't you come to me first?"*[105]

Dr. Myles Munroe states, *"We must be careful not to set-up idols in our lives, however subtle they may be. An idol is anything we give higher priority than God. Our car, clothing, wife or*

---

[105] Warren, The Purpose Driven Life, 154

children. The displacement of God from His rightful position in our lives. *"*[106]

Six months later, the boss who pushed me out, claiming I didn't know what I was doing, was fired for falsifying his numbers. The supervisor who replaced me, received all the glory, and was promoted to manager three months later, faced a similar fate and was also dismissed for the same offense.

God showed me the importance of trusting Him. I learned to release my concerns and let God handle them. I reflected on what the boss had told me: "UPS always takes care of its mistakes."

Mark Batterson asks, ***"What are you holding on to? Or maybe I should ask. What are you not willing to let go of? If you aren't willing to let go, then you don't control whatever it is that you are holding on to. It controls you. And if you don't throw it down, your staff will forever remain a staff. It will always be what it currently is. But if you have the courage to throw down your staff, it will become the lightning rod of God's miraculous power, not because you threw it, but because of the One who'll change it.***[107]

---

[106] Munroe, (Understanding the purpose and power of PRAYER, 179
[107] Batterson, All In (You are one decision away from a totally different life), 132

I had taken my eyes off of Jesus. My goal had become pleasing others. I reflected deeply on that revelation. I am grateful to the Holy Spirit for revealing this truth to me. I reinstated Jesus as the head of my life and realigned my priorities. I continued to work diligently, trusting that Jesus would handle the rest.

My depression lifted. I found happiness and satisfaction within myself. I no longer cared about who got promoted or when I would be promoted. I surrendered these concerns to God.

My focus shifted to Jesus. I was genuinely happy and content. It no longer mattered to me who received promotions; I was at peace. My aim was no longer to please my bosses but to please God. I had been looking at it all wrong.

Dr. Munroe says, "Your belief is evidence that you trust God. He is not impressed by how many scriptures you quote or how long you pray. He is moved and convinced when you believe what He has told you, and when you prove it by acting on it. Belief is trust in action."[108]

The Holy Spirit reminded me that by pleasing God, everything else would fall into place. My promotion would come,

---

[108] Munroe, (Understanding the purpose and power of PRAYER, 188

and the fairness I desired would manifest. By the end of that year, I was promoted to manager. Praise God!

Even the way I was promoted was unusual. Our head of Human Resources had a reputation for never promoting anyone who had worked under him. He was one of the most arrogant individuals I had ever encountered.

Firstly, he never spoke directly to supervisors; you had to go through your immediate manager. Secondly, he was known as "pretty-boy" because his shirts were meticulously pressed, and his hair was always perfectly styled. He never visited our other sites and didn't even know how many buildings he oversaw.

One day, he walked up to my desk, tapped on it, and said, "I need to see you in my office, now." Concerned that I had done something wrong, I followed him immediately. My coworkers watched as all eyes followed us to his office. He sat behind his desk without inviting me to sit, propped his feet up, and said, "So, you want to be a manager."

I replied, "Yes, I do." He slapped his hand on the desk and said, "Okay, you're a manager," and then laughed. Believe it or not, I had to ask him for the details—who, what, when, and where. And, believe it or not, he gave me all the wrong information about my new assignment. Nevertheless, I was promoted.

Immediately, challenges arose. Everything that could go wrong, did go wrong during the first five months of my promotion. Firstly, I was sent to the wrong operation—a building thirty minutes further away from where I should have been.

I got a new boss who was also new to our district. He was a stranger to me, and I to him. My performance was evaluated against the previous year's production numbers for the same period, which, unbeknownst to me, were completely fabricated. They were inflated, unrealistic figures.

As if that wasn't enough, we experienced the worst winter in several decades with thirty-eight ice or snowstorms. There was a storm every five to six days. My commute to and from work became a nightmare. As a newly promoted manager, I had every excuse to fail.

Despite these challenges, I knew how the Preload operation should be run. Though the location was different, the fundamental principles of operation remained the same as all other preloads. Above all, I remained confident in who I was and Whose I was.

The song that the Holy Spirit placed in my heart was:

I Don't Feel Noways Tired

I don't feel noways tired. I've come to far from where I started from. Nobody told me, nobody promised me that the road

would be easy but I don't believe He brought me this far to leave me.

by Rev. James Cleveland

I believe that hymns and songs of praise can open portals to transport us to a place where the very essence of God exists. The right notes and chords must be struck within us, enabling our soul to access this special place. But what happens when the music stops? The aperture of that portal diminishes, though it never fully closes.

Pastor Rick Warren writes, "When the music stops. We don't praise God to feel good, but to do good. Your goal is not a feeling, but a continual awareness of the reality that God is always present."[109]

The right music will consistently open that portal wide, inviting us in to enjoy the presence of the Lord time and again. What happens if you never hear the music? You'll sense the vibrations and recognize the presence of the Lord nearby. Of course, music isn't the only portal to Jesus; baptism is another, and salvation is yet another. Some may argue that these are the sole portals to our Savior.

---

[109] Warren, The Purpose Driven Life, 90

Throughout this ordeal, I never lost my faith or confidence. I continued to pray and praise God, even as my production numbers plummeted. By spring that year, my new boss had grown increasingly dissatisfied with me. He expressed doubts, suggesting that promoting me may have been a mistake. He felt I wasn't prepared for the managerial role.

Each morning, there was a conference call I should have been on, but no one informed me. I was focused solely on finalizing my operation. Unbeknownst to me, the other managers were blaming me for most, if not all, of their operational issues. Without attending these calls, I couldn't defend myself. They had the new boss's ear all to themselves, and he was considering demoting me.

Another song that sustained me was, God Favored Me by Hezekiah Walker. It goes like this: ***God favored me in-spite of my enemies. I can't help but give God the glory. When I think about my story. And I know that God favored me because my enemies did try but couldn't triumph over me. Love is patient, caring and love is kind love is felt most when it's genuine. When I think about all that I went through I still came out on the winning side. I know He favored me because my enemies did try but couldn't triumph over me. For greater is He within me than he that is in the world. They whispered, conspired and told a whole bunch of lies but God*** *favored me. My character my, my integrity, my faith in God, He favored me. Everything was in question, but God favored me!*

God protected me. He fought my battles. He protected my reputation. Hallelujah! Time and time again God did not let those weapons formed against me prosper.

Mark Batterson states, *"We live in a culture that celebrates talent more than integrity, but we've got it backward. Talent depreciates over time. So do intellect and appearance. You will eventually lose your strength and lose your looks. You may even lose your mind. But you don't have to lose your integrity. Integrity is the only thing that doesn't depreciate over time. Nothing takes longer to build than a godly reputation. And nothing is destroyed more quickly by one stroke of sin. That's why it must be celebrated and protected above all else."*[110]

I made it through a very tough winter. That spring, I was summoned to my manager's office. He said, "Do you realize that your productivity is thirty to forty pieces per hour less than last year?" He asked for an explanation. "As you know," I replied, "my operation has four sections. To match or even come close to last year's numbers, one of those sections would have to be eliminated."

---

[110] Batterson, All In (You are one decision away from a totally different life), 146

"So, what are you trying to say?" he inquired. "Nothing specific," I clarified, "just that reducing hours from one of those sections would be necessary." He understood my implication without further explanation. My production numbers were being compared to figures that were fabricated, unrealistic, and baseless.

Shortly afterward, I was called to his office again. This time, he said, "I've spoken with my colleagues about you. They had nothing but positive things to say. Instead of demoting you, I've decided to swap you with my other night manager. I'll bring him here and send you to his building in the Bronx."

"This way," he continued, "I can determine if you are truly the issue." I agreed, asking, "When do we make the switch?" He replied, "Immediately. We have an audit scheduled here next week, and I prefer you not be here." It was clear he was displeased with my performance. This statement alone conveyed his true feelings. I was confident in my abilities, but wondered what else he had to judge me by.

Thus, I began my new assignment in the Bronx, at the building I should have been initially assigned to. The manager I swapped with was a man of integrity. I trusted his numbers and now we were comparing apples to apples. My performance slightly exceeded his. Within a few months of the switch, both managers I had previously worked under, who had blamed me for everything, were demoted.

Several months later, I was called into my boss's office again. This time, he began, "Firstly, I owe you an apology. You were not the problem after all. Due to your outstanding performance here, you have been requested at the main building.

"There is a need for a hub training manager, and they want you," he said. I thanked him and accepted my new assignment. Not only did I receive an apology, but I also landed my dream job, a role that hadn't existed in my district for over a decade. What an awesome God we serve!

My God, the job I had truly desired hadn't been available for over ten years. Now, it was being handed to me on a silver platter. The twilight hub operation was experiencing a 66% turnover rate, losing six out of every ten people hired. I knew exactly what needed to be done. I formed a training team, and within three months, we managed to reduce our turnover rate by sixty percent. Instead of losing six out of ten, we were now retaining six out of ten trainees.

Unfortunately, during this time, one of my part-time supervisors had to be hospitalized for an unrelated issue. To his utter surprise, I visited him in the hospital. It meant so much to him and his family, as I had hoped it would. His situation reminded me of my own many years earlier. When it was all over and he was ready and able to come back to work, I knew that I would be getting back a much more dedicated supervisor. "Take care of your people, and your people will take care of you" had become my mantra.

Due to the efforts of my team, we were now losing fewer than three people out of ten. As a result of this fantastic turnaround, I was invited to participate in the Northeast Region New Full-Time Supervisor Orientation. I had the opportunity to teach selected Human Resources modules to supervisors from New York to Maine and travel within the region. It was a very rewarding experience. God is just so amazing.

Rick Warren says, ***"The Spirit of God uses the Word of God to make us like the Son of God. God's Word generates life, creates faith, produces change, frightens the Devil, causes miracles, heals hurt, builds character, transforms circumstances, imparts joy, overcomes adversity, defeats temptation, infuses hope, releases power, cleanses our mind, brings things into being, and guarantees our future forever!"***[111]

It was October, the peak of the fall season, and I remember driving home from work one morning. I was on a parkway in Yonkers, New York. It was a beautifully bright, sunny day. All of a sudden, I "saw nature's colors." God had removed the scales from

---

[111] Warren, The Purpose Driven Life, 186.

my eyes. For what seemed like the first time in my life, I saw God's beauty in nature. I noticed the reds, yellows, greens, oranges, and browns—essentially, God's beauty. Why had I not noticed these colors and this beauty before? My view of nature, for the first time, was ineffable.

J. Oswald Sanders states that, ***"Eyes that look are common; eyes that see are rare. Vision involves optimism and hope. The pessimist sees difficulty in every opportunity. The optimist sees opportunity in every difficulty."***[112]

Had I allowed my job to absorb me so completely that I could not even recognize God's beauty? He removed my blinders and wanted me to recognize and acknowledge His work, His art. He wanted me to know that He put this here for our enjoyment. And if His eye is on the sparrow, I know He watches over me.

What a beautiful planet He has given us. I began to thank Him not only for blessing me and my family but also for surrounding us with such beauty. I began to sing as tears streamed down my face:

Great is Thy faithfulness,
Morning by morning new mercies I see;

---

[112] Sanders, J. Oswald. Spiritual Leadership (Principles of Excellence for Every Believer). (Moody, 2007), 57

All I have needed Thy hand hath provided;
Great is Thy faithfulness, Lord, unto me.

Mark Batterson states, ***"Man's chief end is to glorify God, and to enjoy Him forever. We exist for one reason and one reason alone: to glorify God, and to enjoy Him forever. It's not about you at all. It's all about Him. It's about glorifying God in whatever circumstance you find yourself in. Anyway. Anywhere. Anyhow. Whenever. Wherever. Whatever. There is no circumstance in which you cannot glorify God."***[113]

At our church in the Bronx, Trinity Baptist Church, there is a point during the service when the pastor asks the standing congregation to accept God's goodness and His blessings. To do this, while standing, you would lift your arms with your elbows remaining by your sides and open your hands, palms facing up. By doing this, you acknowledge God and accept His blessings.

I never did this. I did not do it because none of the other men around me did. I'm ashamed to admit this, but I was watching them. The only men I did see doing this were the deacons, and I expected them to do it because of their position within the church.

---

[113] Batterson, All In (You are one decision away from a totally different life), 119

Seemingly, all of the women did it. I'm embarrassed to admit this. What a juvenile excuse—I didn't do it because you didn't do it. Thank God the Holy Spirit dealt with me concerning this.

As pastor T.D. Jakes puts it, the difficulty that I had was my, ***"unwillingness to express what they feel and, in their inability, to yield their own pride to the power of God."***[114]

One Sunday morning, I decided to acknowledge God and openly accept His blessings. The church was packed, with Sandy and the girls standing beside me. Just as I started the motion to lift my arms, the Holy Spirit took over, and I began to shout and praise God. I had assumed the posture of allowing God to have His way.

It was only when I began to stop shouting that I could hear myself praising God. When I stopped, you could hear a pin drop in the church. A hush fell over the entire congregation. The silence was deafening. Just my motion to acknowledge God's goodness was enough for my spirit to rejoice.

Author J.D. Greear says, ***"But wait, you say, don't I have to ask Jesus for salvation? What if I assume the posture but don't say the prayer? Again, the posture of repentance and faith are in themselves a cry for salvation. He hears the cry of your posture***

---

[114] Jakes, T.D. So You Call Yourself A Man? (Albury Publishing, 1997), 73

even if you don't voice the prayer. Nowhere does the Bible say we have to voice a prayer to be saved. The posture of repentance and belief saves. "[115]

One day, after going shopping in my neighborhood, I parked in an outdoor municipal parking lot. While returning to my car, a young teenage girl approached me and asked for a ride. I told her which direction I was headed, and she said that was fine. I agreed to drop her off near her destination.

Shortly after getting into my car and driving off, she said, "Mister, do you want to do something?" I was so saddened that my heart sank. I then realized that this young girl was prostituting herself. As we drove along, I began to tell her about my church. I said, "You know, I go to a wonderful church not too far from here. It's called the Trinity Baptist church."

As I continued to talk about my church and the goodness of Jesus Christ, she began screaming for me to stop the car. "Stop the car!" she yelled. "Stop the car!" She opened her door before I could come to a complete stop, jumped out of my car, and ran down the street in the opposite direction.

T.D. Jakes states that, *"The very presence of Jesus torments demons. If you are in a truly anointed worship service, demons*

---

[115] Greear, Stop Asking Jesus Into Your Heart, 45

scream out and flee from people who are calling out to the name of Jesus. Nobody has to touch a person or pray a long prayer over a person with unclean spirits. The very atmosphere of worship is a torment to demon powers. Worship is the key to your deliverance."[116]

Demons will flee at the name of Jesus. There is power in the name of Jesus. Every knee shall bow. My God, my God! Satan was at it again, but when does he ever stop? It was the same method, but this time, instead of being on a riverbank in Lumberton, I was in a parking lot in the Bronx. And the next time, it could be in the choir loft or in my Sunday School class. Remain vigilant at all times.

Benny Hinn declares that, *"Satan's plan of attack is this: Every demon that has left will pay a return visit – to see if the opportunity is still available. And if he is given a chance, he will bring others with him. It's a frightening situation, but one that you can avoid by staying completely, totally filled with the Holy Spirit…"*[117]

I used to be a heavy cigarette smoker. I started smoking at age fourteen, continuing with the permission of Aunt Lou, who was also a smoker. By my mid-thirties, I was smoking well over two packs of cigarettes a day. I was clearly overweight and in poor

---

[116] Jakes, So You Call Yourself A Man? 143
[117] Hinn, Good Morning Holy Spirit, 147

health. I had been deceived by Satan into thinking that I enjoyed smoking. I would tell myself that I enjoyed smoking and that I was never going to quit.

Thanks be to God; Satan is a liar. I came to the realization that this habit was literally killing me. My daughter, Jillian, having taken a health course in school, cried and begged me to quit. I began trying different methods to quit, such as the patch and a program called Cigaress.

I was contemplating hypnosis but knew I could not quit on my own. I was not strong enough. I was weak and disgusted with myself for not being able to quit, but thanks be to God, I was strong enough to ask for help. The Holy Spirit led me to call on the One who holds all power in His hands.

While at work one day, I was sitting alone in an empty room, smoking. As I sat there hunched over in my chair with both elbows resting on my knees, I became displeased with myself for not being able to kick this harmful habit. As I mulled over my inability to quit, I remembered attending a small southern storefront church in my hometown many years earlier.

I remember the pastor saying that sometimes to change a situation you must talk directly to the situation. Remembering that, I began talking directly to the cigarette and while looking at it I said, **"You know, this does not make any sense. Satan, you have**

tricked me into thinking that I enjoy you, while with each puff that I take you are literally sucking the life out of my body." Still looking at the cigarette I said, **"Satan, I denounce you, I rebuke you in the name of Jesus. And Father, I ask that you repair any damage done to my body because of my smoking."**

I stood up, raised both my open hands to God, and said, "It is done." I knew right then and there that I had been delivered from cigarette smoking. I was at peace and knew that I would never smoke another cigarette again in my life. **I knew, that I knew, that I knew!** It has now been over twenty-five years, and I remain smoke-free. I've had several operations to help restore my health. Hallelujah and Amen!

Dr. Myles Munroe states that, ***"Satan is the prince of darkness, and he became the god of this world when he successfully tempted Adam and Eve to reject God's ways. Yet, through Christ, we have been delivered from Satan's dominion, out of the realm of darkness. That is why, even though we continue to live in a fallen world we do not belong to it. We belong to God's kingdom. Because we have been delivered from Satan's dominion, he no longer has authority over us. Rather, we have authority over him in the name of Jesus."***[118]

---

[118] Munroe, (Understanding the purpose and power of) PRAYER, 56

For many years, I did not share my deliverance from cigarette smoking with anyone. People who knew me could tell that something was different, and those close to me realized that I was no longer smoking. I didn't tell people because I was embarrassed to admit that Jesus had delivered me. I can hardly believe I'm saying this, but there was no other reason.

One day, while sitting in a church in Greenville, NC, people were giving testimonies of what God had done for them. The Holy Spirit said to me and, I quote, ***"I did not deliver you from cigarettes for you to keep it a secret."*** I stood up and gave my testimony to that congregation just as I've given it to you. Praise God!

Mark Batterson asks, ***"Why do we act as though our sin disqualifies us from the grace of God? That is the only thing that qualifies us! Anything else is a self-righteous attempt to earn God's grace."***[119]

A co-worker once asked me, "Curtis," he said, "what do you think you are doing wrong, having to undergo all of these operations?" For a split second, I thought perhaps I was doing something wrong, or maybe I was being punished.

---

[119] Batterson, All In (You are one decision away from a totally different life), 65

In that moment, the Holy Spirit spoke to me. He said, "I'm only doing what you asked me to do—to repair the damage done by your smoking." What a revelation! Hallelujah! I told my co-worker that I wasn't doing anything wrong and that God was simply fulfilling what I had asked Him to do. I thought to myself, don't let Satan get it twisted!

This was not the first or only time that God spoke directly to me. Years earlier while angry with my wife I flirted with a woman at church. I justified my actions because of my anger. The Lord, knowing my intentions, spoke to me directly and said, "you will not touch one hair on this woman's head." When God speaks to you, you know it. I did not pursue her any more.

Mark Batterson states that, ***"God tests us for two primary reasons. First, it's an opportunity for God to prove Himself to us. Second, it's an opportunity for us to prove ourselves to God."***[120]

If your wife does something that you do not like, undisciplined men will use this action as an excuse to act out. If someone hurts us, we want to hurt them back. We want to get even so that we can feel better about ourselves. We feel that we can handle it on our own and attempt to do so on our own terms. But let

---

[120] Batterson, All In (You are one decision away from a totally different life), 42

us remember whatever we justify, we cannot repent of. Learn to pray about it and trust that God will give you guidance and He will.

Prayer and trust in God builds character and enables the fruit of the spirit to manifest itself. After some time, others will see the result and effectiveness of God's love, mercy and grace through your new Christ-like attitude and behavior.

According to author Benny Hinn, *"The first manifestation you can expect of a Spirit filled life is this: your speech will be different, you'll have a new song in your heart, you'll start giving thanks to God for all things, you'll become a servant. Your heart will yearn to help people."*[121]

My son asked me, "Dad, how do you know when God speaks to you?" I replied, "When the Lord speaks to you, you will know in your spirit that it is Him. It is a voice like no other voice you have ever heard. You will know. Your spirit will know." I used to say my prayers at the foot of his bed, wanting him to see his father praying.

Author Benny Hinn says, *"Then I heard a voice that I knew must be the Lord. It was ever so gentle, but it was unmistakable."*[122]

---

[121] Hinn, Good Morning Holy Spirit, 94-95
[122] Hinn, Benny. Good Morning Holy Spirit, 7

I went on to say that His voice modulates. It may be strong and stern, or it may be soft and soothing. It could be instructive or directive, but whatever its mode, you will undoubtedly know that it is the Lord. Your spirit will recognize it.

As a child, my son Justin loved playing with his Matchbox-sized toy cars. He had over fifty of them. One day, with a serious look on his face, he said to me, "Dad, when I grow up, I want you to buy me a Lamborghini." I looked at him and thought, the nerve of this kid asking me for something so lavish.

However, the revelation for me was that if he believed he could ask me, his father, for anything and receive it, why don't I believe I can go to my Father in Heaven with the same confidence and ask Him for anything I desire? Hallelujah!

One clear, starry night, I remember lifting Justin as a baby above my head toward the sky and saying to him, "Behold the only one greater than you." As he got older, I used to worry a lot about his personal safety, particularly as he waited for his school bus in the mornings at the bottom of our driveway. Even though we lived in a "safe" neighborhood, I constantly worried about him.

One night, I had a dream. I dreamed that while watching him wait for his school bus, a big truck came barreling over the hill, hitting him and mutilating his body. It was a horrific accident. I just knew he had been killed instantly. There was no way he could have survived that impact. I could not believe my eyes.

As I looked on in horror, I felt a tap on my shoulder. I looked down and saw Justin standing beside me. He said, "Dad, why are you crying?" I replied, "But Justin, I just saw you get run over by that truck. You could not have survived that accident." He said, "Dad, look at me."

"I'm fine," he said, as he began to turn around slowly, showing me his entire body. I looked at him from head to toe. There was not a scratch on him. He said again, "Dad, I'm fine." That was the Lord letting me know that, no matter what it seems like, He (God) is still in control and has the final say. In your Bible, read the book of Daniel and see what King Nebuchadnezzar thinks about God's sovereignty! Hallelujah!

Norman Geisler says, ***"While prayer cannot change the nature of God, it can be used by God to implement His will to change people and things. While prayer is not a means to get our will done in heaven, it is a means by which God gets His will done on earth. Things do change because we pray, for a sovereign God has ordained to use prayer as a means to the end of accomplishing***

these things. But if we believe God will do these things even if we do not pray, then there is no need for prayer."[123]

There was one other time when I had a visual manifestation, and it took place at work. I suspected that there was something unusual about a particular employee. I didn't know him well, but there was something very unsettling about him. One day, as the two of us were passing each other in a hallway, he changed—or morphed, which is a better word—into someone else.

J. Oswald Sanders states, ***"The perils of spiritual leadership are especially subtle, more so than for other callings. The leader is not immune from temptations of the flesh, but the greater dangers are in the realm of spirit, for the enemy Satan never fails to exploit the advantage in any area of weakness."***[124]

For a split second, in the twinkling of an eye, he transformed into someone who was extremely, extremely feminine. The Holy Spirit allowed me to see him for who he really was. Wow! Things may not always be what they appear to be, and when they are not, the Holy Spirit will help you decipher them. I don't remember ever seeing him again. Why did the Holy Spirit allow me to see this?

____

[123] Geisler, Norman. Chosen But Free, 142
[124] Sanders, J. Oswald. Spiritual Leadership (Principles of Excellence for Every Believer). (Moody, 2007), 155

Dr. Myles Munroe, ***"God says, 'You aren't supposed to live by what you see, but by what I told you' (see 2 Corinthians 5:7). We know that in all things God works for the good of those who love Him, who have been called according to His purpose (Romans 8:28). Everything works for my good, no matter what it is, because I'm called according to God's purpose and will. It is God's will that I live confidently in the knowledge that He calls 'things that are not as though they were' (Romans 4:17). If I live only by what I see, I'm living in sin. Everything that does not come from faith is sin (Romans 14:23). Faith grows out of one thing – the word of God."***[125]

At one of my many work locations, my union shop steward engaged me in a conversation about Jesus. He was married and living with his wife and son in a very nice home. According to him, things were getting progressively worse at home. He was also having problems at work and needed to be disciplined several times. He was a womanizer, and I suspected him of having an affair with one of my female technicians.

He spoke vaguely of a "church" that he attended. I told him about the goodness of Jesus and encouraged him to pray, assuring him that God does answer prayers. He shared with me about his wife

---

[125] Munroe, (Understanding the purpose and power of) PRAYER, 193

and how they were not getting along, and he mentioned that his son was doing very well in school.

Then he looked at me and said, "I gave Jesus two years. After that, I was done. He did not help me. Nothing changed."

I said, "You cannot put Jesus on the clock. So, because you feel that He did not resolve any of your problems in two years, you stopped believing?"

"Yep," he said.

I responded, "God does not operate like that."

He eventually moved out of his home. Shortly after this conversation, he told me that he went by his house to see his son. He said he was disappointed in his wife's appearance, noting that she had not had her hair done and looked bad.

I wanted to call him an idiot and smack him across the back of his head. Instead, I said, "She is probably worried about how she is going to pay the mortgage and keep food on the table without you being there. She's got a lot to worry about now." He was very pompous and arrogant.

As I continued to pray for him and his family, the Lord gave me a message to deliver to him. God said, ***"He thinks that he is in control. Until he stops and acknowledges Me for who I am he will*** *lose everything."* I wondered how I was going to deliver that message. It had nothing to do with his work. What if he refused to meet with me? I thought of all the reasons why I could not deliver God's message.

God removed all my excuses and paved the way for me to deliver His message. I had to finalize some union business with him. After meeting with him and his shop steward, I asked to speak with him privately. To my surprise, he agreed. We went back into my office, just the two of us.

Dr. Myles Munroe states that, ***"Your belief is evidence that you trust God. He is not impressed by how many scriptures you quote or how long you pray. He is moved and convinced when you believe what He has told you, and when you prove it by acting on it. Belief is trust in action."***[126]

I said to him, "I have a message from the Lord for you."

He asked, "What did He say?"

I delivered the message. He requested that I repeat it while he wrote down each word that the Lord said: **"He thinks that he is in control. Until he stops and acknowledges Me for who I am he will lose everything."**

---

[126] Munroe, (Understanding the purpose and power of) PRAYER, 188

He asked, "Is that it?"

I said, "Yes."

And he replied, "Thank you," before leaving my office. Several weeks later, I was removed from that work location. The last I heard, he had been fired and had since died.

Mark Batterson states that, ***"God tests us for two primary reasons. First, it's an opportunity for God to prove Himself to us. Second, it's an opportunity for us to prove ourselves to God."***[127]

UPSer's are hardworking individuals. I found part-time workers to be particularly interesting because of the myriad reasons they chose to work part-time. One young man, who ended up being an excellent employee, left the job at UPS because his child support payments were too high.

After deductions from his pay, he had very little money left. He would receive a check for fifteen or maybe twenty dollars. He told me that it was not worth working under such conditions. He was willing to work but not willing to work through a system that was so inequitable.

---

[127] Batterson, All In (You are one decision away from a totally different life), 42

So, he quit and said he would never work another job on the books again. The way the system was set up discouraged him from working, and I'm sure many others like him. Whatever his initial agreement with the court was, it left him with very little pay. Thus, he quit, probably never to take another "legal" job again. He would begin to live in the shadows of life, weaving and bobbing, hoping never to be discovered again. However, he did not want to shirk his responsibilities; he was just asking to be treated fairly. Now, everybody loses, and the situation worsens.

Another employee was there solely for the medical benefits. He used to own his own construction business, but when the economy took a downturn, so did his business. He said that the medical benefits were his primary reason for working at UPS. Many others were there for supplemental reasons. They had full-time jobs and needed additional income, benefits, etc., and still others had disabilities.

I had to manage a super-diverse workforce: full-time, part-time, male, female, union, non-union, clerical, administrative, and of course, the supervisors and specialists. All were multi-cultural, multi-racial, and many were multi-lingual. It has always been a rewarding experience to help someone.

I didn't just manage their work; I helped manage people's lives. I let people know that they mattered. If someone was having a problem and was genuinely trying to resolve it, I would ask, "How can I help you? What is it that you need?" They told me they were not used to being managed in such a positive manner. I allowed the Spirit to lead me. Yes, this was my ministry.

Time and time again, God would make my enemies my footstool. He let no weapon formed against me prosper. Those who lied and cheated on me were exposed, and their gains were short-lived.

One of my more rewarding activities was being appointed to the district's promotion panel. It was comprised of five managers from various strata within the organization: two managers from Operations, one from Human Resources, one from Business Development, and one from Industrial Engineering.

Our promotion process had several steps, and sitting before our panel was the final step. It must have been a little intimidating, I'm sure. Candidates would sit before us, and each of us was allowed to ask two questions from a script of possible questions. To keep the playing field level, candidates were not to receive any coaching from any UPSer familiar with the promotion process or have any prior knowledge of the panel questions.

UPS prided itself on promoting from within the organization. These candidates already worked for UPS and sought the opportunity to be promoted to a full-time supervisor position. On this particular day, the panel had three candidates to interview—one Black, one Hispanic, and one White—all male.

The Black and Hispanic candidates went first, in that order. Both were nervous, struggled with finding the right words, and had difficulty delivering appropriate answers. The White candidate was excellent. It was obvious to me that he had been coached—and coached well.

I expressed my concern to my fellow panelists, but they all disagreed with me. Of course, if this were true, it would have given him a huge advantage over the other candidates and would disqualify him. Nevertheless, it was the White candidate who was promoted.

Later that week, I happened to run into a manager who asked me about the performance of one of the candidates, the White guy. I said that he did very well. He replied, "I know; I coached him a lot for that interview." I knew it, I said to myself.

These are not the advantages that minority candidates receive. I knew that the kid had been coached. His answers were too crisp, clean, and polished. My partners seemed to have expected no less from the White candidate.

They could not or would not see the uncanny perfection in his performance and were quick to dismiss the other candidates as weak and unqualified. The White guy clearly had an unfair advantage. Was he the best candidate? We will never know. My prayer was:

According to Leslie Copeland, *"Through prayer, we gain wisdom, direction, and peace. Prayer also prepares us to fight the kind of spiritual battles that we will undoubtedly face. The actual act of praying matters more than the time, place, and format for our prayers."*[128]

---

[128] Copeland, Christ-like Leadership, 28

<u>Nothing but the Blood</u>

During one of my assignments, my boss (Fixer #3) did everything she could to discourage me and discredit my work. She went out of her way to make life very difficult for me. If we passed an audit, she wanted to know why my team was not at 100%. Nothing I did was good enough for her. Even after I was removed from her division, she followed me to my new work location, demanding a meeting with me and my new boss.

She was relentless, but there wasn't anything she could do to harm me. My new boss asked me why she was behaving this way. I could not provide an answer. She got to speak her piece, and my new boss assured me that what she had to say did not sway him one way or the other. He wanted to get to know me for himself, and I respected him for that. Shortly after I left her division, she was demoted.

Each year, those supervisors and managers recommended to receive company stock—nearly everyone—would meet with their district manager in his office. Present at these meetings were also your department head and the district controller, making a total of four people. This was very intimidating for most people, as you were meeting with the person whose signature was on your paycheck.

Supposedly, if you sold any of your stock, you would not be eligible to receive stock the next year. My immediate boss for this particular meeting was the district Human Resources Manager. We filed in and out of the district manager's office in alphabetical order. The last person out would tell the next in line to go in.

I was the last person in my department to be seen due to my last name. As soon as I entered the room, the district manager met me at the door and started yelling at me for selling some of my company stock the year before. He was yelling at me, right in my face. I took a step back from him and held both my hands in the air until he stopped.

I made my way to my seat. My boss and the district controller said nothing. At one time, the company did everything it could to discourage selling any of your stock. As a private company, if you sold stock, you were not viewed as a true UPS partner and could be denied stock the following year. This was no longer the case since UPS was no longer a privately held company.

I could not believe the verbal assault I had just received from the man whose name was on my paycheck. I listened to what he had to say. He stood up to shake my hand to dismiss me, but I refused to shake his hand and said, "Now I have something to say."

Pastor Timothy Keller tells us that **"Apostle Paul is rejecting verbal bullying (using the force of one's personality or witty and cutting disdain); applause generating statements that play to a crowd's prejudices, pride, and fears; and manipulative stories or** *techniques that overwhelm the audience with shows of verbal dexterity, wit, or erudition.* "[129]

Now, this ex-Marine was both furious and embarrassed. He ripped his glasses from his face and flung them across the conference room table. They landed on the floor, and he sat back down. I told him that I had no regrets about selling my stock. I said that what I did was right for me and my family.

I told him that if I had to do it all over again, I would make the same decision. Selling my stock, I said, didn't make me any less of an employee or a loyal partner. If anything, it made me a stronger employee and a more dedicated partner.

Benny Hinn tells us, *"Do you realize that the power of the Spirit can so infill you that you fear absolutely no one? It's possible to establish such a communion with Him that even addressing the leader of a nation would cause no apprehension. The Spirit will lift your head, square your shoulders, and instill in you an unexpected confidence.* "[130]

I left the room without shaking his hand. As the last person from my department to be seen, my boss stood up to leave with me.

---

[129] Keller, Preaching, 17.
[130] Hinn, Good Morning Holy Spirit, 117.

The district manager pointed his finger at him and demanded that he not move. I exited the room and waited for him.

After roughly twenty minutes, he came out. We walked back to his office together. He said, "Well, Curtis, I have never seen him this mad before, but that is his problem. After all, it is your stock. He should not be asking those personal questions anyway. But I have to say, you really stood your ground. Good for you," he said.

Mark Batterson says it best, ***"But no matter how you slice it, the fear of God is the beginning of wisdom, and the fear of man is the beginning of foolishness."***[131]

However, deep down inside, I knew this would not be the end of it. Rumors had already begun to spread the next day about how I had given the district manager a piece of my mind and refused to shake his hand. How dare I speak up for myself?

This district manager was a very proud and arrogant man. He took great pride in his military service, as he should. He was an ex-Marine and made sure everyone knew it. He literally walked around with his chest puffed out. He was a tall man with broad shoulders, purposefully intimidating.

----

[131] Batterson, All In (You are one decision away from a totally different life), 143

I knew that my verbal exchange with him in front of his subordinates would not sit well with him. I was not afraid of him, and he knew it. He was not my God; he was a bully, arrogant, and full of himself. I was neither disrespectful nor impressed. I only spoke the truth. How he chose to deal with it was entirely up to him.

I was not afraid to speak up for myself; I never was. I was also prepared to deal with whatever consequences might arise from speaking up. I believed in and trusted God to take care of me. So, I continued to speak the truth and be honest in my dealings with everyone. I did not know of anyone who had been fired for being honest.

I likened this district manager to King Nebuchadnezzar. He saw himself as the golden statue that everyone should bow down to and worship—narcissism at its finest. After all, it was his name on my paycheck. When I failed to bow down to him, he would soon cast me into his fiery furnace, which was considered operations.

Three months after my encounter with him, I was removed from my comfortable job in Human Resources and placed in operations. I was not surprised and pretty much expected it. The retaliation had begun, and my response was, "Bring it on." I didn't believe that God had brought me this far to leave me.

Operations was viewed as the toughest of all the jobs, and by all accounts, it was. Several of his hand-picked managers were revered as his henchmen. My colleagues warned me that the person I was going to work for was tough and the district manager's right-hand man. His hand-picked managers were supposed to be feared, ruling with an iron fist and having the complete support of the district manager. They were his "fixers." But God was my fixer.

The manager I replaced in my new assignment was not well-liked, and her departure was welcomed by everyone. She had a terrible reputation among people and was also narcissistic. It was common knowledge among those of us in management that she had a military background and was promoted quickly to manager because of it. This, of course, reflected well in the eyes of our district manager, who was an ex-Marine himself. She would later be promoted again and become one of his direct reports, giving her even more power.

Returning to operations was no big deal for me. I had managed various operations except for that of a center manager, a role that terrified me. It was an area of the business in which I had little to no experience. I remember how difficult it was for me to become a driver. I never got to learn the delivery end of the business and naturally grew to fear it. The last thing I wanted was to end up as a center manager.

Working nights in the hubs, on the preloads, and local sorts shielded me from that experience, which was fine with me. In this new assignment as Local Sort Manager, I exceeded all expectations and forged an unexpected alliance with my new "fixer" boss.

Of course, this was not supposed to have happened. This was the man who was supposed to make me suffer or quit. At a minimum, he was supposed to make my life miserable. My operation ran beautifully. King Nebuchadnezzar had failed again. It ran so well that this "fixer" boss thanked me and said he could sleep nights now that I was there. God took care of me.

A year and a half later, I was transferred to another one of his "fixers." This time, it was a job I had always feared the most.

Napoleon Hill states, ***"Your, 'other self' will remain in charge and continue to direct you as long as you rely upon it. Keep doubt and fear and worry, and all thoughts of limitation, entirely out of your mind."***[132]

Craig Groeschel says, ***"One of the enemy's greatest tools is fear."***[133]

Managing full-time package drivers was a job for which I had neither training nor experience. To make matters worse, I was given this assignment during the busiest time of the year, the fall.

---

[132] Hill and Lechter, Outwitting The Devil (The Secret to Freedom and Success), 29

[133] Groeschel, Craig. it (How Churches and Leaders Can Get it and Keep it). (Zondervan, 2008), 115

This new manager was also tough, arrogant, and hand-picked by "King Nebuchadnezzar," the district manager. This was his "fixer #2," but I knew this division manager. I was the first manager he met when he came to visit our district. I had to authorize his entrance into the building, and I'm sure he remembers that.

By far, this was the most challenging assignment I had ever faced. Seasoned managers who knew what they were doing struggled during this time of the year. I'm sure "King Nebuchadnezzar," my district manager, felt that this assignment would finally be the one to do me in. I didn't know the job, the people, or the territory; I wasn't being trained and was working fifteen to sixteen hours every day for months.

Perseverance

Two frogs fell into a can of cream,

Or so I've heard it told.

The sides of the can were shiny and steep;

The cream was deep and cold.

"Oh, what's the use?" said No. 1,

" 'tis fate – no help's around.

Good-bye, my friend! Good-bye, sad world!"

<u>Nothing but the Blood</u>

And, weeping still, he drowned.

But No. 2, of sterner stuff,

Dog-paddled in surprise,

The while he wiped his creamy face

And dried his creamy eyes.

"I'll swim awhile, at least," he said –

Or so I've heard it said –

"It wouldn't really help the world,

If one more frog was dead."

An hour or two he kicked and swam.

Not once he stopped to mutter,

But kicked and swam, and swam and kicked,

Then hopped out via butter!

By T. C. Hamlett

My two supervisors hated each other, and my office clerk was a nasty, arrogant woman. She had a very poor attitude and pretty much told my supervisors what to do. I did not step into a good situation.

To make matters worse, I was given an additional operation to run—the local sort. I prayed a lot, asking God to bless my operation and my staff. Once again, God sustained me, and I thanked Him for it. I made it through the toughest and busiest time of the year. I gained the respect of my drivers and staff. There were only two managers in this facility. The other manager coached and encouraged me. His presence made a difference and kept me going. God made a way again.

In the spring of the following year, "fixer #2" had a meeting with me. He said that I was not learning the job fast enough and mentioned that a position had become available back at the main building. "I am not telling you that you must take it," he said. "But if you choose to stay here with me, things are going to get much more difficult for you. The choice is yours." I told him that I wanted to return to the main building. However, what he did not tell me was that I had been requested by the new district manager.

"King Nebuchadnezzar," my former district manager, had retired. The new district manager and the new regional Human Resources manager had requested me as their employee relations manager. "Fixer #2" did not tell me this. I didn't know it at the time, but "fixer #2" could not have kept me there even if he wanted to. He made it seem as if this was all due to his grand benevolence. It was all God. We serve an awesome God.

It was a no-brainer; I ended up going back to Human Resources. For the first time ever, the regional and district HR managers were Black. Not to mention that the district Employee Relations Manager was also Black—that was me. Those were some of the best years of my UPS career, not because we were all Black, but because we all shared the experience of being Black. My platform to help people was so much bigger. God had enlarged my territory; He had given me access to every full-time management person in the district. Hallelujah!

I began to use my platform as the District Employee Relations Manager to send out words of encouragement to the entire full-time district staff. I wasn't sure if I could do it, but I was led by the Spirit. I was able to reach hundreds of my colleagues. My source was the book *Think on These Things: Meditations for Leaders* by John C. Maxwell. This book was given to me in the summer of 2003 by a friend at work. I was at a place in my life where I wanted to do more for the Lord.

My first email list included all of the managers, division managers, and the district manager. Any meaningful blowback would have come from one of them. I began to send out a message each week. There was no blowback at all, so I included all full-time supervisors. I praised God that it was accepted. I was given access to every full-time management person in the district, over 300 of them. My God!

Week #1:

"What enters our mind and occupies our thought process will somewhere, sometime come out of our mouth."[134]

Week #2:

"People are known not by how they act when they're in control, but by how they react when things are beyond their control."[135]

Week #3:

"Here's a truth that's important to consider; just as a tree can't produce fruit that's not of its kind, neither can we. In other words, we can produce in our lives only fruit that's consistent with our character. No person is such a deceiver that he or she can produce consistently what he or she does not believe or embrace."[136]

---

[134] Maxwell, Think on these Things (Meditation for Leaders), 14
[135] Maxwell, Think on these Things (Meditation for Leaders), *30*
[136] Maxwell, Think on these Things (Meditation for Leaders), *38*

<u>Week #4:</u>

"I love the story of the mule who fell into an old dry well many feet deep. All efforts to rescue him were fruitless. Finally, the owner of the mule, supposing that the poor creature was severely injured by the fall, decided it would be more merciful to kill him than allow him to starve to death. Unable to think of a better way of dispatching him, he had a truckload of dirt thrown in onto him. Instead of allowing himself to be buried alive, the mule quickly shook off the dirt and pressed it down with his feet, thus raising himself a few inches above his original position. Another load was thrown into the well with the same result.

"Slowly but surely, inch by inch, the mule ascended until the well was filled within a few feet of the top. Then, as complacently as if nothing strange had happened to him, the mule stepped out on firm, safe ground. It may offend a few people to look at a mule for a lesson in living. But some people have never learned what that mule already knew – that the very setback originally designed to finish a person off, when properly used, can become the thing that brings him or her out on top."[137]

---

[137] Maxwell, Think on these Things (Meditation for Leaders), *120*

<u>Week #5:</u>

"Monday morning is the only time I can stand up and say, 'So far this week I haven't made a mistake.' Last week's mistakes can be corrected this week. Last week's sorrow can become this week's joy."[138]

The only person who objected was Satan. He attacked my body with a heart attack after my fifth week of sending out the messages.

One evening, I was awakened with what I thought was indigestion. I could not get back to sleep, so I got up, showered, shaved, and got ready for work. I still didn't feel great but was not bad enough to stay home. I arrived at the office and met with my boss.

My boss said, "You don't look good. Are you okay?" I told him it was just indigestion.

We then went to our regular morning meeting with his boss. His boss said, "Curtis, you look like crap. I think you should get checked out," and my boss agreed. I called my doctor, who could see me in a few hours. I left work and went straight to his office.

---

[138] Maxwell, Think on these Things (Meditation for Leaders), *132*

After arriving at his office, I was placed in a waiting room and asked to remove my shirt. When my doctor entered the room, he asked me about my symptoms. Without examining me, he instructed me to get dressed and go over to the hospital emergency room.

The hospital was literally across the street. I wanted more information. "What do I tell them? What do I do?" I asked.

He calmly replied, "Don't worry. They will be expecting you."

Philip Yancey states that, ***"Fear, like pain, serves as a warning system, only with the added benefit of functioning in advance of harm."***[139]

I got dressed and drove over to the hospital. I parked my car and arrived at the emergency room minutes later; yes, they were waiting for me. Still not knowing exactly why I was there, blood was immediately drawn from me. I sat there, not feeling any better or worse.

The doctor returned and said, "Mr. White, I'm sorry to inform you that you've had a heart attack." I was admitted on the

---

[139] Yancey, Philip. Where Is God When It Hurts? (Zondervan, 1990), 55

spot. They found the blockage and placed one stent. Was God present? Absolutely!

Philip Yancey writes, ***"Clear your mind and reflect for a moment on Jesus' life. He was the only person in history able to plan his own birth. Yet he humbled himself, trading in a perfect heavenly body for a frail body of blood and sinew and cartilage and nerve cells. The Bible says there is no temptation known to man that Jesus did not experience. He was lonely, tired, hungry, personally assaulted by Satan, besieged by admirers, persecuted by powerful enemies. The fact that Jesus came to earth where he suffered and died does not remove pain from our lives. But it does show that God did not sit idly by and watch us suffer in isolation. He became one of us."***[140]

My second night in the hospital was restless. I was doing well and decided to get up and walk around the floor. As I pushed my IV pole down the hall, I could hear cries for help, patients moaning, and calls for the nurse. As I waded through this gauntlet of pain and suffering, I thanked God for my condition and prayed for the others. For my own sanity, I knew I had to get out of there. I was released the next day.

---

[140] Yancey, Where Is God When It Hurts? 224-225

<u>Nothing but the Blood</u>

I've had many jobs while working for UPS. The most difficult jobs were in operations, and the only one I never held was that of center manager. It was the job I feared the most because it was the one I had the least amount of experience in. It was a job I had managed to steer clear of for over thirty years, and now I had it. You don't realize just how much you need Jesus until that's all you have.

Some five years later, at a luncheon for retirees, this particular manager asked to speak with me privately. She said she wanted to apologize for the way she had treated me. She said, "I was only doing what I was told to do!" She had received her marching orders from that district manager who had flung his glasses across his conference room table after I refused to shake his hand—the district manager I had dubbed "King Nebuchadnezzar." My God, my God. She knew she was wrong. God had convicted her. She needed to clear her conscience. Wait on the Lord; God will fight your battles.

My brother Robert's health was getting progressively worse. Not long after his visit to our home in Yonkers, he became incapacitated. He had lost a lot of weight and had become very fragile. His hair had become straight, likely a result of his cocktail of drugs.

He would get encouraged if his T-cell count rose. This count had become the barometer for how well he was doing. I began taking him to his doctor appointments. He could no longer walk or stand on his own, so I had to pick him up and carry him to my car. He had house attendants with him throughout the night. I would visit him daily.

This began to take a toll on my health. I wasn't getting enough sleep, and it started to affect my job performance. I sent an email to my boss.

It read as follows:

Original Author: White, Curtis; 10/03/96 19:29 hrs

Good morning,

My brother, Robert White has advance AIDS. He is not expected to see Thanksgiving. His wishes are that he be allowed to die at home. He has been provided with 24hr home care provided that I can be with him when an attendant doesn't come. This has not been a problem in the past but will be now should I have to care for him on either shift. This will reduce the # if hours that I work, here. I will only work a few hours tonight because he was re-examined and admitted to the VA hospital on 23rd Street (10th fl.) today. He will be released the latter part of next week. In effect, being sent home to die. I don't anticipate having to be totally absent from work until the time of his death at which you will be promptly notified. He is single, lives alone and I am his only family member in New York. When he does die there will be no viewing of the body and my family will hold a private funeral service.

Thanking you in advance for your understanding.

Curtis

The response was the following:

Curtis,

You have my heartfelt sympathies. I know how it feels to suffer this type of loss. Take care and keep in touch.

Mike

I needed this kind of response. My personal experiences with UPS up to this point had not been empathetic at all. This allowed me to exhale, take a deep breath, and give my full attention to my brother, Robert.

So, what was my responsibility as a Christian brother? **"My responsibility is to dispense grace, to show him how tenderly Jesus treated people with sexual sins, to assure him of God's love and forgiveness. In short, my role is to move his focus away from the backward glance and direct it forward. Even his guilt is a signal. He can lie in a hospital bed all day and grovel in his sins. Or he**

can bring that guilt to God, who has promised to put confessed sin behind him, 'as far as the east is from the west'."[141]

The next job I was tapped for was Employee Relations Manager. The Human Resources Manager, my department head, had the corner office. It was a beautiful office with a panoramic view of Midtown Manhattan.

From this office, my department witnessed the collapse of the Twin Towers on 9/11. It was from this office that I saw the second plane hit. Shortly after this catastrophe, my boss had to move closer to his boss, who was on the floor below us. One of the other managers in the office claimed that office immediately. His attitude was as if he were entitled to it.

We got a new department head who decided that the office should be occupied by the Employee Relations Manager—that was me. The manager who had claimed that office had to move out and relocate to an office beside the elevators, which was one-third the size.

He had a problem with that and was not happy, but there was nothing he could do about it. The new department head did not care. I could not believe that I was blessed with such a beautiful office.

---

[141] Yancey, *Where Is God When It Hurts?* 203

And again, this was all God. However, my blessings extended beyond the office.

John C. Maxwell tells us, ***"What enters our mind and occupies our thought process will somewhere, sometime come out of our mouth. It's been said, "Be careful about what you set your heart on, for you'll surely get it."***[142]

We were ready to buy our second home and chose a real estate agent registered in Northern Westchester, where we wanted to live. We were looking for new construction, and she took us to a new development not far from one of my favorite fishing spots.

The homes were nice, but they were in the open with few trees around. Finally, within the same development, we were shown a home almost entirely under some high-tension power lines. We were definitely not interested in that.

I remember asking the agent, "Do you have any other new single-family construction to show us?" She replied, "There is one other place, but I think the office closes in a few minutes. It's on the other side of the county. I'm not sure if we can make it in time." I said, "Let's go for it."

---

[142] Maxwell, Think on these Things (Meditation for Leaders), 14

God had it all set up for us. We arrived just at closing time, and the person showing the home acted as if he had been waiting for us. As we entered the model home, which also served as his office, the last family was leaving. We were now the only ones there. He welcomed us warmly and told us to take our time. He answered all our questions and explained everything.

He let us know what was available and was absolutely wonderful. He encouraged us to leave a deposit to secure a lot, which we did. The next day, as we walked the lot, I found myself drawn to a different one that wasn't ours. I remember Sandy calling to me, "Honey, what are you doing over there? That's not our lot—besides, it's twice the size of the one we got."

"I know," I said. "I just like it better over here."

Norman Geisler states that, ***"God is before all things, God created all things, God upholds all things, God is above all things, God knows all things, God can do all things and God accomplishes all things. This complete control of all things is called the sovereignty of God."***[143]

Sandy had taken a five-year sabbatical after the birth of our third child. Justin was a good child, and she didn't mind taking him with her everywhere she went. She regularly met with builders and

---

[143] Geisler, Chosen But Free, 13-14

interior designers, always with Justin in tow. Sandy meticulously reviewed and studied our blueprints, and she noticed a faint, thin line down the middle of our driveway. She inquired about it.

We were informed that it was a shared driveway—a concept that had never crossed our minds. In our section, there were only three homes but just two driveways. We hadn't been aware of this, nor was it something the builder had openly shared. One of the homes had already been purchased, and as fate would have it, it wasn't the one with the private driveway.

However, the sales agent did let us know that another family was interested in the remaining property—the one with its own private driveway. He mentioned that they had failed to leave a deposit and would decide on Monday if they wanted to take it. If we wanted to, we could switch our deposit to that property right away, which we did. It was now ours.

This property had a private driveway, more land, and was also more expensive, but still within our means. Hallelujah! Sandy's discovery of such a minor detail made a monumental difference in our happiness. Again, I credit the Holy Spirit for guiding us. Now I understand why I was standing on that other lot in the beginning— it was meant for us.

We absolutely did not want to share a driveway. We wouldn't have purchased that property for that reason alone. What a find! Once again, thank you, Holy Spirit. That could have easily been overlooked—and it was. We would have been devastated, and the only one who knew that was the Holy Spirit.

This was the most exciting time of our marriage, outside of getting married and having the kids. After making the switch, we were ready to break ground. It would take nine months before completion—it was like having another child. We were having our own home built to our specifications. What a blessing! Financially, UPS had been very, very good to us.

Our children are blessed and doing well. Our oldest daughter was accepted into Columbia University at the age of sixteen. Her sister was accepted to John Jay College of Criminal Justice, followed by their brother, who was accepted to Mercy College in Dobbs Ferry, N.Y. They all earned their degrees and are doing very well. To God be the glory.

"Pray for them without ceasing. Perhaps one of the best ways we can love our children is by interceding for them with God. When my children were young, and even still with my eight-year-old. I enjoyed our bedtime ritual of reading a story and saying our prayers before the lights were turned off and they closed their weary eyes for a good night's sleep. And even though it embarrasses some of my image-conscious teenagers, I still like to pray for them in their presence, aloud. I want them

to know that I hope for them and that I'm praying for their futures. And I want them to experience my faith in action, establishing a spiritual legacy that they can continue with their own children. So often we may feel powerless in our desires and attempts to shield and protect our kids, but we can always pray for them and entrust them to God's care. Yes, my friend, it takes incredible reserves of courage, patience, perseverance, and love to be a father. But as a man who is seeking balance in his life, discovering more of who he is and where he's going, you have it in you to be available for your children and to take the most incredible risk of all with them: loving them as your Father in heaven loves you."[144]

My new manager's boss was a bully. The three of us would meet each morning in the district manager's office. He was a young, tall, good-looking guy who had moved up the ranks fairly quickly to reach his level in the company. It was said that he was the brother-in-law of one of the board members, and he firmly supported his HR manager, who was my boss. They knew each other well, so my boss had a lot of clout.

Our new district manager really enjoyed addressing his managers and supervisors. One of my responsibilities was to set up these meetings, make them exciting, different, and provide some

---

[144] Jakes, He-Motions, 287

really nice gifts. From start to finish, it was all on me. During one such meeting, the air conditioning was out, making the room hot and uncomfortable. He was sweating.

After addressing the group, he called me out into the hallway and let me have it. I had never been spoken to so harshly before. One of my administrative assistants happened to witness the incident and later tried to make me feel better. I was having a bad day. The situation was out of my control. The maintenance department had thought they could have the air conditioning repaired and running before the meeting started, but that didn't happen, and I had no other options.

From that point on, he would threaten to assign me tasks that I was clearly unable to do, enjoying himself at my expense. However, he never brought it up again. I had to go out to his home once to pick something up. He had a beautiful house on a golf course in an exclusive neighborhood in northern New Jersey. He introduced me to his wife and daughter, and they were both very nice. I later discovered that his daughter had some kind of cancer.

This was my boss's boss, the man whose name was on my check. I had never been moved to give a particular gift to any of my managers, whether for Christmas or any other occasion. I had purchased *The Purpose Driven Life* by Pastor Rick Warren for someone else, but the Holy Spirit pressed upon my heart to give this book to him—my boss's boss.

Benny Hinn declares, *"How are you led by the Spirit? You become familiar with His voice. You recognize it. You respond to it. And the more you fellowship with Him, the deeper the relationship becomes."*[145]

I wrapped the book and planned to leave it in his office without seeing him. That didn't happen. As fate would have it, he and I met alone that morning without my boss. I handed him the book, and he opened it immediately, right in front of me. He called out the name of the book and the author. "I'm familiar with Rick Warren," he said. "My wife is a big fan of his. Thank you."

That was it. We never mentioned it again, but I'm sure it was what he needed.

Mark Batterson states that, *"The lesson of Lucifer's fall is this: whatever you don't turn into praise turns into pride. Instead of deflecting praise to God, Lucifer let it feed his ego. It was the sinful desire to be lifted up that led to Lucifer's downfall."*[146]

---

[145] Hinn, Good Morning Holy Spirit, 65
[146] Batterson, All In (You are one decision away from a totally different life), 44

Within a year, he was fired. This happened shortly after my heart attack, and I had been moved to another building. I was told his firing had something to do with money, as it almost always does. It's extremely rare for someone at his level to be terminated. In my over thirty years with the company, this had happened just one other time. God is so amazing. I couldn't have given him a better gift. I prayed for him and his family.

We got a new Region Manager, who happened to buy a home in my neighborhood. Knowing this, my district manager and my boss asked me to personally deliver a welcome package to his home. The package was large, packed with various cheeses, crackers, grapes, meats, and wine. I told him it was from the Metro New York district staff but didn't specifically mention my district manager's name.

Our new Region Manager and his wife were both surprised and very gracious in receiving the welcome package. They offered me to stay and have dinner with them, but I declined. My district manager was furious when I told him that I didn't specifically mention his name.

He couldn't believe it. He saw this as his opportunity to get in good with his new boss. The Region HR manager had instructed me to say the welcome package was from the Metro New York

District staff and not to mention my district manager's name specifically, but I couldn't tell my district manager that.

The building we worked out of was huge, occupying an entire city block—avenue to avenue long and street to street wide. It had two entrances for employees: one was the east lobby on Eleventh Avenue, and the other was the west lobby on Twelfth Avenue.

The building was only eight stories tall, and that was only at the west end. The region offices were on the eighth floor, the district offices on the sixth and seventh floors, and the mechanical and automotive shops on the fifth floor, which led out to the roof. The centers of operation were on floors one through four.

The employee parking garage was in the basement, with access only from the east side of the building. The Region Manager would sometimes enter the building on the east side, take the elevator to the fourth floor, and walk across the floor to take the west side elevator to the eighth.

My center was located on the fourth floor and was the last center before reaching the west elevators. He would come through during the busiest part of the morning and often give me a fist bump or some other acknowledgment whenever he came through. I was the only manager he knew.

Word spread quickly that we had that kind of relationship. But unbeknownst to them, I was the first manager he met from our district and probably one of the very few to have ever been to his home. Because of this, he favored me. God is so amazing!

Benny Hinn tells us that, ***"The first manifestation you can expect of a Spirit filled life is this: your speech will be different, you'll have a new song in your heart, you'll start giving thanks to God for all things, you'll become a servant. Your heart will yearn to help people."***[147]

After my heart attack and stent placement operation, I returned to work several weeks later, but not to my previous role as the Employee Relations Manager. They wanted me to take it easy, so they gave me a position closer to home with much less responsibility. Even so, my new boss was relentless. She hounded me about everything. I surmised that she was still doing the bidding of the former district manager, the one I had embarrassed when receiving my stock.

After all, he had promoted her. Even though he had retired, she remained focused on his objective concerning me—either to demote, fire, or make me quit. I believe she was another one of his "fixers," and she would be "fixer #3." The Holy Spirit helped me

---

[147] Hinn, Good Morning Holy Spirit, 94-95

realize where her unprovoked hostility was coming from, and I did my best to ignore her.

She continued to bark, threaten, and make my life as miserable as I would allow her to. I wasn't intimidated and continued to praise God. With only months left until my retirement, I figured I would be allowed to finish out my time where I was and not be moved again.

Pastor Rick Warren says this about fear, ***"Fear is a self-imposed prison that will keep you from becoming what God intends for you to be. You must move against it with the weapons of faith and love. Self-worth and net worth are not the same."***[148]

Unfortunately, that's not what happened—I was moved again. I had to face my biggest fear of all: I was put in charge of a package center, once more. It was a job in which I had less than six months of experience, and the one I feared the most. Why was I placed in this position just months before my retirement? Everyone who knew me was appalled by this decision.

I felt like Daniel, thrown into the fiery furnace or the lion's den. It was only by the hand of God that I performed as well as I did.

---

[148] Warren, The Purpose Driven Life, 28-29

To God be the glory! Months after I left her division, she was eventually demoted.

Times Square! I was named the Times Square Center Manager. This operation was one of the most highly profiled within our district because of its high-profile customer base. They chose me, with no real center manager experience, to manage deliveries to the "Crossroads of the World." This was either a very cruel joke or a true testament to my demonstrated managerial skills.

One of the main reasons Times Square is so iconic is the sheer number of theaters along Broadway, in Lincoln Center, and in the Theater District. Then there's the Diamond District on 47th Street, which boasts the largest concentration of diamond and jewelry-related companies and retailers. An estimated 90% of diamonds in the United States pass through the 47th Street Diamond District. Additionally, there's Restaurant Row, a diverse array of culinary options from around the world, as well as a vibrant nightlife, located on West 46th Street between 8th and 9th Avenues—a culinary journey for generations.

Rockefeller Center is a national historic landmark in the heart of Midtown Manhattan. It's home to the Top of the Rock Observation Deck, NBC Studios, Radio City Music Hall, and much more. This complex is noted for the large quantities of art present in almost all of its buildings, its expansive underground concourse, its ice-skating rink,[149] and its annual lighting of the Rockefeller Center Christmas Tree.[150]

Broadway is not just a street name that runs north to south across Manhattan Island; it's also used to refer to the Theatre District, where Americans flock to watch plays and musicals. As you can see, a mistake here could be heard around the country, if not the world.

Who made the decision to put me in such a high-profile location, and why? I wasn't qualified to manage such an operation. I continued praying and getting to know my drivers. I needed God more than I'd ever needed Him before. This was my furnace; this was my lion's den.

Mark Batterson states that, ***"In God's kingdom, calling trumps credentials every time! God doesn't call the qualified. He qualifies the called. And the litmus test isn't experience or expertise. It's availability and teachability. If you are willing to go***

---

[149] An ice rink (or ice-skating rink) is a frozen body of water and/or an artificial sheet of ice where people can ice skate or play winter sports.

[150] The Rockefeller Center Christmas Tree is a large Christmas tree placed annually in Rockefeller Center, in Midtown Manhattan, New York City, United States.

when God gives you a green light. He will take you to inaccessible places to do impossible things."[151]

I began my new assignment by getting to know my employees. I introduced myself personally to each of them, one-on-one. It wasn't a terribly large group; I dispatched, on average, about forty drivers per day. My drivers were a very "UPS typical" group.

They came from different countries, with diverse religions, backgrounds, and experiences. They were a great bunch of people. I was surprised to learn how little they knew about me, which helped put my mind at ease. I was starting with a clean slate. As I got to know my employees, the Holy Spirit guided me to those I should minister to.

Pastor Rick Warren tells me, ***"You'll never know that God is all you need until God is all you've got."***[152]

Many scenes from my life flashed across my mind, and like in the poem *Footprints in the Sand*, I asked why. "Why, Lord, during the low periods of my life, when I needed You most, were You not there for me? When my father abandoned us, when my mother died, when I was hungry, when I suffered injuries, when I was sick, when I was molested, when I was frightened and alone—when I was

---

[151] Batterson, All In (You are one decision away from a totally different life), 107

[152] Warren, Rick. The Purpose Driven Life, 194

blinded by Your goodness and could see only one set of footprints, thinking they belonged to me alone." His answer was, "The times you have seen only one set of footprints, my child, are when I carried you." Hallelujah!

God doesn't call the qualified; He qualifies the called. I couldn't go out and perform their jobs, nor did I pretend that I could. I told them, "You all have a very difficult job, and I admire the professionalism with which you perform it every day. There isn't anything I can teach you."

So, let's not talk about your job, but rather about why you do what you do. What does this job mean to those you love, to the ones you kiss goodbye every morning? They had never heard anything like this from any of their previous managers.

I had three full-time supervisors whom I knew nothing about: one female and two males. The female was new to operations, having recently been downsized from our customer service department. She had two small children and had been with UPS for nearly ten years. It was either learn operations or look for employment elsewhere. The same fate befell another female supervisor in finance, who also, with no other option, became an operations center supervisor.

One of my male supervisors had an alcohol problem, while the other was my lead supervisor, running the center. He was the most knowledgeable, energetic, and level-headed, definitely ready for a promotion to manager, though he claimed not to be interested.

There were ten other center managers like myself in my division. I knew all of them, and none were female. Several of the full-time supervisors were female. My female supervisor did not know how to drive a manual transmission, which limited her effectiveness. One of my first directives from my new boss was to teach her how to drive our vehicles.

I had to teach her how to drive a manual transmission. She was not the first female I had trained in this skill. She was a quick learner, and the training went smoothly. She was extremely grateful and could now contribute more to the team. I prayed for my management team, encouraged them to be their best, and acknowledged all of their accomplishments.

All center managers had to meet each morning in our boss's office. Everyone knew that I had never run a package center before. The managers had their own clique. The Puerto Rican manager and I were not part of it. The clique often ate breakfast and lunch together, and rarely did either of us receive an invitation to join them. It didn't bother me, but I was disappointed; I hadn't expected this.

These managers had been in their roles for many years. In most cases, it was all they had ever done. I had much more diverse experience due to the various positions I'd held over the years. I noticed that their management styles were quite uniform.

They all worked similar hours and were on their way home by 3 p.m. each day. They seemed to think and act alike. At our morning meetings, I didn't say much because I didn't know much. I just sat back and observed everything.

Our boss, the division manager, seemed fair. He went out on the road with me one day. We did a lot of walking, and I had some difficulty keeping up with him. It was clear that he was annoyed by having to be out there with me. Clearly, someone had instructed him to provide me with some kind of training. I learned absolutely nothing from him, but he got to check that box.

I already knew basic things like reducing package selection time and knowing at least five stops ahead. Always carry your keys on your pinky finger with them pressed into the palm of your hand— these were some of the things I remembered from being a driver supervisor for six months thirty years earlier. I had no knowledge of the current methods or technology.

I continued to build relationships with my drivers. I talked to them about their families and their lives. I held small group meetings every day in my office, and my drivers loved it. For once, it wasn't all about the job; it was about them.

I attended the wakes of their loved ones, ordered family Bibles when appropriate, and made sure to personally give them out. They got to know me, and I got to know them. What was important to them became important to me. My supervisors knew how to run the operation, so I let them manage it.

This wasn't about me. One of my drivers and I ministered to the union business agent as he broke down and cried out for help in my office. Yes, God was using me. This was my ministry.

I successfully taught my female supervisor how to drive a manual transmission. She was very grateful and was able to contribute more effectively to her co-workers. Her self-esteem soared, and her colleagues gained more respect for her. My supervisor with the alcohol problem struggled to keep it under control, but he managed to do so during my tenure.

The most disappointing moment was with my lead supervisor, who was brimming with potential. He was terminated for stealing computers. I was shocked. He was more than ready for a promotion, so why had he thrown away such a promising career? I never got the chance to ask him.

Pastor Rick Warren states that, ***"On the path to spiritual maturity, even temptation becomes a stepping-stone rather than a stumbling block when you realize that it is just as much an occasion to do the right thing as it is to do the wrong thing. Temptation simply*** *provides the choice. While temptation is Satan's primary weapon to destroy you, God wants to use it to develop you. Every time you choose to do good instead of sin, you are growing in the character of Christ.* "[153]

My center was running smoothly, and my boss didn't bother me much. Each month, we had to attend a managers' meeting with thirty to forty managers present. At these meetings, recognition was given to the best-performing center in the district.

Certain indices determined the rankings, such as late air frequency, safety—whether your center had any auto accidents or personal injuries—and production S.P.O.R.H. (stops per on-road hour), which measured how quickly drivers were delivering. As the rookie center manager, I was being compared to managers who had been in this job for decades.

At my very first meeting, I was called up and presented with a plaque for the best package center in the district for that month. Some managers laughed, and many attributed my win to the previous manager's legacy.

The following month, my center was again number one in the district. There was slightly less laughter this time, but I was still not taken seriously. In the third month, I was called up once more.

---

[153] Warren, The Purpose Driven Life, 201

Being number one for three months in a row, people began to take notice.

I knew it was all God. It was always all God! Here I stood in the midst of my greatest fear, knowing that the Lord is my strength and my salvation. Whom shall I fear?

Benny Hinn tells us, *"Do you realize that the power of the Spirit can so infill you that you fear absolutely no one? It's possible to establish such a communion with Him that even addressing the leader of a nation would cause no apprehension. The Spirit will lift your head, square your shoulders, and instill in you an unexpected confidence."*[154]

I knew I hadn't achieved this success on my own, as I didn't know how. The other managers were genuinely surprised and amazed. According to them, this wasn't supposed to happen. To my surprise, my immediate boss never congratulated me for any of my monthly wins.

In the fourth month, it was a tie between me and another center manager for first place. Before the meeting, I was asked if it would be acceptable to give the award to the other manager simply because I had won so many times consecutively. Imagine that! We serve an awesome God. I agreed, and it was never announced that

____

[154] Hinn, Good Morning, Holy Spirit, 117

there was a tie. Shortly thereafter, I retired on April 1, 2010, after 37 years of service.

Looking back over my life, I can truly say I've been blessed and I have a testimony.

Aunt Lou passed away on August 31, 2011. I found her unresponsive in her bed at home around 4:00 in the afternoon. We had plans to go to the movies that day to see "The Help." When she failed to meet me downstairs, I used my set of keys to enter her apartment. I could hear her television blasting from her bedroom.

When I entered her bedroom, she was sitting on the edge of her bed, slightly slumped to one side. She had taken half of the rollers out of her hair and was in the process of putting on her pantyhose. Thinking she might be asleep, I touched her.

She was as cold as ice. I jumped back in horror and quickly realized she was dead. I immediately called 911 and then my wife.

She must have died sometime that morning. She still had rollers in her hair and was putting on her pantyhose. I arranged for her body to be flown back to Lumberton. The funeral was held at True Believers Church, with Pastor Ellie Baker presiding.

Bernardette passed away on January 19, 2020. Like our mother, she died in the same month she was born. And like her brother Robert, she chose to be cremated. Despite our many disagreements, she lived life on her own terms, and only she has to answer for that. Her funeral was held at Central and Worley Mortuary Chapel, with Pastor Ruby Mitchell and Evangelist Clara Mae Bostic presiding.

Dr. Jefferson states that, ***"The difficulty is we are dealing with the choice between heaven and hell and many of us are not really aware of that; and many of us don't believe that is the case. The sinfulness of our human condition has blinded us to the reality of sin and its consequences of eternal damnation. We have devised our own way of thinking and eternity is not a part of it. Some of us are so accustomed to sin that we are not aware of what it has done to us."***[155]

It takes a special person to do what Aunt Lou did for me and my sister Bernardette. What did she do? Here was a single young woman living in New York City, free to come and go as she pleased, with no obligations to anyone. Yet she chose to take in a little boy and a little girl whom she barely knew and raise them.

Can you imagine the conversations she must have had with her friends? "Lou, you won't be able to do the things you used to do. Girl, you must be crazy. Lou, it's not going to be easy. You don't

---

[155] Jefferson, One Night In Bethlehem, 110

know what you're getting yourself into," and so on. Despite all the negativity, she did it anyway.

It was an unselfish love. I was explaining this to the responding police officers while standing in Aunt Lou's living room. I said that Aunt Lou gave up her life to raise us. The officer replied, "No, son, she didn't give up her life—she found her life. Her life began when she took you and your sister in."

How do you repay such a debt? Aunt Lou never asked me for a dime. She never put me on a guilt trip by saying things like, "After all I've done for you." From a very early age, I knew the best way to thank and repay her was to stay out of trouble, go to school, and stand on my own two feet.

Aunt Lou retired about fifteen years ago. My personal mission has been to make her as comfortable as possible. We often held hands, and each time I held her hand, it was a thank you. It wasn't about what I could or couldn't buy for her. I took her to all her doctor appointments—that was a thank you. When I suggested we visit her sister in Baltimore, that was a thank you. When we sat together in complete silence, that was a thank you.

Aunt Lou, I only hope I've made you as proud of me as I am of you. You didn't have to do what you did, but you did, and I say thank you.

It is through God's grace and mercy that we've made it through, and I'm living this moment because of you. Thank you—I love you.

I ask God why I've been so blessed. I've certainly been no angel. Yet You have always been there, patiently waiting for me to acknowledge and accept Your presence.

Author Norman Geisler says, *"One of the great motivating factors in the Christian life is the assurance of salvation. Thank God, the Bible assures us that we can know that we have eternal life (John 5:24; 1 John 5:13). And nothing can separate us from the love of Christ (Rom. 8:36-39). Even if we are faithless, God remains faithful (2 Tim. 2:13). These and numerous other passages of Scripture inform us that true believers are eternally secure."*[156]

J.D. Greear adds, *"But for all of its difficulties, salvation is also wonderfully simple. Salvation is simple in terms of how people obtain it. Part of the mystery at work is that God took the complex notion of salvation and in His genius made it understandable enough for any man or woman to grasp."*[157]

---

[156] Geisler, Chosen But Free, 148
[157] Greear, Stop Asking Jesus Into Your Heart, xiv

So, How Do You Know Without a Shadow of Doubt that You Are Saved?

Author Norman Geisler explains it this way, *"There are no conditions for God's giving of salvation; it is wholly of grace. But there is one (and only one) condition for receiving this gift – true saving faith. There is absolutely nothing in man that is the basis for God saving him. But there was something in God (love) that is the basis for man's salvation. It was not because of any merit in man but only because of grace in God that salvation was initiated toward man. Man does not initiate salvation (Rom. 3:11), and he cannot attain it (Rom. 4:5). But he can and must receive it (John 1:12). Salvation is an unconditional act of God's election. Man's faith is not a condition for God giving salvation, but it is for man receiving it. Nonetheless, the act of faith (free choice) by which man receives salvation is not meritorious. It is the Giver who gets credit for the gift, not the receiver. Why, then, does one person go to heaven and another not? Because God willed that all who receive His grace will be saved and that all who reject it will be lost."*[158]

Dr. Myles Munroe goes on to say that, *"Your belief is evidence that you trust God. He is not impressed by how many scriptures you quote or how long you pray. He is moved and*

---

[158] Geisler, Chosen But Free, 185

convinced when you believe what He has told you, and when you prove it by acting on it. Belief is trust in action. "[159]

Repent and believe in Christ Jesus

What is repentance? **Repentance** is the regret for past wrongdoings and feeling remorseful about what you have or haven't done. However, it also involves showing and proving that you are actively trying to change and improve. Jesus Himself made it clear that repentance is essential, urging people to turn to God and ask for forgiveness for their sins.

Rick Warren states that, *"Your first step in spiritual growth is to start changing the way you think. Change always starts first in your mind. The way you think determines the way you feel, and the way you feel influences the way you act. To be like Christ you must develop the mind of Christ. The New Testament calls this mental shift REPENTANCE, which in Greek literally means "to change your mind." You repent whenever you change the way you think by adopting how God thinks – about yourself, sin, God, other people, life, your future, and everything else.* "[160]

True salvation always results in good works and a changed life. Faith is the means of salvation; good works are the fruit. Where

---

[159] Munroe, (Understanding the purpose and power of) PRAYER, 188
[160] Warren, The Purpose Driven Life, 182

good works are absent, saving faith is also missing. True faith consistently produces good works, and when the Holy Spirit controls our lives, He will produce this kind of fruit in us:

Love, **Joy**, **Peace**, **Patience**, **Kindness**, **Goodness**, **Faithfulness**, **Gentleness**, and **Self-Control**.

Dr. Jefferson goes on to say that, ***"Jesus, His birth, His life, His ministry, His death and resurrection, were all a part of God's plan to save sinners who heard the message of salvation and believed. Remember, it was God who loved the world and because of that He devised a plan to save sinners without going against the sinners will. He accepted only those who came to Him believing the gospel indicating their hearts were touched and their minds were made up to accept His invitation to salvation and eternal life with Him in Heaven."***[161]

What do I believe? I believe in God and in Jesus Christ. I believe He suffered and on the third day rose again. I believe He is seated at the right hand of God, and I believe in the Holy Spirit… In essence, I believe in the Apostle's Creed.

―――――――――――――――――

[161] Jefferson, One Night In Bethlehem, 112

Apostle's Creed

I believe in God, *the Father almighty,*
creator of heaven and earth.

I believe in Jesus Christ, *his only Son, our Lord,*
who was conceived by the Holy Spirit
and born of the virgin Mary.

I believe He suffered *under Pontius Pilate,*
was crucified, died, and was buried;
he descended to hell.

I believe the third day he rose *again from the dead.*
He ascended to heaven.

I believe He is seated at the right hand of God the Father
almighty. From there he will come to judge the living and the dead.

I believe in the Holy Spirit, *the holy Christian church,*
the communion of saints, the forgiveness of sins,
the resurrection of the body, and the life everlasting.

Amen!

BIBLIOGRAPHY

1. **<u>Batterson, Mark. All In (You are one decision away from a totally different life). Zondervan, 2013</u>**

   Mark Batterson is the lead pastor of National Community Church, a multi-campus church with seven locations in Washington, DC. He is the author of several bestselling books, including *In a Pit with a Lion on a Snowy Day*, *Wild Goose Chase*, and *Primal*. Mark and his wife, Lora, reside on Capitol Hill with their three children.

2. **<u>Copeland, Leslie. Christ-like Leadership. Judson Press, 2022</u>**

   Leslie Copeland, DMin, MBA, serves as the Chief Operating Officer for the National Council of the Churches of Christ in the USA. An ordained Baptist minister, she has extensive experience with faith-based organizations, including roles as the director of the Ecumenical Poverty Initiative and the director of Ecumenical Advocacy Days for Global Peace with Justice.

Bibliography

3. **<u>Geisler, Norman. Chosen But Free. Bethany House, 2001</u>**

   Dr. Norman L. Geisler is the President of Southern Evangelical Seminary in Charlotte, North Carolina. He is the author or coauthor of more than sixty books and hundreds of articles and has spoken or debated nationwide and in numerous countries.

4. **<u>Greear, J. D. Stop Asking Jesus Into Your Heart. B & H, 2013</u>**

   For years, J.D. Greear felt isolated in his struggle to find assurance of salvation. However, after numerous conversations with Christians of all ages, he has concluded that a lack of assurance is widespread. J.D. is the lead pastor of The Summit Church, a multi-site congregation in Raleigh-Durham, North Carolina. He and his wife have four children.

5. **<u>Groeschel, Craig. it (How Churches and Leaders Can Get it and Keep it). Zondervan, 2008</u>**

   Greg Groeschel is the founding and senior pastor of LifeChurch.tv. He, his wife Amy, and their six children live in the Edmond, Oklahoma, area, where LifeChurch.tv was established in 1996.

6. **<u>Hill, Napoleon and Lechter, Sharon. Outwitting The Devil (The Secret to Freedom and Success). Sterling, 2011</u>**

Napoleon Hill (1883-1970) was an American author and entrepreneur best known for *Think and Grow Rich*, published in 1937, which has become one of the bestselling books of all time. His teachings have influenced generations of success seekers and set the standard for modern motivational thinking.

Sharon Lechter is the co-author of *Three Feet from Gold* and the international bestseller *Rich Dad Poor Dad*, along with fourteen other books in the Rich Dad series. She is also a national spokesperson for the National CPAs Commission on Financial Literacy and the founder of Pay Your Family First, a financial education organization. Additionally, she created *ThriveTime for Teens*, an award-winning financial life and money reality game. Sharon is currently focused on expanding the global knowledge of Napoleon Hill's principles and teachings in collaboration with the Napoleon Hill Foundation.

Bibliography

7. <u>**Hinn, Benny. Good Morning, Holy Spirit. Thomas Nelson, 1990**</u>

Benny Hill is respected as a pastor, teacher, evangelist, and author, effectively ministering both from the pulpit and through television. As the founder and pastor of Orlando Christian Center, an interdenominational church in Florida, he leads a congregation of more than 7,000 attendees each week. He also hosts a daily half-hour television program broadcast across America.

8. <u>**Jakes, T.D., He-Motions. G. P. Putnam Son's, 2004**</u>

He-Motions brings clarity and hope to men, helping them strengthen their relationships with themselves, the women in their lives, and their Lord. It offers solutions for women as they relate to the men they love, bringing both closer together and closer to God.

Bishop T.D. Jakes is the founder and senior pastor of The Potter's House church in Dallas, Texas. His church is one of the fastest-growing in the nation, with an interracial congregation of more than 28,000 members.

9. **Jakes, T.D. So You Call Yourself A Man? Albury Publishing, 1997**

> Bishop T.D. Jakes is the founder and senior pastor of The Potter's House church in Dallas, Texas. He is a highly celebrated author, conference speaker, and nationally televised pastor. His messages of hope and deep healing are filled with God's wisdom and compassion, transcending barriers worldwide.

10. **Jefferson, Bobbie. Elusive. Omnibook, 2018**

> The author of several books, she is a mother of seven and grandmother of ten. Her ministry took her to West Africa, where she worked with her husband for eight years. Called by God and entrusted as a missionary, she dedicated herself to teaching His word and sharing the good news of the gospel.

11. **Jefferson, James T., One Night In Bethlehem. It Is Written, 2023**

> Pastor Jefferson, as he prefers to be called, has a remarkable and diverse history. He has accepted invitations to speak at a variety of congregations, including Baptist, Methodist, Apostolic, Seventh-day Adventist, and non-denominational groups. He holds four degrees, including a

doctorate in ministry from Glad Tidings Bible College in St. Louis, Missouri. Pastor Jefferson is the Founder and President of Grace School of Ministry.

12. **<u>Keller, Timothy. Preaching. Penguin, 2016</u>**

Many Christians, including pastors, struggle to communicate their faith in a way that demonstrates the transformative power of the Christian gospel. Timothy Keller, founder of Redeemer Presbyterian Church in New York City, is renowned for his insightful, accessible, and erudite sermons. His preaching has inspired millions in their Christian lives and has been instrumental in bringing many to faith.

13. **<u>MacArthur, John. Twelve Extraordinary Women. Nelson, 2005</u>**

John MacArthur, author of 150 books, is the pastor-teacher of Grace Community Church in Sun Valley, California, and president of The Master's College and Seminary. John and his wife, Patricia, have four married children and thirteen grandchildren.

14. <u>**MacArthur, John. Twelve Ordinary Men. Nelson, 2002**</u>

John MacArthur, author of 150 books, is the pastor-teacher of Grace Community Church in Sun Valley, California, and president of The Master's College and Seminary. John and his wife, Patricia, have four married children and thirteen grandchildren.

15. <u>**Maxwell, John C., Think on these Things (Meditation for Leaders). Beacon Hill Press, 1999**</u>

John C. Maxwell speaks full-time for Injoy, a Christian leadership organization he founded in Atlanta in 1985. He has pastored for 26 years, including serving as pastor of Skyline Wesleyan Church in San Diego. He is the author of more than a dozen books.

16. <u>**Munroe, Myles. (Understanding the purpose and power of) PRAYER. Whitaker, 2002**</u>

Dr. Myles Munroe was an international motivational speaker, bestselling author, lecturer, educator, and business consultant. He was the founder and president of Bahamas Faith Ministries International and the founder, executive producer, and principal host of several radio and television programs broadcast worldwide. Dr. Munroe and his wife,

Bibliography

Ruth, travelled together as seminar speakers and were the proud parents of two children, Charisa and Myles Jr.

17. **<u>Sanders, J. Oswald. Spiritual Leadership (Principles of Excellence for Every Believer). Moody, 2007</u>**

J. Oswald Sanders served as a consulting director for Overseas Missionary Fellowship and conducted an international preaching ministry. He was awarded the Order of the British Empire for his Christian service and theological writing. His numerous books include *The Incomparable Christ*, *Spiritual Discipleship*, and *Spiritual Maturity*.

18. **<u>Warren, Rick. The Purpose Driven Life. Zondervan, 2022</u>**

Rick Warren is often referred to as "America's most influential spiritual leader." He founded Saddleback Church in Orange County, California, one of the largest and most well-known churches in the world. Additionally, he established the Purpose Driven Movement, a network encompassing tens of thousands of churches across all denominations in 160 countries. Rick Warren has also trained over 350,000 pastors globally.

19. **<u>Yancey, Philip. Where Is God When It Hurts?</u> <u>Zondervan, 1990</u>**

Author Philip Yancey delves into the many perplexing and challenging issues surrounding the mystery of pain, whether physical, emotional, or spiritual. With sensitivity and compassion, his unique book helps us understand why we suffer and offers guidance on coping with our own pain, as well as assisting others in dealing with theirs.